Manuel Lucena Salmoral

AMERICA 1492

PORTRAIT OF A CONTINENT
500 YEARS AGO

Facts On File
New York • Oxford

Facing the title page, this Sinú ceramic statuette from the Museo del Oro in Bogota displays the artistic wealth of the peoples living outside the territory of the high cultures. The simplicity—not without tenderness—of the mother's face, with eyes in the shape of coffee beans, contrasts with the complexity of the design of the skirt, the adornment of the collar, the armlets and the container that she carries on her head.

AMERICA 1492

Copyright © 1990 Anaya Editoriale s.r.l., Milan/Fenice 2000 s.r.l., Milan

Facts On File, Inc.   Facts On File Limited
460 Park Avenue South   Collins Street
New York NY 10016   Oxford OX4 1XJ
USA   United Kingdom

Library of Congress Cataloging-in-Publication Data
Lucena Salmoral, Manuel.
America 1492 / Manuel Lucena Salmoral.
    p. cm.
ISBN 0-8160-2483-9
Includes bibliographical references
    1. Indians of North America—History. 2. Indians of Mexico—
    History. 3. Indians of North America—Social life and customs.
    4. Indians of Mexico—Social life and customs. I. Title.
E58.L88 1990
970.01'1—dc20   89-77029
                                                 CIP
A British CIP catalogue record for this book is available from the British Library.

Text design by Manuel Franch
Jacket design by Bruno Binosi
Composition by Facts On File, Inc.
Printed by Amilcare Pizzi S.p.A. Cinisello Balsamo (Milano)
Printed in Italy

10 9 8 7 6 5 4 3 2 1

This book is printed on acid-free paper.

Created and produced by Grupo Anaya, S.A.
Executive director: Antonio Roche
Editorial director: Pedro Pardo
Managing editor: Manuel Gonzáles
Editing: Estrella Molina
Photographic research: José María Marcelino
Original art: Jordi Clapers
Maps: Andrés Sánchez

Duodecimo dia
sol

endecimo dia
aua

decimo dia
aguila

nouenodia
tigrree

octauodia
caña

terdecimo dia
pedernal

an aqui este signo
utes hobres mas no
undir a nadie

AMERICA 1492

PORTRAIT OF A CONTINENT 500 YEARS AGO

Table of Contents

6

Lintel 41 in Yaxchilán, Chiapas (Mexico), now in the British Museum in London, has this bas-relief in limestone depicting the monarch Jaguar-Bird dressed for the battle he commanded on May 9, 755 A.D. Of the cities of the Classic Maya period, Yaxchilán has some of the best war iconography, with depictions of warrior-kings, military equipment and bloody sacrifices. This is possibly due to Yaxchilán's strategic location on the Usumacinta River, as well as to the fact that it was on the route of the merchants who traveled from the north to the central lowlands of the south. Jaguar-Bird ascended the throne in 752, after defeating his many enemies in battle, and died in 768, at the age of 57.

Foreword

In 1541 the viceroy of Mexico, don Antonio de Mendoza, was in a tight spot. Spain had asked him to supply a pictorial account of the way of life of the Aztec Indians. He had not been asked for an exhaustive book on the subject but for scenes and pictures reflecting everyday life.

Don Antonio gathered together the best native artists available and had them paint scenes depicting how the native peoples had eaten, dressed, studied, worshiped and spent their leisure time before the arrival of the Spaniards. It was now up to him to do his duty and comply with the rather unusual caprice of the Spaniard who had had the idea of getting to know *Las Indias* (Spanish America) through pictures, and so avoid making the trip.

The artists worked hard, using their old illustrative techniques, and managed to fulfill their duties without intruding too much on the natives. Their work is perhaps the greatest illustrative testimony of the Amerindian peoples and makes up the third part of the so-called *Mendoza Codex*, now in the Bodleian library in Oxford. The first part deals with the history of Mexico and Tenochtitlan and the second with the tribute the natives had to pay to the Spaniards.

By 1549 the work was finished and ready for shipment to Spain. Ten days before it was taken aboard ship, someone remarked that without any kind of text explaining the pictures, no one from Europe was likely to understand the paintings. Scenes familiar to all those who lived in Mexico, such as Indians playing ball or a father reprimanding his children, would be incomprehensible across the Atlantic. So an accompanying written account of native customs was hastily charged to a Spaniard, who understood Nahuatl (the Aztec language). The person chosen was a mysterious missionary of whom we know only that his Christian name or surname began with "J"—the letter he shyly wrote on his contribution to the codex. The Reverend J took great pains with his work and in fact used two types of text on the sheets: The first was a short note on each figure appearing in each picture, and the second was texts similar to what we would now call captions. These were more detailed and discussed the content contained in the images. This work fell into the hands of French pirates who captured the Spanish ship and subsequently into those of the writer and traveler André Thevet, who was able to enjoy what Philip II of Spain would never get to see. The codex then changed hands several times until it finally reached the library in Oxford.

This book does not go beyond what Mendoza had set out to achieve. It attempts to give to the contemporary reader an idea of the everyday life of the Amerindian before the European invasion. Nor does it surpass the work of the Reverend J, who supplied the explanations to the pictures. There remains, however, great difficulty in doing a work of this sort. The absence of a written language—with the exception of the Central American languages— the indifference of Europeans to the life of those they considered savages, the wanton destruction and burning of books suspected of containing the devil's teachings (as happened with the Aztec and Maya manuscripts under Juán de Zumárraga and Diego de Landa), and five centuries of iconoclasm are difficulties that have put an end to virtually all testimony of the times. What is left are fragments of that everyday life, in no way representative of the whole of Spanish America but at least of a substantial part of it. Much of what is left is monotonous and repetitive to our Western minds, and it has been necessary to leave out or remove parts in order to make this book more readable. This book has been written with aims similar to those of Viceroy Antonio de Mendoza: to offer to readers living at the end of the 20th century a picture of the everyday life of the pre-Columbian American.

Civilization
and barbarity

America offered a vigorous contrast between civilization and barbarism, which to Europeans were expressed in extremely fine objects made of gold and
abominable cannibalistic customs. Left: A Taino
breastplate of gold from the Museo del Oro in
Bogota. Above: A scene of cannibalism in Brazil,
from the History of America (1849), by Belloc.

The Amerindian's world

To the pre-Columbian American peoples, "civilization" meant their particular world, the territory under their control. Inca, Aztec and Maya each considered themselves the only culture in which barbarism did not exist. Those most guilty of ethnocentricity were the Inca, who believed not only that the civilized world did not exist outside their empire but also that their culture had sprung up spontaneously like a divine gift from the sun. The chronicler Garcilaso de la Vega repeats the typical Inca belief, which he received from the lips of his uncle, who told him that before the Inca there had existed peoples who "had lived like wild, stupid animals, without religion, nor law, without village communities, without a roof over their heads, who neither tilled nor sowed the land, who neither dressed in clothes nor covered their flesh because they did not know how to use cotton or wool to make clothing. When they did gather together it was in twos and threes, living in caves and rock openings and caverns in the earth; like animals they ate herbs and tree roots and wild fruit, which they considered their own, and human flesh. They covered themselves with leaves and tree bark and animal skins. Others went naked through the world. All in all they lived like deer and savages and even as regards women they were like animals since women were not taken as wives and they could not distinguish between one woman and another." A similar impression is conveyed by the chronicler Francisco de Avila, who described the ancestors of the Inca as "savage, wild men."

Father Sun took pity on the men for living in such conditions and decided to send the Inca a "morning star." He sent two children of his own solar flesh, a man and a woman, "to bring them rules and laws by which to live with reason and in society; so that they could live in houses and villages, know how to till the land, grow plants and corn (maize), raise cattle, reap their benefits, and those of the fruit of the earth, like rational beings and not like animals." Thus appeared the Inca.

Nor were there any civilized peoples outside the *Tahuantinsuyu*, or Inca empire, where through lack of organization barbarism was perpetuated. Garcilaso speaks contemptuously of

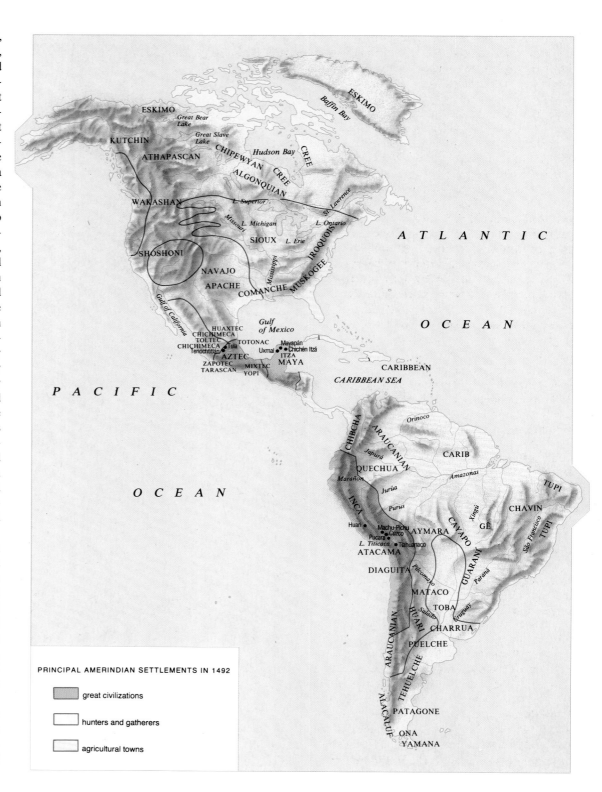

PRINCIPAL AMERINDIAN SETTLEMENTS IN 1492

great civilizations

hunters and gatherers

agricultural towns

the lack of culture among the South American aborigines at the end of the 16th century, since "the teachings of the Inca had not reached there: many of them (the nations) are today as barbaric and wild as they were one and seventy years ago when the Spaniards entered Peru." Before the Inca—nothing. Without the Inca—nothing.

The Aztec tried to erase from their collective consciousness the legacy of a "barbaric" people, which sharply contrasted with the extremely high degree of civilization they managed to achieve over only a few hundred years. Thus they joined with the Toltec civilization, a race of warriors and artists from whom they considered themselves to have descended, and attempted with the new generations to erase the memory of their miserable arrival in the Valley of Mexico as a primitive people, despised by the cultured Culhuacan, the Xochimilco, the Chalco and other peoples who now paid tribute to them. Around 1427, in the reign of *tlatoani* ("speaker") or King Itzcoatl there was a purge of records of the historical and religious traditions of former times, the aim being to eradicate all testimony to such practices. Some of Friar Bernardino de Sahagún's informants, who revealed to him the wonders of the Aztec culture, commented:

"They kept their history.
But then they burnt it,
when Itzcoatl reigned in Mexico.
They took a decision,
the Mexican lords said:
it is necessary that the people
not know the pictures (codices).
Those who come into contact with them could
be corrupted,
and the country could change
since many lies are kept there,
and many men there are regarded as gods."

Itzcoatl's supreme counselor, Tlacaelel, ordered those codices referring to things that, in the opinion of the lords, it was "necessary that the people should not know" to be burned. Then he helped the oligarchy devise a new history of the Aztec, one more in line with the greatness of the nation. Thus, of the time before the Aztec virtually nothing remains, only the Toltec myths.

Indios Mecos, Barbaros.

11

The Aztec empire bordered on the north with the territory of the Chichimeca people, whom they considered backward and barbaric. The Chichimec, or more simply Mec, were the Pame group who lived in the mountainous area to the southeast of San Luis de Potosi and the areas bordering the Tamaulipa and Queretaro territories, having previously extended to Guanajuato and Mexico. The Chichimeca were always a danger for the colonizing Spaniards, who were greatly attracted by the silver mines to the north of Mexico. They sent soldiers to exterminate the Indians and then missionaries to evangelize and civilize the remainder. By the 18th century they were viewed with a certain tolerance, as we can see in this painting from the same century, now in the Museo de América, in Madrid.

The northern frontier of the Aztec territories bordered with other Nahuatl-speaking nations such as the Chichimeca, whom the Aztec regarded as barbarians. Even farther afield were other, even wilder barbarians called the "Teochichimec," who lacked housing and covered themselves with animal skins. Little did the Aztec know that they had inherited *peyotl* or peyote, the famous hallucinatory drug that they made so much use of, from these people. Nor did they know that some of those northern peoples such as the Yuman were assimilating certain of their customs and had begun to decapitate their enemies and dance with their trophies to celebrate their victories. Civilization and barbarism—two topics that have been discussed incessantly—coexisted.

To the Maya as well neither man nor civilization had existed before them. Real men, that is, born of the maize, like themselves. Before the Maya there had only been pseudomen such as those that, according to the *Popol Vuh*, the sacred book of the Quiché Maya, had been made of clay, sticks and straw.

What had actually existed in the Americas before the time of the Inca, Aztec and Maya? There was, in fact, a great deal of human activity that preceded these civilizations. Before the high cultures there had been a lengthy process of virtually independent cultural evolution lasting possibly 40,000 years, perhaps, as some archaeologists claim, as much as 100,000. The first inhabitants came from Asia by way of the Bering Strait (a land bridge during some periods of the last, or Wisconsin, glaciation), bringing with them only an elementary lithic culture. The most advanced peoples hunted mammoth, early ancestors of the horse and llama (all of which had disappeared by 7000 B.C.), using flaked flint weapons. The more primitive cultures did not even know how to hunt and so ate fruit and wild berries, which they broke open with stones.

Later men came from Australia, Melanesia, Polynesia and possibly from Japan, but these brought few technological innovations with them. The introduction of ceramics in Valdivia (Ecuador) is attributed to Japanese fishermen from Kyushu and Honshu, but there are those who believe that ceramics was invented by the American peoples. A range of advances made in the old Euro-Asian-African world contributed to many aspects of Amerindian culture, among them basketry, agriculture, the domestication of animals, the calendar, pictography, numerical reckoning, textile making, even the invention of the house, the village and the town. The cultural steps in this development are called the Paleo–indian, the Archaic, the Formative, the Classic and the Post-Classic periods. Only two large areas on the continent, Mesoamerica (the southern half of Mexico and Central America) and the central Andean region (from the north of Ecuador to the north of Chile), managed to go through a

Micaylcuitl

12

Micaylcuitl or the god Tezcatlipoca, seen in this print from the Veitia Codex, *presided over the festivities on the Day of the Dead, when the Aztec wore mourning in memory of their deceased relatives. The Aztec military conquests turned their culture into an extremely complex one, absorbing aspects and rituals from all the subject peoples in the empire. Proof of this complexity was evident in their religion, with gods such as the one seen here having different sym-bols and names associated with colors and the points of the compass. Thus there was Tezcatlipoca, the red god of the west, the god of springtime and of vegetation; Tezcatlipoca, the blue god of the south and the god of war; Tezcatlipoca, the black god of the north who was a sun divinity; and Tezcatlipoca, the white god of the east who was god of the arts.*

The Mexicans held great festivals in honor of Quetzalcoatl, the feathered serpent, whom we see in this copy from the Veitia Codex. Quetzalcoatl is related to the Aztec civilization and to the eastern region. The Mexicans attempted to personify him as an individual who taught them the benefits of civilization—deeply rooted in the Maya culture—and afterward left for the east, saying that he would one day return. On their arrival, Cortés and the Spaniards were considered the fulfillment of this prophecy.

process of uninterrupted and progressive evolution and form civilizations with true *civitas*, or cities, from the Classic age (1st to 10th century A.D.). Their technical, artistic, intellectual, political, social and religious achievements were then adopted, ordered and systematized by the Aztec and the Inca.

Surrounding the Inca, Aztec and Maya was one of the most complicated human mosaics in the world, made up of small units of men, languages and cultures. There were Indians of almost six feet (1.80 m.) in height like the Kiowa or the Sioux, in contrast to others of four and a half feet (1.40 m.), such as the Motilone. There were peoples with long or round heads, with prominent sharp noses or flat snub noses, with thick lips or thin lips, yellow or copper-colored complexions, with black or white hair, with or without the Mongoloid spot, etc. Anthropologists and prehistorians faced with this human diversity finally concluded that the continent shows signs of Mongolian, Indonesian (including original Indonesian), Australian, Polynesian, Melanesian

and other origins, and that subsequently this human diversity grew even greater as a result of environmental phenomena lasting for centuries.

Another riddle for scholars is that of linguistics; Athapaskan, for example, is made up of around 40 different languages. If the Tower of Babel ever existed, there is no doubt that it was built somewhere in the Americas. And the cultures? How many were there? We have no inventory of some that have disappeared without a trace, but what we do know about others allows us to assume that this so-called barbaric world was as rich as, if not richer than, the high cultures, although we hold the latter in greater esteem because we have been able to witness their traditions—a privilege we have not been granted for the vast majority of those other Amerindian cultures, lost over the centuries. Let us now take a look at America in 1492, when the Europeans encountered these two unfamiliar groups: on the one hand the great empires and, on the other, the larger remaining cultures, consisting of the hunting, gathering, fishing and agricultural societies.

The origins of American man

In America there are no traces of man's evolution. Unlike Africa, Asia and Oceania, there are no remains of Australopithecus, Sinanthropus or Pithecanthropus, nor even of the more modern European Neanderthals. Consequently, America is a continent populated by true Homo Sapiens who arrived there from the Old World. The questions of how, where, and when have given rise to numerous scientific theories. The first traces of human beings on the continent are chipped-stone projectile tips, made by hunters about 13,000 years ago. Other stones that could have been used for crushing have also been found and have been dated at around 40,000 years, but they are so rough that there is some doubt as to whether they were actually tools made by humans. We also know that the culture of the first settlers was similar to that of the Paleolithic culture in the Old World and that they populated North America before going on to South America.

Thus, America was populated about 13,000 years ago by a wave of hunters who reached the northern hemisphere, who were probably preceded by another wave of gatherers following the same route about 40,000 years ago. These migrations took place during the last or Wisconsin Ice Age, between 50,000 B.C. and 9000 B.C.

Archaeological evidence suggests that the first settlers came from Asia across the Bering Strait, which separates Asia and America at a distance of only 56 miles (90 km.). During an ice age the strait would have become a landbridge due to a drop in the level of the ocean. It was not only Asian man who emigrated but also the flora and fauna: the mammoth, the bison, the deer and the moose are of Asian origin. Later, more migratory groups came from Australia, Polynesia and Melanesia by the transpacific route (stopping at Easter Island) or by the South Pole route (Tasmania, the Aucklands, Campbell, Macquarie and Esmeralda). Finally, new Asian migrations arrived. There is no doubt whatsoever as to the arrival of the Inuit, in contrast to that of Japanese fishers in Valdivia (Ecuador), who are believed by some to have introduced ceramics around the year 3000 B.C.

From sages to warriors: the Maya

The Maya, Aztec and Inca empires were a source of amazement to the Spanish *conquistadores*, who could not conceive of how or when they had developed. Later colonists, especially the missionaries, managed to unravel part of the mystery by asking the Indians themselves. This oral history concurred with more or less official versions. With this information and by means of extensive modern research, we have discovered a good deal about the development and splendor of the empires, though little about their origins; these are still enshrouded in the mists of legend.

The Maya were the oldest and the most brilliant of the peoples. When we speak of the Maya it is necessary to make a distinction, since there were two Maya: one very ancient people who lived mainly in the lowlands of Guatemala and the other, modern or Post-Classic people who controlled the Yucatán Peninsula. The former were the "sages," the latter the "warriors." The ancient Maya tamed the jungle, sowing it with city-states like Tikal, Palenque, Calakmul, Copán and others, and invented a system of writing made up of idiograms and phonetic symbols, which even now have not been completely deciphered. They invented a 365-day calendar, a linear chronological system, the corbel vault and many other technological marvels. These ancient or Classic Maya flourished mainly between 250 A.D. and 900 A.D. Among other things they are famous for their temples with their long stairways and crenellated constructions, their many-roomed palaces, their ball games, steam baths, astronomical observatories, roads, stelae and altars. The decline began at the end of the 8th century, the empire falling in the 10th century, with the last Maya monument erected in 909 A.D. The reason or reasons for the fall are unknown, although many hypotheses have been put forth, including soil exhaustion, changes in climate, peasant revolutions, volcanic eruptions, epidemics, psychotic depression due to anxiety, and civil war.

One segment of the remaining ancient Maya subsequently immigrated to the highlands of Guatemala and the Yucatán Peninsula, taking their great culture with them. There they settled in an arid, calcareous land where water was scarce and had to be brought above ground using

The steles like the one in this photograph, known as number 4, from Piedras Negras (constructed in 667 A.D.) and now part of the collection of the Museo de Arqueología y Etnología in Guatemala, are the finest manifestation of the art of the Classic Maya in stone-carving. They are monoliths of an average height of four meters depicting carvings of hieroglyphics, human figures such as priest-kings, and dates. These dates are the most important aspect, for the steles were erected once every 20 years to mark the end of the regular periods of the Maya calendar.

enormous natural and artificial wells. Villages such as those that later became Chichén Itzá, Kabah and Labná grew up around the wells.

At the beginning of the 10th century, Yucatán was invaded by several waves of northern peoples. One of the most important of these groups was the Toltec who came from their capital city of Tula and were led by a chieftain who had taken the name of Kukulcan, which means the Feathered Serpent. The Maya chroniclers place this event in 987 A.D. We know that Tula was not destroyed until 1168 by the Chichimeca, so perhaps the Toltec emigrated before the disaster. The Toltec settled in Chichén Itzá, merging their cul- ture with the existing Maya culture. These were the new, or warrior, Maya.

Chichén Itzá was rebuilt to be much more grandiose than Tula. Its warriors' temple, for example, was larger and more beautiful than the one in Tula, although its layout is reminiscent of its antecedent. Other buildings worthy of note

This bas-relief dating from 776 A.D. depicts the last governors of the city of Copán. They are seated cross-legged and wear a kind of oriental turban on their heads. From left to right are Governor 1, Governor 2 and Governor 16 or Yac-Pac. The ruins of Copán (now in Honduras) were discovered in the 16th century by the judge of the high court of Guatemala, Diego García de Palacio. They are particularly interesting for their inscriptions on astronomy as well as for the famous temple to the planet Venus. The priests of Copán were able to calculate eclipses of the sun with complete accuracy, and it is thought likely that it was they who fashioned the ritual year of 260 days, which was later adopted all over Mesoamerica. The city must have been a center of confluence for currents of thought and contains beautiful sculptures, steles and altars. In 782 A.D., Yax Murciélago (Yax Bat) ascended the throne, but he was an ineffectual monarch, and it was under him that the city's fame was finally diminished.

were the Kukulcan temple and the court with its hundred columns. Common to the architecture in general are columns shaped like descending snakes with the head near the ground, atlantes and figures such as Chac Mool, with the receptacle for sacrifices on its belly, and the jaguars and eagles that ate the hearts of its victims. These motifs came from the north and clearly show the influence of the Nahuatl-speaking peoples. However, we also find innumerable characteristics of the Maya culture, with which the Toltec had mixed, such as a circular astronomical observatory known as the Snail, ball courts (the main one decorated with bas-relief scenes depicting this

ritual sport), the characteristic sundials, the use of mosaics to decorate the façades of buildings, and renderings of Chac, the ancient Maya rain god. The most remarkable product was the fusion of Toltec urban architecture with Maya decorative art.

Chichén ruled the Yucatán territory for perhaps two centuries, establishing a powerful centralized state thanks to a combination of military might, from the Toltecs, and trade, from the Maya. The cities of the new Maya empire could not survive by farming only the arid land irrigated with the water from the natural wells, so they obtained the food they needed from trading and

the tribute paid by the peoples they had conquered. Brought to the cities were vast amounts of corn, kidney beans, pumpkins, chili peppers, sage seeds and cacao as well as wood, cotton, henequen, pigments, and luxury goods such as jade, turquoise, pyrites, alabaster, amber, copper and gold. The merchants controlled an intricate network covering the south of Mexico to the north of Central America in which they moved around with ease thanks to the vast dissemination of the Maya language.

The predominance of Chichén ended in tyranny, the two cities of Izamal and Mayapán forming an alliance in the 12th century to bring about

---

The creation of man (Maya)

The traditional oral tale of the origins of the world and of man, later compiled in writing in the *Popol Vuh*, the sacred book of the Maya, is one of the most beautiful stories in Amerindian literature.

It begins: "This is the story of how all was still, all quiet, in silence; there was no movement, no sound, and the whole of the sky was empty. This is the first story, the first speech. There were no men yet, nor animals, nor birds, nor fish, nor crabs, nor trees, nor stones, nor caves, nor ravines, nor grass nor forests. Only the sky was."

After making the dawn in the sky, after creating the earth and the animals, the Creator and the Maker formed man out of clay, but: "They realized it was not right, because it melted, was soft and had no mobility or strength, it fell down, was

watery, could not move its head, its face fell to one side." It became wet and "it could not stand."

So they made a man out of wood. "It looked like a man and spoke like a man, so they populated the earth with it...But these men had no

souls or minds; they did not remember their Creator or their Maker...They had no blood or consistency, no liquid or fat." That is why the men of wood were annihilated, destroyed by a deluge: "A flood came from the heart of the sky, it was a

great flood that fell on the heads of the wooden dolls."

Then the Creator and the Maker shaped man out of straw, but these men "could not think, did not speak with their Creator and their Maker." Then resin fell from the sky and "emptied their eyes." Presently, small animals, utensils like the *comales*, pans and the stones from the hearths rose up against the men, so that the terrified men of straw "ran to and fro; they wanted to climb to the roofs...up the trees...to go inside the caves." But they were destroyed. However, "It is said that their offspring are the monkeys which now inhabit the forests." So there were no real men until the Creator and the Maker made man out of corn, and then the real men, the Maya, came forth.

Chichén Itzá, in Yucatán, symbolized the new splendor of the Post-Classic Maya and was constructed by the Itzá in emulation of ancient Tula. On the right of this photograph we see the ruins of the Temple of the Warriors, which contains bas-reliefs and paintings recounting the military campaigns of the Itzá— evidence of the onslaught of Mexican militarism in the Maya area. Also pictured is the impressive patio of "the thousand columns" and in the background

the Castle or Pyramid of Kukulcan, formed by nine bodies flanked by a stairway whose beams ended at ground level in heads of the feathered serpent.

This fresco from the collection of the Museo de Arqueología y Etnología in Guatemala was created by the painter Antonio Tevedaf in 1959. It reproduces the wall paintings of Uaxactún depicting the arrival of ambassadors, each bearing gifts for the sovereign of the city. Uaxactún was one of the earliest Maya cities and possesses the oldest building and stele in all of Maya civilization. The stele dates from 328 A.D., when the city had its first known king.

Uaxactún, which developed in the shadow of Tikal, holds the key to the formation of Maya art and architecture, as well as the evolution of its socio-political structures. During this period both religious and political power were under the control of one person, the priest-king, and alliances were forged between cities.

its downfall. Warriors of the alliance took Chichén and destroyed it, the city's old inhabitants, the Itzá, fleeing to Peten, where they lived until the beginning of the 18th century.

The victors established Mayapán as the new capital of the area, though with less success than its predecessor since many city-states managed to remain independent. It had been founded in 1100 A.D. and was the last of the great Maya cities. It was surrounded by a wall 5.5 miles (9 km.) in length encompassing some 4,140 buildings, 140 of which were used for ceremonial purposes. Although it has characteristics of both Toltec and Maya, it was actually the continuation of the cultural symbiosis that had taken place previously in Chichén Itzá. Its main temple was practically a copy of a Chichén castle and its astronomical observatory was similar to the Snail. Some 2,100 of its buildings served as dwellings for a population estimated at around 12,000.

The kings of the Cocom dynasty, who governed in Mayapán, gathered around them a regional aristocracy, which gave them political and economic control over the area. The strength of the dynasty, however, lay in the army, which was made up of mercenaries, many of whom came from Mexico, home of the great warriors. With their help, supremacy over Yucatán was preserved until 1441, when revolts put an end to the reigning dynasty. There then sprang up 17 provinces or independent states, none of which were of any particular importance. The result was a resplendent decline resulting in a gradual breakdown of the old trade networks.

By the middle of the 15th century the Maya population had abandoned the cities and were now living in rural areas where ancient customs and some trading links were still upheld. Chichén Itzá, Uxmal and various other cities were by now deserted, and this was what Hernán Cortés found in 1524 when he crossed the area on his way to Honduras, using a map drawn up by Maya merchants.

The mask of the mysterious lord of Pacal

With cold seashell and obsidian eyes, this Maya mask has watched with indifference the passing of more than 13 centuries, from the splendor of the Maya empire until the present day. A jade mosaic made on a wooden frame, which rotted away hundreds of years ago, it was made to cover the face of the lord of Pacal, who was the most important governor the city of Palenque ever had. All records of the lord of Pacal (or "Handshield") were lost until about 30 years ago, when Maya hieroglyphic writing began to be deciphered. He was born on March 6, 603 A.D. and died on August 3, 684. Living to the age of 80, he came to power at the age of 12 and governed his native town practically all of his life. The lord of Pacal was the eldest son of the noble lady Zac Kuk, daughter of Kan Ik, founder of the dynasty. Pacal the Great (there was another Pacal, his uncle, who never reigned) ruled Palenque when it was at the height of its splendor, becoming lord of the southwestern Maya territories. In 633 hegemony was strengthened due to a pact with the Tortuguero, made, signed and ratified through a marriage of convenience accepted by the lord of Pacal.

Pacal the Great exercised an extravagant caprice by having his tomb built during his lifetime, in the manner of the Egyptian pharaohs. Measuring 28 ft. by 23 ft. (9 m. by 7 m.) the walls were covered with stucco and carved with reliefs representing men who were perhaps the new lords of the night or perhaps his ancestors. Finally, he gave the most extravagant order of all: the building of a pyramid-temple above his tomb, which would become famous for its inscriptions and keep watch over his remains.

All the great Maya archaeologists, including Sylvanus Morley— who explored Palenque at the beginning of the century, digging up Maya remains—never suspected that the tomb of the lord of Pacal was under the very ground on which they were standing. The tomb was finally discovered in 1957, when the Mexican archaeologist Alberto Ruiz was working in the Temple of the Inscriptions and became interested in the enormous flat stones covering the temple floor. Beneath them he found a stairway filled with gravel, probably intended to stop looters from gaining access, which led to a burial chamber. A great triangular stone impeded access to the chamber, where an enormous rectangular stone

measuring almost 13 ft. (4 m.) and covered with carvings and inscriptions referring to the lord of Pacal was found. This stone covered a stone sarcophagus containing the body of the ancient ruler of the town. He was surrounded by a wealth of jade objects: the face was covered by a life-size jade mask, there were disks of jade and precious stones to adorn the ears, tubular necklaces of beads and jade rings on his fingers. As was typical of the Late Maya, the Aztec and the Chinese, a piece of jade had been placed over the mouth. By the body were two small jade figures, one of which represented the sun god.

The treasures of the lord of Pacal were taken to the Museo de Antropología in Mexico. The most important piece was the mask, which had covered the face of the great lord of Palenque for 13 centuries. On New Year's Eve, 1987, this masterpiece of Maya art was stolen. In the course of the next few years, the thieves made several unsuccessful attempts to take it out of Mexico, and it was finally recovered by the Mexican authorities in 1989, intact but for a few missing pieces of mosaic. Very soon now, the cold seashell and obsidian eyes will again indifferently watch the men of the late 20th century.

The most feared of all the peoples: the Aztec

The Aztec were the most warlike nation in pre-Hispanic America. They succeeded in conquering the Mesoamerican area between the Atlantic and Pacific coasts and from central Mexico to the south. Ten million souls lived in an area governed from a capital called Tenochtitlan, built on several islets in lakes situated 7,218 ft. (2,200 m.) above sea level. When the Spaniards entered the capital they said that it reminded them of old tales of chivalry, as the capital did not seem real but like something in a dream.

Whereas the Maya have been compared to the Greeks, the Aztec may be compared to the Romans since they succeeded in conquering all of Mesoamerica. Paradoxically, this warrior nation was also the most civilized in North America. To the Aztec we owe the existence of words such as aguacate (avocado), chocolate, chili, cacao, copal, tomato, ocelot, etc., used, though sometimes modified, in languages all over the world.

Since most books and records on the ancient history of the Aztec were burnt in the time of Itzcoatl, the origin of the Aztec, although relatively recent, is lost in myth and legend, some of which are contradictory. What may be deduced from the legends is that the Aztec were a primitive, warlike (their greatest deity was the god of war), Nahuatl-speaking people who lived in the arid southwestern area of North America, from where they were forced to emigrate in order to survive. After wandering for many years they arrived in the central valley of Mexico, where they found excellent land, of volcanic origin, irrigated by an abundant water supply (which came from the snow-capped mountains nearby). This place must have seemed like paradise, and they decided to stay. However, the valley was already occupied, and had been for a long time, by a great many civilized peoples. Thus, being very capable warriors, the Aztec offered their services as mercenaries to the various nations. The city of Culhuacan accepted and allowed them to settle in Tizaapan, an uninhabited area infested with poisonous snakes. To the amazement of their patrons, the Aztec ate the snakes, thus adding to their reputation as barbarians.

The lord of Culhuacan allowed them to trade with his people and even agreed to give his daughter to their chieftain, Huitzilopochtli, when asked for her hand in marriage. The Aztec killed the princess, flayed her and used the skin to dress one of their priests, who then performed the ceremonial dance celebrating the marriage to their god. The lord of Culhuacan, however, had no capacity for understanding the religious symbolism and was appalled at the death of his daughter. Culhuacan declared war on the Aztec in 1323 and banished them from the land.

Defeated and pursued, the Aztec took refuge on a deserted islet on Lake Texcoco where the only vegetation was cactus and reeds. They were obliged to feed on larvae, worms, flies' eggs and whatever else they could find, and these ingredients actually became a part of the Aztec diet, even when food was abundant. It was here that, according to legend, they found a sign sent to them by their god Huitzilopochtli—an eagle perched

20

The Aztec masons created an amazing art employing only rough tools of stone, wood and cane, using emery and sand for polishing. They made frameworks of wood, stucco or bone and arranged in them tiny precious stones to form mosaics of great beauty. No one knew the origin of such a tradition, though they called this craft toltecayotl *or "belonging to the Toltec," for the Aztec supposed that it came from Tula, the mythical city of civilized man. In fact this was not the case, for it had arisen in an earlier Mesoamerican culture as we can see in this mask from Teotihuacan. The face is a mosaic of turquoise stones, and the teeth and eyes are of shell. The mask is now in the British Museum, London.*

The famous Calendar Stone, now in the Museo de Antropología in Mexico, was carved toward the end of Aztec dominion during the reign of Motecuhzoma Xocoyotzin. It was discovered in the Zócalo, or main square, of Mexico City in the 18th century. It is almost 13.2 ft. (4 m.) in diameter with the face of the sun god or Tonatiuh in the center. He rules over the present era, which is that of the fifth sun. All around him we see the symbols of the four suns or ages, which preceded this era and ended in catastrophe. Surrounding this section is a wheel with the signs of the 20 days of the month, and around this a further circle with the glyph representing the turquoise or jade, as a precious thing, out of which extend the sun's rays. The final two external circles are formed by great fire serpents, which symbolize time. This calendar was installed in the sacred precinct of Tenochtitlan so that everyone would remember the necessity of offering blood sacrifices to the gods. In this way the gods would remain forever vigorous and have the strength to go on sustaining the world, as well as the movement of the sun.

on a prickly pear with a snake in its beak. And it was also here that in 1325 Tenochtitlan, the city of the Tenoch or Tenochca, was founded. Tenochtitlan flourished and by the time the Spaniards arrived almost two centuries later had become a magnificent city. We shall discuss Tenochtitlan in the next chapter; let us just mention at the moment that it had an enormous center with 78 buildings (temples, palaces, schools, ball courts, etc.) and 108 districts in which lived a population estimated at between 150,000 and 300,000.

Thirteen years after Tenochtitlan was founded, the city of Tlatelolco was built nearby and soon became quite prosperous. The dominant state in the region was Azcapotzalco, to which both Tenochtitlan and Tlatelolco paid tribute. In 1367 the Aztec managed to persuade the son of the lord of Culhuacan, Acamapichtli, to go to Tenochtitlan as their ruler. Acamapichtli was their first *tlatoani*, or king. His son married (this time in a more conventional manner) a princess from Azcapotzalco and tribute was consequently lowered. In 1427 the lord of Azcapotzalco attempted to destroy Texcoco but was defeated by the Aztec. The following year the Triple Alliance between the cities of Tenochtitlan, Texcoco and Tlacopan was formed. It was Itzcoatl's, the *tlatoani* of Tenochtitlan's, greatest triumph. The lords of the other two cities in the federation would also be great Aztec leaders, though to a lesser degree than the lord of Tenochtitlan. From then on there began a series of military conquests that gave the Aztec absolute control over the Valley of Mexico.

In 1440, Motecuhzoma Ilhuicamina, or Motecuhzoma the Elder, was proclaimed *tlatoani*. Motecuhzoma undertook far-reaching political, social and religious reforms and created a true bureaucracy with which to govern the growing empire. He launched his armies to the southwest, taking territories in Chalco, Oaxaca and Tepeyacac. Motecuhzoma died without leaving an heir and was succeeded by his grandson, Axayacatl (1469–1481), who continued the conquest and annexed the rival sister city of Tlatelolco, thus joining the two cities and making Tenochtitlan-Tlatelolco the greatest single city in Mesoamerica. Expansion continued under Axayacatl's brother, Tizoc (1481–1486), who according to some historians was poisoned by military leaders who considered him to be inept at war. The next king was Ahuitzotl (1486–1502), whose southern campaigns conquered territory as far as the Isthmus of Tehuantepec. Ahuitzotl also began improvements to the city such as the second aqueduct and in 1487 consecrated the great temple, which had been under construction for some years, in an ostentatious ceremony in which it is claimed thousands of human sacrifices were made.

After Ahuitzotl, Motecuhzoma Xocoyotzin, or Motecuhzoma the Younger, whom the Spaniards called Moctezuma, became *tlatoani*. Like his namesake, he was also a great reformer. He strengthened the power of the *tlatoani*, giving the title a certain degree of sacrosanctity, brought the nobility to the palace and added oriental pomp to court ceremony. Motecuhzoma is said to have relegated the *tlatoanis* of Texcoco and Tlacopan to the background. He was obliged to allow the Spaniards to enter Tenochtitlan and sadly saw his city and Aztec territory occupied by intruders. He died in 1520 in an accident (the Spanish chroniclers claim he was killed by a stone thrown at Cortés and his escort). His successor, Cuauhtemoc, ruled during the period of the conquest.

The basis of Aztec power was the fighting capacity of its excellent warriors and the terror they instilled in their enemies. Apart from obtain-

Folio 36 of the Azatitlan Codex, *in the Bibliothéque Nationale in Paris, depicts the capture of Tlatelolco in 1473. The warriors of Tenochtitlan, armed with swords, climbed up the steps of the* teocalli *or main temple of the sister city and killed Mocuihuis, the king. Here we see him rolling down the steps. Axayacatl watches the scene from the majesty of his throne. What was the cause of this war? Undoubtedly it was the attempt by Tenochtitlan to gain hegemony in the valley of Mexico. As in all conquests, there are always pretexts to hide the truth. It was said that Mocuihuis had ill-treated his wife, sister to the powerful Axayacatl, who decided to wreak vengeance.*

ing prisoners, the wars also enabled them to seize the food supplies of the peoples they defeated. Great amounts of tribute paid in food and valuable objects maintained the splendor of the empire. Two-fifths of the tribute went to Tenochtitlan, another two-fifths to Texcoco and only the remaining one-fifth to Tlacopan.

The long wanderings of the Aztec

According to legend, the Aztec came from a place called Aztlán (probably in the southeast of the present-day United States), in the 12th Century A.D., following the advice of their god Huitzilopochtli. He spoke to them in the shape of a hummingbird, saying *tiui*, or "go." Then they started on their long wanderings, which lasted two centuries, until they finally arrived in the Valley of Mexico, where they were looked on with contempt by the peoples who had already settled there.

The legend, as recorded directly in the 16th century from the Aztec by the chronicler Bernardino de Sahagún, tells of how their god offered to lead them. "I will lead you and show you the way," he said to them. "And immediately, the Aztec started on their way here. And the places where the Mexicas passed through exist, are marked, and are named in the Aztec language. When the Mexicas came, they were certainly wandering aimlessly, they were to be the last. On their way they were not made welcome anywhere. Everywhere they were reproached. No one knew their faces. Everywhere they were asked, 'Who are you? Where do you come from?' Thus they could not settle anywhere; they were expelled and pursued by all. They came through Ichpuchco, through Ecatépec, through Chiquiuhtepetitlan and soon after to Chapultepec, where many settled. Realms already existed in Azcapotzalco, Coatlinchan and Culhuacan, but Mexico did not yet exist. There were only prickly-pear fields and reed-grasses where Mexico now stands."

Huitzilopochtli, god of war, to whom human sacrifices were made, is represented here on a page from the Veitia Codex. *He was probably the first god of the Aztec and the one who accompanied them on their long wanderings from the north of Mexico to the lakes. His idol was to be found in the main temple of Tenochtitlan, next to that of Tlaloc, who was the god of rain.*

Primitive dwellings

Pre-Columbian dwellings underwent a long process of development lasting 5,000 years, from their first appearance with the Chilca (Peru) in the Archaic period. In Mesoamerica and the Andean region, the house was conceived of as an urban dwelling since the Formative period, these dwelling sites developing from the beginning of the Classic period into towns and becoming more and more complex until they began to form large cities like Tenochtitlan and Cuzco. Outside these areas development was slower, with the dwelling being adapted to the economic life and geographic environment of its inhabitants—mostly farmers, hunters and gatherers. Here it is necessary to distinguish between the sedentary and the seminomadic peoples. The first group generally made their dwellings out of adobe and vegetation, while the second used mainly skins. The most rudimentary structure was a simple windbreak consisting of skins, as used by the Botocudo of Brazil, the Seri of lower California and the inhabitants of Tierra del Fuego. Somewhat more sophisticated were the awnings of the Tahuelches (figure 3), which were made with guanaco skins. More advanced was the hut or cabin, normally circular in shape with a straw roof, as found in both North America (Algonquians) and South America (El Chaco tribes). A form of dwelling perfectly adapted to nomadic life was the tepee of the Omaha (figure 4), used widely by the Indians of the Plains. This consisted of a conical tent on four posts with a flap near the top, which was drawn back to let out smoke. The igloo of the Inuit (figure 1), forming a false vault with blocks of ice, was another example of perfect adaptation to function and environment. Completely different were the earth houses covered with straw, such as those made by the Wichita of the Caddo group (figure 2), the semisubterranean dwellings of the Pawnee and the large communal cabins, called *bohios* or *caneyes*, of the Taino of the West Indies (figure 5). The lake dwellings of the peoples of Florida, Guayana and Maracaibo were erected for defensive purposes, while social organization (clan cohabitation) led to the development of great communal houses, such as those of the Iroquois, the circular dwellings with the conical palm-leaf roof of the Karib, the communal dwellings of the Vaupe tribes with their enormous roof sloping down to the ground (figure 7), the rectangular *maloca* of the Tucano and the magnificent cedar dwellings of the Haida, characterized by a large totem pole in the middle of the main facade (figure 6). Truly complex forms built by the Pueblo Indians consisted of stone and adobe rooms built one on top of the other (figure 8), accessible by a series of outside ladders.

1

2

3

4

5

6

7

8

An empire beneath the sun: the Inca

The Inca established the greatest but also the shortest-lasting state in pre-Hispanic America. They briefly controlled what is today Colombia, Ecuador, Peru, Bolivia and the northern half of Chile. The Inca civilization lasted a little more than three centuries and their empire less than one, during the century before the arrival of the Spaniards. Within their realm, which they called the world (*Tahuantinsuyu* in their language), between 15 and 30 million people lived at one of the highest elevations on earth (the second highest after the Himalayas), on a sort of long island with the Andean mountain range and the Pacific Ocean on either side and the Chilean deserts and the jungle at each end. It was like a lost world in the Andes, and it has often been said that their habitat, with its unnavigable rivers, its deserts and uncultivatable peaks, was the least suited for the sustenance of a civilization. However, the Inca had a powerful ally, and this was the cultural experience of their Andean and coast-dwelling ancestors (Chavín, Tiahuanaco, Nazca, Chimú, Huari, etc.), though they failed to take full advantage of this.

The historical origin of the Inca is even more mysterious than that of the Aztec and in the same way is told of in myths and legends reflecting the cultural process of a migratory people who spoke Quechua and burst into the Cuzco region. We also owe to this people the existence of a large number of words used in languages all over the world: alpaca, coca, condor, guano, llama, pampa, puma and quinine, to name a few. It is possible that the Inca came from an arid, mountainous region, found good, arable land when they reached Cuzco, and so decided to stay. In order to do so they had to fight and defeat the people already living there, who probably spoke Aymara. One of their legends refers to the mythicized episode of Mama Ocllo, the wife and sister of Manco Capac—the first Inca leader—which tells of this event. The arrival of the Inca in Cuzco is thought to have taken place around 1100.

With Sinchi Roca (which means hero and warrior), Manco Capac's successor, there begins a line of legendary monarchs who fortified the Inca settlement in Cuzco and made it possible to control territory extending as far as Titicaca. The Inca very probably benefited from the influence

26

The kero *or Inca wooden vase was shaped like a truncated cone and often carved in the shape of a head, either human or animal. The animal most frequently represented was the puma. These vases were sometimes decorated by carving out the designs with a pointed tool and filling in the spaces with resinous paint. On other occasions they were painted on the surface, as in this example from the Museo de Arqueología y Antropología in Lima. Here we see* the figure of a harpist in a headdress and a number of little figures that seem to dance on the neck. Few keros *from the pre-Hispanic period remain, most of those still in existence are from colonial times.*

of the Tiahuanaco and Huari or Wari cultures, which at that time were at their height. According to the Peruvian archaeologist L.G. Lumbreras, the Inca state arose as a consequence of the struggle for power between the lords of Cuzco and the neighboring Huari and Chanca. The lords of Callao in Titicaca formed alliances with the Inca because of the great economic ties existing between them, thus playing a very important role.

The history of the Inca empire begins in 1438 with Pachacutec. Pachacutec, whose name means "transformer of the world," prevailed as a general in the wars against the Chanca, a fearsome people from the northwest who invaded and at one point threatened to put an end to Cuzco and the Inca. Pachacutec was named *Sapay Inca* or "The (One) Inca," and he launched a series of military conquests to the north as far as present-day Ecuador.

In his final years he left military operations to his son, Tupac, while he gave himself up to organizing the area he ruled and began by ordering a map of the area made in clay. Pachacutec had the brilliant idea of integrating conquered peoples into the empire instead of turning their territories into occupied provinces. He did away with the tribute system and replaced it with the Inca regime of production and distribution. In order to do this successfully, it was necessary to organize each production and consumer unit, and the decimal system was devised. Pachacutec is also credited with having reformed the agricultural system by dictating the times for sowing and harvesting. In order to carry this out he had columns set up all over the empire so that the position of the sun and the stars could be accurately calculated.

Pachacutec died in 1471. Tupac Yupanqui succeeded him and became another great conqueror. He extended the southern border down to the north of Chile and on the coast succeeded in dominating the powerful Chimú kingdom, which had hastened to help its allies in Cajamarca when the Inca had attacked. In order to defeat the Chimú it was necessary to cut off the aqueducts taking drinking water to the Chimú from the mountains. Tupac Yupanqui also had rafts built in order to take possession of some of the ocean islands (possibly the Galapagos). It has been suggested that the Inca under Tupac Yupanqui reached Oceania, where a legend is told of men who came on rafts from the east. However, this great Inca failed in his attempts to tame the Amazon jungle, and in order to curb invasions from that front finally had fortifications built on the edges of the gorges that descend to the jungle.

Huayna Capac (1493–1527) suppressed some attempted revolts within the newly integrated provinces. He took Guayaquil and extended the northern frontier as far as the Ancasmayo River (southern Colombia). He also had to defend the eastern frontier from attacks by the Chiriguano, a Guaraní tribe that made an incursion into Inca territory in 1524 in search of objects made of gold and copper. It seems that among the Chiriguano there was a white man called Alejo García, a survivor of the shipwrecked Solís expedition to the Plata River. The invasion of the European *conquistadores* had begun.

Huayna Capac is a figure enshrouded in mystery. For some still unknown reason, he left Cuzco and had a great palace built in Tomebamba (Cuenca, in Ecuador), where he lived out the last years of his life surrounded by his 200 wives. It is claimed that his reason for leaving was a princess from Quito, but this is a rather facile expla-

28

One of the most impressive cities of the Inca domain was Machu Picchu, which served as the last refuge for the Inca Manco after the Spanish conquest and was not discovered until 1912. It is situated at 8,250 ft. (2,500 m.) above sea level, on top of a ridge in the Andes mountains, facing in the direction of the Atlantic. It is, in fact, a huge fortified city, dominated by its ceremonial Great Square. On its eastern side are numerous dwellings, grouped together and built all

on the same plan, with a central patio and four or five rooms around it. To the west of the Great Square are the so-called Casa de la Ñusta, the fortified military tower and the Temple of the Three Windows. To the northwest of the city itself is the main temple. Further on is the Intihuatana or "the place where the sun moors." Machu Picchu has been the subject of a number of careful archaeological reconstructions, as can be seen from these photo-

graphs, taken half a century apart. The one on the left was taken by Martin Chambi in 1935 and shows the city as it was found 23 years before. The photograph on the right was taken in February 1989.

nation, since he could easily have had her brought to the capital. His son Atahualpa also lived in Tomebamba, while Atahualpa's brother, Huascar, who was heir to the throne, stayed in Cuzco. Huascar had the support of the priesthood and Atahualpa that of the generals. It is possible that Huayna Capac left the capital because of friction between the civil and religious powers over how the empire should be organized. Huayna Capac's aim must certainly have been the decentralization of Cuzco. According to certain accounts he died suddenly as he was opening a box full of black nocturnal moths and butterflies, while according to others he died from an unknown illness that was sweeping the country from the coast to the interior, killing nobles and commoners alike; the Spanish *conquistadores* had brought smallpox to the continent.

Huascar was proclaimed Inca in Peru and invested by the priests with all the Inca's powers, but Atahualpa rose up against him. A terrible civil war raged between 1528 and 1532, when Atahualpa finally defeated his brother. Atahualpa should then have marched swiftly on Cuzco to be proclaimed Inca but showed no interest in doing so, which again would seem to confirm the existence of friction between the civil and religious powers. In 1532 he set off from Quito for the south to fight invaders who wore red wool on their faces and were causing trouble within the realm. He was in no particular hurry to stop them, however, since he had arranged a meeting with them in a city where he had decided to go to take thermal baths. The name of the city was Cajamarca, and it was here that the Inca empire—an empire that had lasted 94 years, from the coronation of Pachacutec in 1438 until the Cajamarca disaster in 1532—was to fall.

The Inca had no tradition in goldsmithing and so resorted to bringing skilled Chimú artisans to Cuzco to set up a school. The result is that Inca goldsmithing is closely connected to that of the coastal tradition, being, in fact, hardly distinguishable from it. Such is the case of this Venus, in the Frías style, now in the Brüning Collection in Lima. Here we see the general features of a head, enormous in proportion to the body, with an inexpressive face. The arms are extended and the feet very solid, to serve as a good base for the piece to rest on.

Also in the Chimú goldsmithing tradition are these two gold and silver figurines of females from the Museo de la Universidad in Cuzco. The figure on the left weighs 524 grams and is of gold; the one on the right weighs 440 grams and is of silver. The chroniclers frequently spoke of Inca representations of Inti, the sun, and Quilla, the moon, in the temples, but these were melted down and in any case were not common. It is difficult to understand why deities such as the gods of thunder, lightning, the earth or even the moon never accompanied the bodies of important persons, as in other cultures. It may be that there was an enormous gap separating the world of religious belief and the world of the dead. What is more common is to find human figures such as these on funeral urns: naked women with pointed breasts, long hair, stylized faces and crude bodies resting heavily on thick legs.

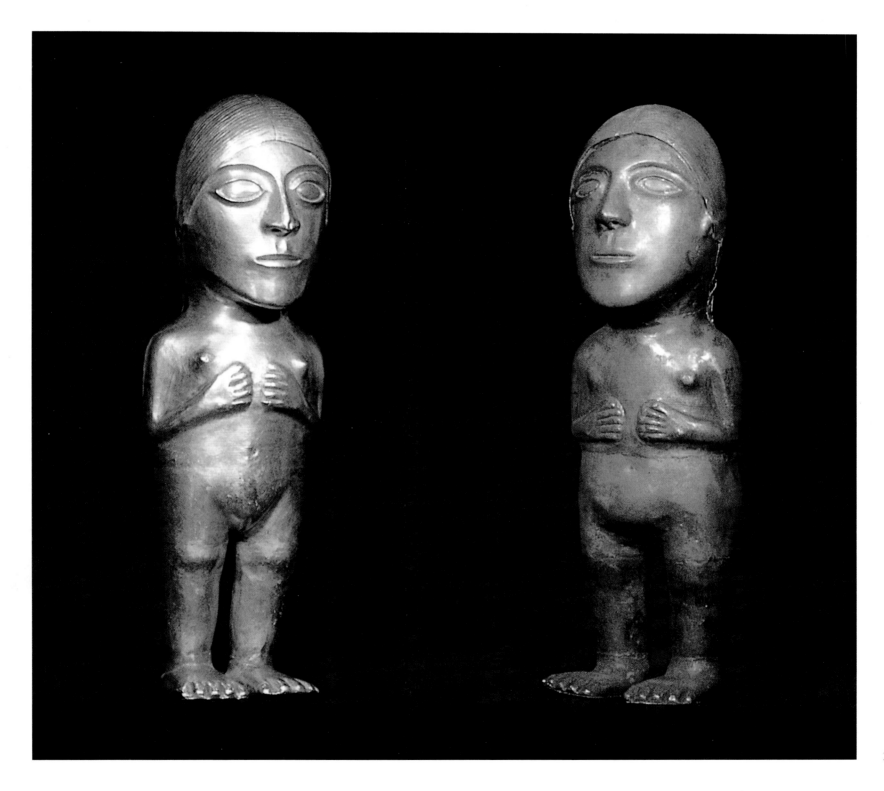

The other peoples

In the gigantic mosaic surrounding the high cultures, men had adapted extraordinarily well to their environment. The peoples clung to their age-old methods of survival through inertia and a general reluctance to try new methods. Thus they continued to be hunters, gatherers, fishers and farmers—ways of life that went went back thousands of years. Extensive farming had been widespread for almost 3,000 years (intensive farming was only recently practiced, and only in areas where water was plentiful, the Spaniards later settling there). Gathering had been the standard way of life for 9,000 years, and the Asiatic immigrants had lived on subsistence hunting 13,000 years earlier. In the greater part of America the people lived on what nature had to offer,

and so hunters, fishers and gatherers spent their whole lives in search of their daily nourishment; thus there was little time for spiritual pursuits, for creativity or reflection. The inability to monitor time, to produce literature or to advance technologically was nonetheless compensated by their communion with nature—a virgin nature that always provided Man with enough, though no more than enough, to survive. Many of the peoples had no words for concepts such as palace, street, city or wheel; on the other hand, they had 40 or 50 words to distinguish between different types of trees, flowers, ferns and butterflies.

To the Eskimo the hunt meant life or death. The *Inuit* or "men," as they called themselves, did not realize that on the earth—or, rather, on the

ice—other peoples existed, since they did not see them. Neither did they hunt all the year round. The main hunting season began when the days started to grow shorter (from August 21) and the first ice began to form. But the special hunt took place when the sun disappeared altogether (October 21) and the great darkness, which would last for four months (until February 21), arrived. The big hunt took place by moonlight, when, on the newly formed ice, they hunted walrus, white whale and narwhal. In order to catch seals, they had to wait until the ice was packed. Then the Inuit spread out over the ice wearing silent bearskin footwear, in search of the holes through which the seals came up to breathe. There they listened and waited. When the seal appeared,

32

Hunting was normally a group activity, with leaders and group members having specific tasks to carry out during the hunt. By the end of the 15th century it was virtually impossible to find tribes that hunted to the exclusion of all else. The most common method was that of alternating hunting with other activities, such as gathering, fishing and even farming. In this 1564 print by Jacques le Moyne, we see natives of Florida hunting gigantic caymans. The system they *used was first to immobilize the cayman by placing large sticks between the jaws and turning it over onto its back, after which it was killed with various types of weapons, such as the arrow, the lance and the club.*

The great variety of the Amerindian races came as a surprise to Europeans. In these three prints from the work Prints of American Life and Peoples *from the Museo Naval in Madrid, we see a latter-day idealization of this diversity, represented here with an Indian from Patagonia on the left, an Amazon woman in the middle and a Marañón Indian on the right. Like the Marañón River Indian, the Amazon woman carries an elegant bow with a double curve, which looks nothing like those of almost two meters in length used in Amazonia. The Patagonian Indian is holding a* boleadoras *in his right hand and wearing a European-style suit and cape.*

they would throw their harpoons. The seal would disappear under the ice and when it came back up to breathe, they would finish it off with clubs. If the ice was too thick, another *maupok* had to be used. A hunter would sit on a three-legged stool by a hole he believed to be a breathing hole and wait patiently, hour after hour, without making the slightest sound. Two, five or ten hours later the seal would appear and be killed using the same technique.

When the winter weather worsened an Inuit would stop hunting and live on his food stores. It was the time for social activity. He would make visits, attend great banquets, trade stories, make jokes and dance to the music of an instrument made with a seal intestine stretched over a ring of bone. The Inuit had unusual customs, such as that of the guest being able and even being obliged to sleep with the wife of the owner of the house. If the guest had brought a woman with him, then so much the better, and wives would be exchanged.

These holidays ended on February 21, when the lost sun reappeared. The men went to the sea to hunt walrus and perhaps a bear or two. From April 21, there was no night, and the sun shone continuously for four months. The seals came out to warm themselves in the sun, and an Inuit hunted them using the *utok* method, sliding along on the ice on his belly, in imitation of a seal, waving his arms about like flippers and his legs as if they were the tail. At times he would even scratch the ice with a seal flipper, making a sound to reassure the seal, until it came close enough for him to harpoon it. Toward the end of May each Inuit would go back to the interior, where he would catch razorbill in nets made with tendons tied to sticks. These birds were kept in sealskin bags filled with oil and were eaten—bones, feathers and all—once they had decomposed. When the summer came to an end, the Inuit hunted caribou with bows and arrows and then returned to the coast to begin the yearly cycle once again.

South of the Inuit lived the Algonquians, who were great reindeer hunters. They captured the migrating reindeer by using two converging fences made of stones and stakes. The women and children drove the reindeer toward a watery region, where the men lay in wait in their kayaks for the kill. No part of the reindeer was wasted. The meat was eaten, the skin used to make dwellings and clothing, the fat for cooking and to light the dwellings and the bones for making tools. The Dene were also reindeer hunters, and they followed tracks in the coniferous forests wearing snowshoes shaped like rackets to stop them from sinking into the deep snow. They also hunted moose and deer. It was the Dene who invented the sledge, with two boards raised at the front, enabling them to carry loads in comfort.

Farther to the south lived the Iroquois, split up into innumerable tribes, living mainly to the east of the Great Lakes. Although they were farmers they also hunted deer with bows and arrows and even with blowpipes—which were unusual in North America and more typical of the Amazon region.

The Shoshoni, who lived in the Great Basin, were great deer hunters. Although primarily gatherers, they also caught all kinds of animals, such as the rabbit, whose skin they used to make clothing. They caught deer by dressing up in

33

The Indians of the Amazon Basin obtained a high-protein diet from river-fishing. This balanced well with agricultural produce, which in turn was rich in carbohydrates and was the result of adaptation to the consumption of yucca. This print, from Twelve Views of the Interior of Guayana by Charles Bentley (1840), shows fishing with bows and arrows exactly as it was carried out at the end of the 15th century. The Indians used special featherless arrows made of cane (often of bamboo), with a slot in the base for fitting over the string; the tip was of bone or hardwood, sometimes barbed, and the Indian fired the arrow from his canoe or from strategic points along the river. The Indian's skill in following the fish and managing to hit it was inherited from a culture and technique acquired over thousands of years.

deerskins and horns, which enabled them to come close enough to their prey to shoot it with arrows. Curiously, the same method was used by the Indians living in Florida.

The great hunting area in North America has always been the prairies between the Mississippi River and the Rocky Mountains, where enormous herds of bison drew hunters from the Rockies and the northern woods. Contrary to books and films on how the American West was won,

there were not always hunting tribes, warriors and nomads living on the prairies. At the end of the 15th century the prairies were, in fact, virtually uninhabited. On some strips of land stretching westward from the Missouri there lived peaceful farmers, and in what is now the state of Kansas, farmers such as the Wichita tribe of the Caddo had settled. Two of their villages, Quivira and Harahey, were visited by Francisco Coronado on his quest for the mythical city of *El*

Dorado. Coronado also met bison hunters in Arkansas in 1541, one group being the Querecho, who possibly came from the Rockies and then only to hunt. The lack of any native population was the reason the Spaniards showed so little interest in settling the area.

Hunting was equally important in South America. In fact all the extensive farmers and gatherers living east of the Andes, from the Gulf of Maracaibo to El Chaco, also hunted, since it was extremely difficult to survive on one staple (in this area, the yucca). The South American Indians, like the North American tribes, hunted with traps, arrows, dart throwers, and two weapons that were very typical of the hemisphere, the *boleadoras* (ropes tied together with balls at the end) and the blowpipe.

Many peoples, such as the Witoto of the Amazon region, used the blowpipe, made of two pieces of American palm, hollowed and fit to-gether. The wood was covered with strips of bark and a mouthpiece fixed to one end. The hole was then polished using a piece of string first soaked in gum and then rolled in sand. The blowpipe's companion was the dart, made from the back of a palm leaf. A small ball of vegetable wool was placed behind the dart to give it thrust. The tip of the dart was extremely fine and a small notch was made in it so that it would splinter easily on entering the body of the animal. The final, essen-tial addition to the blowpipe was the curare poi-son with which the tip of the dart was smeared, made from the sap of the *strychnos toxifera* plant, mixed with ants and with poisons from other creatures. On entering the bloodstream it caused death instantly by cardiac arrest.

Hunting with darts was silent and did not alert the animals. The din of the monkeys and birds in the jungle would go on while one by one the prey would drop from the branches to the accompani-

35

This print, also by Bentley, of a hunting party of Guayana Indians is an idyllic view of what in all reality was one of the Amerindian's most difficult tasks—hunting in the jungle. The native hunts in a world of deep shadow and darkness, hardly able to see the sky for the trees. Surrounded by creatures that he cannot see but can hear, he searches for tracks over marshy ground covered with dead leaves. The blowpipe, as held by one of the Indians *in the print, is the best companion for hunting in silence, as it does not startle the prey.*

ment of the sound of a slight rush of air made by the native with his blowpipe as he crouched among the bushes. The prey was not disfigured and did not lose blood, making it possible to use the skins or feathers afterward. The use of curare poison is attributed to the Caribbean peoples of Guayana in relatively modern, though naturally pre-Columbian, times. The peoples of the West Indies did not use this method, nor was it used by the peoples of southeastern Amazonia.

In the southern region of South America lived the specialized hunters such as the Patagone and the Ona. The Patagone hunted the *ñandu* or American ostrich by dressing up in ostrich skins, as the Shoshoni would use deerskins. In order to protect their feet, they wore great bags made of hide, which puzzled the Spaniards when they first saw the footprints; it was the Spaniards who gave them the name *Patagones*: big feet. They lured the guanaco (a type of llama) by using live does

as bait. They also used beaters to drive the guanaco into narrow passes and rings of fire. They handled the *boleadoras* with great skill, winding them round the animal's legs to bring it down and then killing it with spears. The Ona lived by hunting guanaco, which they killed with arrows. The hunters camouflaged themselves, covering their bodies with dark paint in spring and light in winter in order to get as close to the animal as possible. They did not use weapons to hunt small

A. Yndio Yumbo de Maynas con su Carga.
B. Árbol de Pitahayas y su Fruto.
C. Árbol del Obo, y su Fruto.
D. Árbol del Mamey con su Fruta entera, y abierta
E. Pájaro Predicador.
F. Loro.
G. Un Monito Comiendo Guineo.
H. Calabazos y Frutas, dentro de la Carga.

36

This scene, painted in 1783 by Vicente Alban, can be seen in the Museo de América in Madrid. It shows a Yumbo Indian carrying cultivated fruit. Fortunately, the influence of the Spanish colonizers is minimal, seen only in the huge machete. In pre-Hispanic fashion the Indian is carrying a fiber basket that contains indigenous foodstuffs, such as fruits from the agave and the obo, as well as pumpkins. Although its name probably comes from the Antilles, the agave

belongs to the cactus family and was found in both cultivated and wild forms in South America at the time when the first Spaniards arrived. Obo is a Taino word and in the Antilles is called jobo. It's a fruit of the genus Spondias and was cultivated all over tropical America. It is a delicacy to the tapir and was therefore used for fattening up pigs. The Yumbo were capable farmers who lived west of what is today the Ecuadorian province of Pichincha. Eth-

nically, they were a subgroup of the Quitu. Sadly, they died out some centuries ago, and nowadays the word Yumbo is used to describe the Indians of the plains.

game, catching *turones* (a type of field mouse), for example, by digging them out of their dens.

In eastern Brazil the Ge people hunted tapir and wild boar with their enormous spears, as well as many other types of animal using arrows made of different kinds of wood, the arrow chosen according to the prey. To catch birds they used arrows with a cross affixed to the head to prevent the arrow passing through the body and destroying the bird.

In the region around Peru, birds were hunted with slings, as may be seen in some pictures from the Azca culture. In the mountains birds were caught with *boleadoras* or with nets held between two sticks. Deer-hunting methods are illustrated on Mochica pottery. The deer was driven into a net and killed with clubs or arrows.

Pre-Columbian cattle-raising was, on the other hand, extremely limited. Apart from the llama and the alpaca, the only domesticated animals were the dog, the turkey or Mesoamerican *guajolete*, and the *curí* or guinea pig. Apparently there were two types of dog, one hairless and another that did not bark. Mesoamericans, especially the Aztec, ate the meat of the dog, although this was not the case in Peru, except among the Huanaca. In the Andean region dogs were used as bedwarmers, for hunting and for sacrifice.

The gatherer peoples inhabited more territory in pre-Columbian America than any other group. Actually, no group lived solely from gathering wild fruit and berries, since the gatherers were usually also fishers or hunters and very often both at the same time. Some were even farmers, as in the case of the Mojave, the Hopi and the Iroquois peoples. During the long hunting seasons the Tunica lived off wild plants such as the plum-date (persimmon) instead of corn, and the Krik off sarsaparilla roots (smilax). In the lower Mississippi region the Natchez and the Chitimacha peoples gathered grassy seeds and water lily seeds, as did the Ojibwa or Klamath. The great gatherer area extended along the North American Pacific coast from the Aleutians to California, though concentrated along the southern strip. There were also many gatherer peoples in Brazil, in El Chaco, on the South American Pacific coast and on the plains of the southern hemisphere.

The gatherers, who had inherited a feeding tradition dating from the beginning of the Recent period (7,000 years ago), had a very limited use of pottery. Pottery did not appear on the American continent until 3000 B.C., and until then the gatherers normally used wickerwork baskets. Such was the case of the Californian Indians, who sifted and toasted their food in utensils made of fiber, and made their baskets and plates of the same material. For cooking they used the hot-stone technique (also used in eastern Brazil), typical of prepottery cultures, where food is placed in an impermeable basket in water over hot stones. Bread was made in the ashes of the fire or on hot stone slabs. The basic food of the Californians consisted of acorns, chestnuts, pine seeds, berries, grass seeds, roots and tubers. Sweet substances were extracted from the sap of the saccharine pine. Seeds were gathered with a wickerwork ladle and roots with a pointed stick weighted with a stone ring. The food gathered was placed in large baskets or in containers standing on wooden frames. It was then washed in water to extract bitter-tasting substances and ground into meal with stone mortars.

The Shoshoni, whom we've seen were hunters, were also great gatherers. Their basic diet was made up of gathered foods, and they knew of more than one hundred species of seeds, roots and fruits. Roots were dug with a pointed stick and seeds were gathered with a fan-shaped striking tool. Roots and seeds were put straight into large baskets. With the peanut, they made a kind of paste that was one of their favorite foods. Apart from fruit, berries and roots they also ate insects. They held communal grasshopper hunts in which grasshoppers were enclosed in a circle and driven to a hollow ten yards wide and one yard deep, where they were caught and then roasted. Ants were a real treat in March, when they were coming out of the larva stage. The women used shell-shaped sifting baskets, in which they skillfully shook the nests to remove all the sand and rubbish, leaving the ants on the bottom. The ants were then roasted and ground on stones and made into a kind of edible paste.

The great gatherers in South America lived in the eastern region of Brazil and in El Chaco. In

37

The pre-ceramics character of the agricultural period is evident throughout America in the prevalent use of baskets, plates and containers made of vegetable fiber. This 18th-century picture in the Museo de América in Madrid shows the kind of basket used by native women to carry vegetable produce.

Brazil the Kaingang and Guayaki peoples gathered araucaria almonds, the nuts and round heads of the palm, pikí and saucaya fruits, and all kinds of tubers. Their favorite food was the honeycomb of hornets' nests, found in tree trunks. The Indians climbed the trees with great skill, using climbing belts made of bark. Those who lived in the Gran Chaco ate the pith of the caranday palm (*Copernicia*), the fruit of the *Acacia* and the *chañar* bush (*Gourliea*) and also made an intoxicating drink from the fruit of the carob tree (*Prosopis*).

The gatherers were normally seminomadic peoples who covered small areas in which they were sure of finding food. They formed groups of no more than 50 and their culture centered around the female, sometimes as a matriarchy with the children bearing the mother's name or the matrimonial residence being in or near the house of the woman's parents.

Just as the gatherers did not live exclusively from gathering, no pre-Columbian people lived exclusively from fishing. Fishing was practiced in combination with gathering, hunting and agriculture. Most fishermen lived on the coast, taking

advantage of the Kuro Shivo current in North America and the Humboldt current in South America.

The first fishermen had settled on the western North American coasts (from latitude 52° N to 54° N) and mainly on the Carlota Islands. Thanks to the Kuro Shivo current, the coasts were rich in marine mammals such as dolphins, seals, sea lions, sea otters and whales, as well as an enormous variety of fish, such as halibut, cod and salmon. Before embarking on a hunt, the Haida had to purify themselves for a whole lunar month. Purification consisted of sexual abstinence, not drinking water, ritual fasting, bathing and the taking of certain medicines. They hunted in shallow waters or on the rocky shores, approaching their prey in their canoes, which were hidden behind screens. They surrounded the animal until it was enclosed in a narrow circle and then attacked it with arrows or harpoons. The Haida had seven different types of canoe, each one used for a specific type of work.

The Haida caught halibut on hooks and dragged them to the shore, where they killed them with clubs. Their main food was salmon,

which they caught in dragnets placed in stream mouths or with darts and harpoons used in waterfalls. They also placed in the rivers a type of palisade with openings, which led the fish into conical traps. If the water was shallow, they built two sluices positioned close together. The salmon were able to jump the first but not the second. During the salmon season all the Haida left their villages and went to temporary camps on the riverbanks. It was there that they held their enormous feasts. They roasted the fresh salmon on spits or boiled them in wooden containers or impermeable wicker bags using the hot-stone technique. When they had eaten heartily, they prepared the food surplus for the winter.

River fishing was practiced in the great American rivers. In Amazonia, poison, as well as arrows and traps, was used in fishing. The poison was obtained from the roots of certain bushes that grew in the jungle; baskets containing the poison were placed in backwaters, and as the poison became diluted in the water, the fish died and

During the brief summer in the arctic region, the Inuit followed the seal and the walrus out to the open sea in his kayac. The Inuit hunter in his waterproof sealskin suit, as one with his sealskin boat, is typical of the northernmost part of America. He appears in this picture from Manners and Customs of the Peoples (Paris, 1814), with his double set of oars (one double-bladed), his harpoons resting on his boat, while ahead nets are being dried. Fishing in the kayac was not particularly common, however, for it was during the summer months that the Inuit spent his time on dry land, hunting caribou.

Salmon fishing was common in all of North America. In this picture, taken from the History of America *by Belloc (1844), Indians from Virginia bake a salmon (one of them is carrying a basket full of fish) in the foreground, while depicted behind them are others catching the salmon using sluices. On the Pacific Coast and especially in the Colombia River region, the Indians were experts. They caught the salmon in the spawning season, held enormous feasts and then dried the surplus fish in the sun for food in the winter.*

floated up to the surface, where they were easily caught. Once dead the fish were not poisonous to Man.

Together with Mesopotamia, Egypt, and the Indo and Hoang Ho valleys, the Americas were the cradle of the domestication of edible plants and one of the greatest agricultural areas. The Amerindian managed to domesticate 120 species of plants, and in the Andean region alone between 31 and 70 edible plants were known. Agricultural areas covered a relatively small part of the continent compared with hunting and gathering areas, but within that area innumerable plants for food and other uses were grown successfully.

The first instance of plant domestication was in the Mexican region around 7000 B.C., becoming particularly significant 2,000 years later when maize—the first American plant equivalent to wheat or rice in the Near and Far East—was grown. Other major plants were the *frijol* or kidney bean (domesticated around 4000 B.C.), the pumpkin and the amaranth. At around the same

time, various types of potato or *papa* were domesticated in the Peru area. Also domesticated were the sweet potato (2000 B.C.), the pumpkin (there are varieties typical of South America and very different from the North American varieties), the *frijol* and canna (2300 B.C.). In the northeast of South America and the Caribbean area, yucca or manioc was grown. There were two varieties of yucca, the sweet (*manihot utilissima*) and the bitter or hot (*manihot esculenta*). The hot variety was eaten mainly in western Brazil, the area covering Colombia and Venezuela, and in the West Indies, where it had probably been taken by the Arawak peoples (Taino).

Agriculture was practiced in its two forms—extensive and intensive. In extensive farming, virtually no advantage was taken of rainwater and the only way of producing more was to increase the cultivated surface area. This was done through clearing land by felling trees and burning vegetation, thus leaving the land ready for cultivation. This system soon exhausted the soil, making it essential to let the land lie fallow for some years while other plots were producing. This led to the people dispersing over greater areas, since

For the European, American gatherers evoked an idea of life in a Heaven on Earth in which all that was necessary for survival was taken from the trees. This picture from The Natural and Moral History of the Antilles of America, *published in Rotterdam in 1658, is a nostalgic view of such an idyllic life. We see an Indian picking fruit from a tree (perhaps a mango) in the company of another, who, adorned with flowers, holds an enormous double-curved bow and carries his quiver on his back.*

four families, for example, would need between 15 and 20 plots to exist on. Most farming was carried out using extensive farming methods in the great southeastern arc of North America (from the south of the Labrador Peninsula to Texas), all of the West Indies, Venezuela, eastern Colombia, the Guayanas and most of Brazil. Here many varieties of edible plants, though mainly maize in North America and yucca in the Caribbean and South America, were grown.

In intensive farming, on the other hand, various methods (irrigation, terracing, fertilizing and others) were used to increase yield per surface area. Intensive farming was probably practiced from around 2,000 years ago and particularly by the Classic cultures, from whom the high Aztec and Inca cultures inherited their techniques. Intensive farming outside the high cultures area was practiced by the Muisca, a Chibcha-speaking people living in the high plateaus on the eastern Andean range in what today is Colombia. The Muisca used terracing in the mountains to increase the area of arable land, this being neces-

sary as part of their territory was still flooded. The soil was good, since it was made up of the sediment of ancient lakes. They grew maize, papa, yucca, arracacha, quinoa, sweet potato, tomato, chili and pumpkin. On the lower levels of the mountains, which they were losing to the attacks of Karib-speaking peoples (mainly the Panche), they grew cotton and many varieties of fruit. The enormous variety of *papas* that grew within these territories has led some prehistorians to believe that the *papa* was actually domesticated in that area, although the general consensus of opinion is that it came from Peru. Agricultural work was performed mainly by the women, who, it was believed, had the ability to transmit fertility into the soil. This belief also enabled the men to engage in other activities, such as hunting and war.

Labourage, Tentes & Navires des Floridains.

40

This print by Jacques le Moyne (1564) depicts the Florida Indians' way of planting. This was done using the same method as that used by countless other Indian peoples. The earth was broken up with an unusual type of hoe, and the women came behind, some making holes with a drilling stick and others dropping seeds into the holes. It was necessary for the woman to do the actual planting, as it was believed that she was fertile, whereas the man was not.

One of the greatest fishing peoples in Mesoamerica was the Tarascan, whom the Aztec called michuaque or fishermen. They lived in what is now the state of Michoacan, in Mexico. Although this people would seem to be pre-Aztec, there is a tradition that they came from the north and accompanied the Aztec until both groups reached Lake Patzcuara, where the Tarascans decided to settle, while the Aztec continued on their journey. The Tarascans were also excellent farmers. This illustration, from the Tudela Codex in the Museo de América in Madrid, shows a Tarascan woman in a long tunic, carrying on her head a bowl full of the fruits of the earth.

Bread, love
and sex

A deep respect for food is evident here in the Moche
vessel at left, where the Andean artist has made full
use of the shape of the peanut to model a figure of a
quena *player whose clothing imitates the wrinkles of
the peanut's shell. Above, from the* Veitia Codex, *is
the complement to food—two men drinking* pulche.

If it doesn't kill you, it won't hurt you

The differences among the types of American cultures discussed in the previous chapter were enormous. It is interesting to see how much three aspects of these cultures—food, sex and love—contrasted with respective practices in Europe in 1492.

There is no such thing as "Amerindian cooking," in the same way that there is no such thing as "European" or "African cooking." It is difficult, however, to find anywhere in the world where food native to the Americas, including the potato, maize, the tomato, the kidney bean and cacao, is not used. Though ways of preparation may differ, it can be said that American food has been decisive in the feeding of modern man. In addition, the Amerindian peoples contributed remarkable advances to the preservation of food.

What did the Amerindians eat in 1492? Well, absolutely anything that would not kill them. From ants to snakes, from smoked salmon to chocolate, turkey, *bagre* (a species of fish) and monkey. All living creatures on the face of the earth, in the seas and in the skies were candidates for ingestion. Thus the Amerindian's diet was much more varied than that of the European living at the same time. The only restrictions were those associated with religion and magic, taboos

forbidding the eating of certain kinds of beasts, such as those considered to be ancestors or cultural heroes. Sometimes the meat of these creatures was exquisite, as was the case of the deer and the tapir, though usually it was the meat of ferocious (the jaguar in Amazonia, the coyote with the Shoshoni) or repulsive animals (snakes) that was forbidden.

It would not be possible to give a complete list of the animals and plants eaten in America, as there were so many, but that is not our aim in any case. (The reader can refer to the previous chapter. Most of those items—those eaten by the gatherers in particular—are not eaten now.) The main products of American farming and cattle raising were incorporated into the diet of the high culture peoples, who took the greatest advantage of past experience. Analysis of the eating habits of these cultures will give us a good idea of what was eaten in general.

44

Every kind of animal, except those that were taboo, was eaten by the inhabitants of the jungle. In this illustration from The Journey to Brazil of Prince Maximillian von Wied-Neuwied, *published in 1860, we see Puri Indians in a rude hut made with palm leaves in the form of a wind-break. The man is resting in a hammock while the woman roasts a small monkey.*

The best example of an omniverous diet is found in the food of the Indians of the subarctic regions, who hunted, fished and gathered. One such example is the Chippewa people of North America. Here we see them at a ceremonial meal, sitting next to a funeral mound containing the body of a dead relative. The illustration is from the First Annual Report of the Office of American Ethnology, Washington, D.C., *published in 1881.*

The Aztec diet was based on corn, the kidney bean, the amaranth and lime-leaved sage. These four items appear in the *Mendoza Codex* as tribute imposed annually on the subject cities. There were several types of maize, varying according to its place of origin. Kidney beans were either black or lilac-colored, large or small, the pods being eaten when tender. Vegetables included pumpkin, *chayote* (a pear-shaped fruit with a large stone), bottle gourd, *quelite*, *quintonile*, mallow and *chichatotl* Other foods were nopal, *cruceta*, *huanzontle* (a variety of *quelite*), maize fungus, sweet potato and *papa*, besides a large number of fruits, among which were sapota fruit (there were many varieties), mamey, custard apple and sousop. Three major crops were the tomato, *ají* or chili pepper and cacao. The first two flavored any food, however insipid it might be. There were many varieties of tomato, including the red tomato or *jitomate* and the green tomato, which had rind. The *ají* or chili pepper, such as the highland type, the *guajillo*, the yellow variety, the *chilhuacle*, and the *piquín*, the *morita* and the *cascabel*, all of which the Amerindians used, are still used today. The chili pepper was one of the first plants to be domesticated in Mesoamerica. It is depicted in a glyph in Monte Albán (on the Mexican Atlantic coast), dating back to before the year 200 A.D. The Aztec demanded chili peppers as tribute and for this reason the chili pepper often appears in the codices. Cacao and vanilla both came from the warmer regions.

Meat came from the two domesticated animals, the turkey and the dog, and also from a variety of game—deer, rabbit, hare, peccary and various types of fowl such as pheasant, *corneja* (a type of crow), turtledove and duck.

From their far-off days as gatherers the Aztec still used some types of wild plants, as well as ants, maguey worms and snails. As an isolated lake people, they began eating a large number of aquatic creatures such as fish, frogs, frogspawn, water snakes, shrimps, water flies (the eggs, too), larvae and white worms. As they spread out over the region they were able to include sea fish, turtle, oysters and crabs in their diet.

Maya food was similar to Aztec except in those foods dating back to the gathering days.

45

Hunting was, above all, a shared experience, with groups of hunters entering the jungle for several days at a time. The members of the group established firm ties with each other through having to share everything. This illustration, from Twelve Views of the Interior of Guayana, *by Charles Bentley, published in 1840, shows these hunters at a makeshift camp in the jungle.*

Intensive agriculture left its indelible mark on the Andes, which were terraced with cultivated platforms so as to best take advantage of the soil and irrigation. The phenomenon is evident along all of the South American cordillera (mountain range) from Colombia to Chile, especially near volcanic terrain, where crop yield was higher. In this photograph we see terraces near Pisac in Peru, in the valley of the

Upper Urubamba. Here the Indians performed a great work of engineering in order to take advantage of the slopes near one of the great Inca fortresses.

The most important food was maize, which according to their creation myths formed part of the flesh of man. They had a passion for cacao, and it was cultivated throughout their territory, including the most prized variety—*xononusco*. It was so exquisite that it was later reserved for the Spanish royal table. The Maya also had a special taste for honey. They were expert beekeepers and made hives from straw or used calabashes or even cooking pots, often keeping them near their houses. They also liked game, and it is believed there were professional hunters employed to supply the communities with food. In the *Trocortesian Codex* in Madrid, a trap for deer and mountain pigs is depicted. The trap is a slip noose tied to a bent-over branch. A box for catching armadillos is also seen.

The variety of food in the Inca empire was enormous though the diet was based primarily on tubers (*papa, ulluca, mashua* and *oca oxalis*), which were grown in the highlands. *Papas* were held in such high esteem in the Peru region that they appear on Chimú and Mochica vessels, where at times they have been given human form—the eyes like those of a human being, the wrinkles like noses and the cracks like mouths. It is possible that they were transported from the mountains to the coast. Quinoa or Peruvian rice, which grew in the underbrush, was eaten with the potatoes, thus adding mineral salts to the dish. Quinoa is 15% protein and its ashes make lime, used today for chewing with coca. The Inca grew maize on the sides of valleys and areas protected from wind and frost. They appreciated maize for its high energy value and because it was easy to care for. Proof of their high esteem for maize is the fact that maize flour was given to the gods as a valuable offering.

A great many foods such as the pumpkin, the broad bean, the chili pepper, the avocado pear, fruits and especially the kidney bean (of which there was a great variety) also came from the coast. Kidney beans are depicted so often on Mochica pottery that it has even been suggested that they were used in a kind of writing. Many other plants and bulbs were eaten, especially the *tumbo* (a type of passionflower depicted on vessels of the Paracas Necropolis style), sweet yucca, the pineapple, the tomato (used less by the

The Inca were masters at terracing mountains. They usually did this in the form of stairways leading up to their cities. The terraces were constructed by gangs of workers, and the cost was frequently covered by the state, which supplied sustenance to the laborers. The mountains were cut out into small terraces held in place by stone walls, the height of which was determined by the inclination of the terrain. A base of refuse was usually placed on the terrace and then covered with soil and fertilizer. It has often been said that arable land was so important to the Inca that they could not conceive of building cities on it.

The range of Mexican edible plants was extremely wide and of great nutritional value. As well as corn, the Indians ate black beans, pumpkin, various types of vegetable (jitomate, miltomate, huahzongli, epazote), seeds (wild amaranth, lime-leaved sage), roots and pulses (sweet potato, jicama) and an enormous variety of fruits (avocado, cherimoyer, mammee, sapodilla, capulin, Mexican sloe, guava, nanche, guamúchil, etc.). Food was seasoned with achiote or vanilla, and most of all with guacamole, which gave the food a very particular taste. Cacao often figured in the Aztec diet and was an indispensable drink at the tables of the rich. This illustration from the Tudela Codex in the Museo de América in Madrid shows some of the edible plants found in the Aztec world.

Fish from the waters of Lakes Tenochtitlan and Tlatelolco was another important source of nourishment for the Aztec, to the extent that fishing was even a full-time profession. In the Florentine Codex in the Biblioteca Lorenziana in Florence, these fishermen work from their canoes in the neighborhood of the Mexican capital. As the lake water was salty, they had to take drinking water with them.

98.

Aztec than the other peoples) and the peanut, which is also given human form on Mochica vessels.

Although the Inca were virtually the only cattle-raisers in South America, meat was not a common ingredient in the Andean diet. The llama was too valuable to be killed, as it was used as a beast of burden and produced wool and dung—a good source of fuel in a region of desolate, arid high mountains, where vegetation was extremely sparse. They did, however, eat the meat of the guanaco and the vicuna, species they had been unable to domesticate. The prey was surrounded by hundreds of beaters and, once caught, shorn with flint or obsidian shears. A certain number of females were then released together with a small number of males; the rest were killed and great feasts held. Any food left over was cut into strips, salted and dried in the sun. The Inca also ate curí

187.

48

Maize was the staple food of the Aztec and was eaten every day in the form of tortilla, atole and tomal. The Mendoza Codex tells of the portions of tortilla—half, one, one and a half or two—which the Aztec ate according to his age. Atole was usually eaten at breakfast time, seasoned with chili or honey. The illustration is from the Florentine Codex.

At certain times of the year a great many birds nested on the lakes near Tenochtitlan, mainly on Lake Texcoco. Some were caught in nets and sold in the market at Tlateloloco, where they were normally bought by the rich. In the Florentine Codex, we see this rendering of the bird-catchers at work.

Xuctexutle, the god of fishing, gave the Aztec abundant supplies of aquatic food, which, except in the case of the Otamies, was normally lacking in the diets of the Indians of the interior. Besides fish they caught frogs, tadpoles, freshwater shrimp, flies, larvae, white worms and ahuauhtli, which was a kind of caviar made from the eggs of water flies called axayacatl. The great military conquests of later years made it possible for the Aztec to eat seafish, turtle, crab and oysters.

or guinea pig and a variety of game, mainly duck. On the coast and around Lake Titicaca large quantities of fish were eaten.

Aztec cuisine

The three basics of Mexican food were the *atole*, the *tortilla* and the *tamale*.

Atole
Atole was made with corn soaked in water containing slaked lime. When the grains became yellow they were put on the fire to boil for a short time, after which they were taken off and left to cool. Then the husks were removed and the grains washed in water until they were white and ready for grinding, at which point more water was added to rinse them, and then they were strained. Finally, they were put back on the fire to thicken. *Atole* could also be made with amaranth and seasoned with chili or sweetened with sugar or honey. It could be eaten hot or cold.

The tortilla
As Sahagún wrote, there were different kinds of *tortilla*. First, there were *tlatonqui*, fit for the tables of great lords and served hot and folded over. According to the chronicler, they were very thin and white. The dough or *mixtamal* was made of the cleanest, best-quality corn. To make them, lime water was put on to boil. When it started to boil, previously washed corn was added. After boiling for a short time, it was taken off the fire, covered, and left to stand until the next day, when it was washed and ground in a mortar. The real *tortilla* was made in a *comal*, a flat earthenware dish with a slightly raised rim, and it was necessary to take a great deal of care with the heat to avoid either undercooking or burning it. The corn flour made a thin, firm pancake, which had to be turned over several times to obtain the best results. The *tortilla* had to be spongy, unlike those described by Sahagún as "very white, thick, large and coarse" that were the result of badly ground corn. The brownish kind of *tortilla* was made using purple or blue corn. Others resembled puff pastry. Small, elongated rolls filled with green tomato and chili sauce were also made.

The tamale
Tamales were a sort of cornmeal pie, usually with a filling of black beans and chili, and sometimes of turkey or dog meat. Turkey was favored over dog, as the habit of putting the former on top and the latter inside shows. The dough for the *tamale* was *nixtamal*, similar to that used for making the *tortilla* but cooked a little longer. The usual filling was of ground black beans, either boiled or stewed, seasoned with chili and sometimes with avocado leaves. The dough was rolled and wrapped in green or dry corn leaves, previously soaked in cold water. Finally it was boiled and served.

The fruits of the earth

The problem of preservation and storage of food was solved using the same methods as in the Old World. Food was frozen, salted, dried and smoked. The only method not used was that of crystallization, not used in Europe either until late medieval times.

Freezing food was common among the peoples of the arctic circle. In the subarctic it was more common to dry and smoke food. The Haida women prepared surplus salmon for the winter using both methods. In the first they skillfully removed the head, slit the salmon open, gutted it, took out the backbone and cut off the tail and fins. They then cut the meat up into long strips and placed it on wooden frames to dry in the sun. The other method was to smoke the salmon over a slow fire. They also made a type of flat cake with the rotten heads of salmon and halibut, cooked with herbs and berries and then pressed into a mass like bread. South of the tropics, it was a common practice to dry food in the sun. Salting

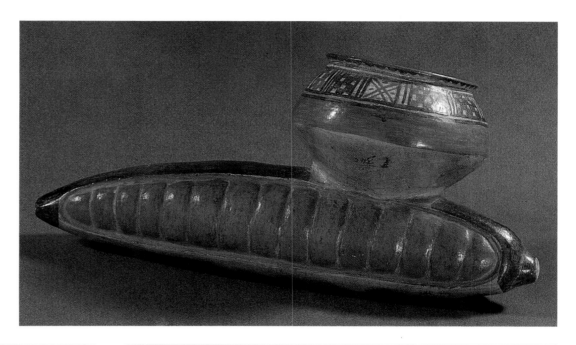

Top: It is uncommon to find pre-Columbian portraits of the guama *or* pacay, *as seen on this container belonging to the Museo De Antropología in Lima. This fruit was rarely grown and was commonly picked in its wild state around the Caribbean and Amazonian regions.* Guama *is the Taino word and* pacay *Quechua. The fruit is sweet and looks like a type of cotton, covering large seeds inside an enormous pod. Above left:* Maize, *or* Zea Mays, *a plant*

of Mesoamerican origin, reached the coast of Peru around 2500 B.C., where it was more widely cultivated than in the Sierra. Carved on this vessel, from the Museo de Arqueología in Lima, is Mama Sara, the fertility goddess who ensured the fertilization of this plant. The ears of corn, ending in humanlike heads, frame a jaguarlike face featuring a mouth with snarling fangs. Above right: The Amerindians in Mesoamerica and Peru were probably the first to

*cultivate the black bean (*Phaseolus*) independently. It soon became part of their staple diet. The Inca used black beans in their games and possibly even in some kinds of writing. They are depicted in different colors and shapes on the white background of this polychrome container from the Museo de Arqueología in Lima.*

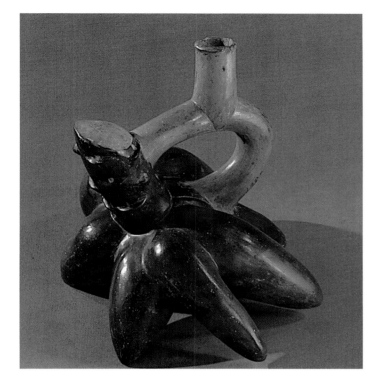

was only practiced in places where salt was abundant.

The reducing of foods to meal, thus making it easier to store and transport, had been common practice since the Archaic period (7000–2000 B.C.). This method was used in Mesoamerica with maize from the moment it was domesticated. The grains were ground using a stone *metate* (quern) or mortar and pestle. In South America and later in the Caribbean a similar process was used with yucca. As we have said before, the two varieties of this tuber were the sweet (*manihot utilissima*) and the hot or bitter type (*manihot esculenta*), the latter being poisonous due to its hydrocyanic acid content. The Guahivo, the Biaroa, the Witoto and other peoples (from the plains of Colombia, Venezuela and Amazonia) and the Taino of the Caribbean extracted the poison using a very complicated procedure. This involved cleaning the roots with a wooden knife, cutting them into pieces, and leaving them in a bowl containing water and a piece of rotten manioc (which caused fermentation) for a day. The pieces of root were then grated on a bamboo

51

Top left: Native to the north of South America, the yucca (Mandihot) was quick to reach the Caribbean, where it became the main ingredient in the diet of the Amerindian. It has been traced in the Andes to 1000 B.C. Its prominence in Inca culture is evident in this vessel, with carvings representing yucca bulbs. It belongs to the Museo de Arqueología in Lima. Top right: It is not known where the sweet potato (Ipomoea batata) was first cultivated. It may

have been in Mesoamerica, in the eastern Andean region or in the Amazon basin. The first archaeological evidence dates from 2000 B.C., on the coast of Peru. The image of the sweet potato and its roots adorns this ceramic cup from Nazca, in the collection of the Museo de América in Madrid. Above: The Inca favored the cultivation of maize, which grew well in the low areas and in the Andes up to 12,540 ft. (3,800 m.), where it gave way to the potato. Maize

was so highly regarded that it was even offered to the gods. In this picture we see two ears of corn made of stone on a polished ceremonial dish of the same material from the Museo de Arqueología in Lima.

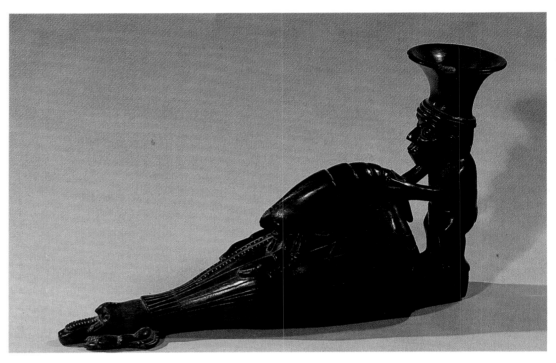

board pierced with palm thorns and the resulting substance placed in a squeezer or fiber press whose upper part was hung from the branch of a tree and a stick inserted into the lower part. The woman then sat on the stick to press the squeezer and extract the poison. The pulp was then dried in the sun and sifted through a wickerwork sieve to make flour.

The Inca used the most advanced technique for preserving foods. In dryer areas *papas* were often covered with straw and with *muña* (a plant belonging to the mint family, with insecticide properties) for up to nine months. The Inca also used the most sophisticated method in the whole of America, which was to transform the *papa* into *chuño* or *moraya*—a technique that had been used in Tiahuanaco and possibly adopted from there by the Inca. The *papas* were made into *chuño* through exposure for 10 days to the daytime sun and the nighttime frosts. They were then covered with a layer of straw and trodden until they released any remaining water. Finally, they were left out in the sun for another 10 days, and great care was taken to cover them at night. In this way the *papa* (now changed into *chuño*) lost a third of its original weight and could be stored more easily. The *moraya* method was similar but was used to extract the bitter taste of the *papa*, which was dehydrated, rehydrated and once again dehydrated.

The Inca used similar techniques with certain edible herbs called *yuyo*, which were boiled two or three times in clean water and then put out in the sun to dry. Preserved foods were stored in maize cane boxes or buried in holes in the ground. Like other Amerindians, they also preserved meat by cutting it into strips, salting it and drying it in the sun.

Fishing from small reed boats, like the famous ones used on Lake Titicaca, often appears in the iconography adorning vessels of the Mochica culture. On this one with a stirrup-shaped handle, the fisherman displays evident feline features. Below the boat are various types of fish. The original is in the Museo Nacional de Arqueología y Antropología in Lima.

There is a strange symbolism on this Mochica bottle. A humanlike winged figure with the face of a monkey and wearing earrings is devouring a fish. Three elements—earth, water and air—seem to have combined in this interpretation of the areas from which the inhabitants of Peru took their food. The original is in the Museo Nacional de Arqueología y Antropología in Lima.

Situated at 12,705 ft. (3,850 m.) above sea level, Titicaca is the navigable lake on earth closest to the sun. Without doubt it holds the key to the mystery of the appearance of the Inca culture, which is some-how bound to the Colla or Aymara who lived in the region during the 13th century, and also to the nearby ruins of Tiahuanaco, the pre-Inca culture that had more influence on Peru than any other.

Everyday food

Meals were largely informal, except perhaps in the high cultures. Food was eaten quickly, without utensils and with very little preparation. Fortunately, the chili pepper and tomato worked miracles in improving taste.

The Inuit did not schedule meals. In fact they had no schedules for anything, since the nights lasted four months and the days another four. They ate when they were hungry and when they were hunting, and when they ate they did so with a vengeance. The Inuit could eat four or five kilos of food at one sitting without upsetting his stomach. This enormous amount of protein enabled him to survive in his environment—in short, to stay alive. He usually boiled his food but also ate meat raw, and since he ate no vegetables this practice guarded against scurvy. He also ate and enjoyed partially decomposed food. Choice dishes for the Inuit were the skin of the narwhal and the white whale, raw walrus liver and the bone marrow of the musk ox. He ate by cramming his mouth full of meat and cutting it off at the lips with a knife.

The Haida, whom we'll use as a typical example of the subarctic peoples, did have set mealtimes. They ate in the morning, at midday and in the evening before nightfall, and the menu might include fish or game. It was common to have halibut and boiled seaweed for breakfast, to eat a hearty lunch of marine mammal at midday and to have whatever was at hand at around six or seven in the evening. Men and women ate together, seated on the ground with the legs crossed, around a mat on which they placed wooden trays of food. Each person had his own eating utensil, usually a large spoon made of wood or horn. It was considered good manners to rinse out the mouth before eating and to drink a mouthful of water after each salty dish.

54

The lush vegetation with its enormous variety of foods that were virtually unknown in Europe gave rise to the idea of a Paradise in which food was easily obtainable. In this French print, the Indians appear surrounded by all kinds of fruit trees on a fertile earth that gives abundant yucca pulses. It seemed that their only labor was to take all that they needed of what bountiful Mother Nature had provided them with in her generosity. This print and the one on the facing page are from the 1741 edition of the Natural History of the Orinoco.

*The bitter yucca (*Manihot esculenta*) was the most common food of the greater part of South America. In order to lower the high prussic-acid content of the yucca to an amount acceptable to humans, the natives subjected it to an extremely complicated process. It was first peeled, then cut, grated and finally pounded. The pulp obtained was then placed in a type of squeezer made of fiber, one of whose ends was tied to a tree and the other to a stick. When the native woman sat on the stick, her weight tightened the squeezer. The flour obtained from this process was* manioc, *which could be eaten mixed with water or used to make* cazabe.

The peoples of Amazonia and northeastern South America who grew bitter yucca had an appalling diet. At around six o'clock in the morning, when the man left his hammock (his wife did so a little earlier), he ate coarse, tasteless cassava bread (made with toasted yucca flour), or simply manioc, the untoasted bread. In order to ingest such a breakfast it was necessary to drink large quantities of water, which is advisable in hot climates. He did not usually eat anything else until evening, though he would perhaps take a handful of manioc if he felt hungry during the day. At around five o'clock he would have the

At Moctezuma's table

The *tlatoani* of Tenochtitlan ate in grand style. According to the chronicler Bernal Díaz de Castillo, so that the king would not feel the cold, "They made for him a fire of smokeless embers from the wood of a tree bark which gave out an exceedingly pleasant smell, and so that it would not give more heat than he wished, they put in front of it a kind of screen carved in gold with images of idols." The ritual of his daily meal was as became a great monarch. He seated himself "on a soft, rich, low seat, and the table, which was also low, was made in the same manner as the seat, and there they set out for him fine white cloths and long kerchiefs of the same material, and four beautiful and clean women held for him to wash his hands some kind of deep basins that they call *sicales*, and below held others that looked like plates, to catch any water that spilt, and gave him his towels...And two other women brought him the *tortilla* bread; when he had commenced to eat, they put a kind of gold painted door in front of him, so that he should not be looked on while eating; and the four women stood far and apart, and around him stood four elderly great lords, to whom now and then Moctezuma spoke and asked things, and to show them great favor gave each one to eat a dish from his table; and it was said that those old men were his near relatives, his counselors and judges, and they ate the dish that Moctezuma gave them standing, showing great respect, never looking at his face."

55

Catching fish with the hands, as depicted in this 19th-century print from Picturesque America, was not so easy as it looked. In some regions of North America, fish were caught during the salmon season using traps or sluices in midstream. This print illustrates how in South America's Amazon region the water was poisoned with the sap of the liana timbu and other plants in an inlet of the river or in some backwater. The dead fish floated to the surface and were thus easily caught. The substance was not poisonous to humans.

same meal as at breakfast, though he would sometimes dip it into a sort of rotten stew made with boiled chili peppers and whatever had been found and thrown into the pot—monkey, parrot, turkey, sow. He only varied his diet with what he managed to hunt.

The Maya had their meals as organized as the rest of their activities. When they got up they had a light breakfast of *atole* (a gruel made of cornmeal) and corn pancakes. When they came home from work at sundown they bathed and ate a large meal of corn pancakes, vegetables and occasionally fish or meat. The men ate first, waited on by the women, who ate together afterward.

The Aztec daily meals consisted of corn pancakes, tamales, kidney beans, amaranth grains and lime-leaved sage. At around ten o'clock in the morning, hours after rising, they had a breakfast usually including a bowl of corn dough with water, either seasoned with chili or sweetened with honey. At midday they ate corn pancakes and kidney beans with chili or tomato sauce. Occasionally they ate *tamales* filled with the meat from game or domesticated animals. They ate quickly, squatting near the fire. Afterward, if they were able, they had a short *siesta*—a healthy

As was common practice in both North and South America, the Indian warrior of the upper Missouri disguised himself in the antlers and skin of a deer so as to be able to get closer to his prey and be sure of hitting the target. Once the deer had been brought down, it was clubbed to death and then dressed. The print comes from Manners and Customs of the Peoples, published in Paris in 1814.

56

The European imagination transformed America into the promised land. The multicolored, fantastic plants that appear in these two prints from the Galerie agreable du monde (Madrid, Biblioteca Nacional) represent, according to the 17th-century mentality, a sum of all the possible kinds of hunting offered by the New World.

pre-Hispanic custom. They had no suppertime, but it was common practice to eat *atole*, amaranth or lime-leaved sage before retiring.

The Inca had only two mealtimes each day, between eight and nine o'clock in the morning and four and five o'clock in the afternoon. Everyday food consisted of dehydrated potato with water, seasoned with *ají* and salt, and very occasionally eaten with jerked meat. They placed the food on fiber mats and ate it in a squatting position.

57

Culinary specialties

The cuisine of the high cultures was considerably refined, especially among the wealthy. The tastiest cuisine was without doubt the Aztec, which used a great deal of aromatic herbs like *epazote, acuyo* or mint, *papalo quelite* and coriander to name but a few. Their main condiment, however, was *mole*, a sauce made with *ají* or chili peppers and green tomatoes, which accompanied a host of dishes. *Guacamole* was made with the same base as *mole* but avocado pear and sometimes coriander were added.

Father Sahagún tells us that the Aztec had seven different types of *tortilla* (pancake), six types of *tamale* (a type of corn roll, usually filled), many different roast and boiled dishes (they did not have oils for frying), twenty recipes for poultry, fish, batrachians (frogs, for example) and insect dishes, and many more using tubers such as the sweet potato and others including the tomato.

The basic ingredient was corn, of which no part was wasted, even the worms that infested it. These worms, called *cinocuili*, were toasted in *comales* (large, flat earthenware pans made spe-

Although maize originated in Mesoamerica, it was soon introduced into the Andean region. The Inca succeeded in cultivating it in areas up to 12,540 ft. (3,800 m.) above sea level on the sides of their valleys and on land sheltered from the wind and frosts. It was appreciated by the Inca for its high energy value and easiness to store. Proof of the esteem in which they held it is the fact that maize flour was offered to the gods as something of great value. In this

photograph are corn cobs on a ceremonial plate used in the Cuzco region and now part of the collection of the Museo de Arqueología y Antropología in Lima.

The Inca used various methods of food preservation, among them the dehydration of the papa, *whereby it was turned into* chuño *or* moraya. *For the former, the* papas *were exposed to the midday sun and night frosts for 10 days. At the end of this period they were covered with a layer of straw and trampled until all the moisture had been removed. In this way the* papa *would lose up to a third of its original weight, making it much easier to preserve.* Moraya *was the result of a similar process, but in this case the* papa *was rehydrated to remove the bitter taste. Here,* chuño *is served on a ceremonial dish featuring the head and tail of a duck.*

cially for cooking corn cakes) and were considered a great delicacy. Corn was used to make *atole*, *tortillas* and *tamales*. Tender *elotes* or kernels were used in soups (with ground tomato, chili peppers and wormseed). They were also eaten roasted or boiled. A favorite delicacy was *exquites*, which was made with grains of tender corn, chili peppers and wormseed.

Kidney beans were also cooked in many different ways: the usual method was to boil them with corn flour, ground tomato, *chipotles* and even boiled avocado pear. *Mole* sometimes gave the dish an intense red color.

Quelite soups were also made, using *quelites* and *jitamote*. Nopals were cooked with corn flour, chili peppers and wormseed. Other dishes were frogs in green chili pepper sauce, frogspawn in yellow chili pepper sauce, winged ants, maguey worms and fish, which were prepared with chili and tomato sauces, and pumpkin seeds with poultry stock. The Aztec ate certain types of flower such as the maguey, the *colorin* and the palm flower, or they used them to cook with, as in pumpkin flower soup.

59

Chocolate, the drink of the gods

Cacao (*teobroma*) was considered by the Aztec to be the drink of the gods. According to legend, Quetzalcoatl stole it from his brother gods and took it to Tula, where he planted it, begging the god Tlaloc to feed it with his rain and the goddess Xochiquetzal to embellish it with flowers. Then he taught the Toltec women how to make chocolate.

The Aztec imported cacao from the warmer regions, usually as tribute. During the reign of Moctezuma, 980 loads—some 48,400 lbs. (22,000 kg.)—were taken to Tenochtitlan annually from Itzapán, Toztlán, Acapetlatlan, Ahuilizpan, and Teoxilocan. It was so valuable that its beans were used as a means of exchange and offered to the gods in sacrifice.

The drink, *chocolatl* or chocolate—which probably means bitter water, from *xococ*, bitter, and *atl*, water—was drunk cold and was made in the following way: The cacao beans were ground in a mortar with a few boiled grains of corn and mixed with water. This was beaten with a spoon or wooden whisk until it was well mixed and frothy. Before it was finally drunk from the *jicara* container, it was again beaten until it was frothy. Aromatic spices such as vanilla and black flower (*vanilla panifolia*) and honey were often added. As a drink, it was indispensable to a good meal and its energy value was well known: Warriors carried it together with their black beans and corn when they went off to war. It would also seem that the Aztec state encouraged the drinking of cacao as opposed to alcoholic drinks, for drinking spirits was considered to be degrading.

stated that the Inca made one particular dish called *locro* with dried or boiled meat, *ají*, pepper, *papas*, *papa* flour and other ingredients. *Chupiera* was a kind of stew made with meat, fish, cereals, tubers and fresh vegetables. The Inca also ate a wide variety of fruits, including the prickly pear and the *tarwi*. The water in which they cooked the Indian fig was effective against parasites.

Naturally, the rich and the high dignitaries ate much better than the common people. Thus, at breakfast time wealthy Aztec drank a cup of cacao seasoned with chili peppers or sweetened with honey. To this strange chocolate were sometimes added grains of tender corn, vanilla and fermented maguey juice. The midday meal was also different from that of the common man: Chocolate was always drunk and meat was often eaten. Great dinners were also given periodically, especially by merchants. As banquets lasted all night, the hosts had to have ready large amounts of food such as corn, kidney beans, chili peppers, tomatoes, turkeys, dogs, cacao, etc., which the women spent hours to prepare. The guests arrived punctually at midnight, ate heartily, and on finishing washed their hands and rinsed out their mouths. After all this they drank cacao, then they smoked, sang and danced, finishing at dawn with one last cup of cacao aromatized with vanilla and honey.

Although sobriety was characteristic of the Inca, the nobles and important persons held great feasts in imitation of the Inca king's table. On some Mochica pottery there are representations of banquets for dignitaries from the coast. All in all, those who ate the best food were the *tlatoani* in Tenochtitlan and the Inca king in Cuzco. Bernal Díaz del Castillo tells us that "Moctezuma's chefs prepared some thirty different dishes…They were placed on small clay braziers so that they might not go cold…and when the time came for eating, Moctezuma would come out with his principal servants and stewards, who showed him which dish was best and with what fowl and things they were cooked, and according to what they said, that was the food to be eaten…And since I heard it said that for his enjoyment they would often cook the flesh of young children, and there was such a diversity of

In Inca cuisine the *ají* or chili pepper also played a very important part but the tomato was even more important. Mushrooms, frogs, fowl and insects also gave flavor to the food. Commonly used were peanuts and peppers. A great deal of corn was eaten, boiled or toasted. Corn flour as well as cinchona, *achita* and *cañahua* were also used for making soups, to which le-

gumes and starch were added. Red kidney beans, cooked or roasted and seasoned with salt and pepper, were also considered a delicacy.

The commonest food in the Andes was dehydrated *papa* flour. Water, *ají* and salt were added to it. Sweet yucca (in Peru the bitter variety was unknown) and oca oxalis were prepared according to the same recipe. Father Bernabe Cobo

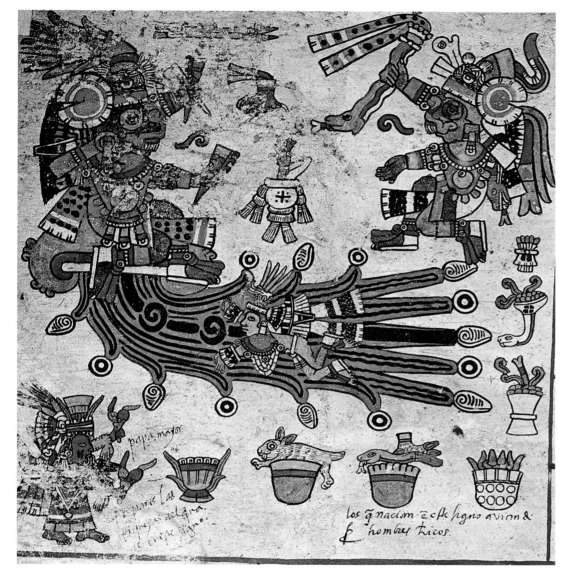

remained resting; and when the great Moctezuma had eaten, then could all those in his guard and many others of his house servants eat."

The Inca king did not fare badly, either. He ate only twice a day, as did all the Inca, but there was never a lack of meat, which was so scarce for the common people, on his table. A favorite meat was llama of less than three years of age or vicuna of less than two; the meat of these animals when mature was no longer tender. He also ate wild duck, *puna* partridge, mushrooms, frogs, snails and fish. The meal began with fruits from the warmer regions, then came food displayed on a woven rush mat laid on the floor. The emperor made himself comfortable on his seat, which was made of wood and covered in fine woollen cloth, and pointed to the food he wanted. Then one of the women from his retinue served him on a plate of clay or of precious metal and held it in her hands while the Inca king ate. What food remained and everything else the Inca had touched would be put in an ark, burnt and the ashes scattered. After the meal, the Inca watched his clowns. Being a clown must have been very difficult, since the king was supposed to remain unmoved and never lose his composure.

cooked foods and other things, we did not know if we were eating human flesh or something else, since daily they cooked hens, turkeys, pheasants, wild and tame ducks, venison, boar, pigeons, hares and rabbits and all manner of fowl and things which live in these lands...Food was served on plates of Cholula clay, one kind red, the other black. While Moctezuma was eating, the men who stood guard in the halls nearby could make no noise or speak loudly. They brought him all the fruits which grew in the land, though he

ate but little, and from time to time they brought goblets of fine gold containing a certain drink made from cacao which they said was for to have access to women; and then we did not look; and I saw that they brought some fifty great jugs made of good cacao with its froth, from which he drank; and the women served him with great deference." The chronicler adds that when Moctezuma had finished eating, the four women who had served him "Lifted the tablecloths, took turns to wash his hands, and showed him great deference...and he

61

*Native to Mesoamerica, the cacao tree (*Teobroma) *was probably first cultivated by the Maya of the Classic period. Their way of growing and drinking it spread to many areas of Mexico and Central America. In this picture, we see the* cacahuaquauitl, *or cacao tree, on a polychrome cup from the Maya Classic period (700–800), which belongs to the Museo Popol Vuh in Guatemala.*

Alcohol, tobacco, stimulants and hallucinatory drugs

The main drinks served with meals in Mesoamerica were water and cocoa. In the Inca regions the alcoholic *chicha* was sometimes drunk, particularly at the tables of the nobles and at the end of the meal. In general, the Indians drank alcoholic beverages to get drunk and ate food for nourishment, the two considered to have no connection. According to Garcilaso de la Vega, the Inca "ate little and were more fond of drinking; they did not drink while eating, but made up for it later by drinking well into the night." This was done only by the rich; the common people were always short of everything.

Chicha was normally made from corn (it was also made from yucca, quinoa, *cañahua*, peanut, carob bean, and even from maguey juice). It was made by old women with great experience who had refined the process. They first chewed the

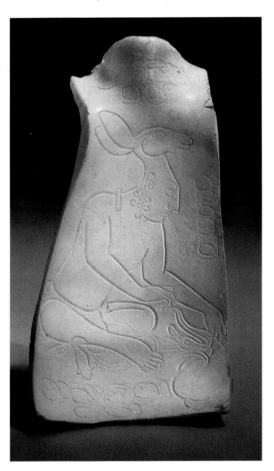

The smoking of tobacco was a typical as well as ancient custom of the lords of Mesoamerica, as may be observed in this delicate drawing on a piece of seashell from the latter part of the Classic Maya period (600 to 800 A.D.), now in the Cleveland Art Museum. The Maya lord, with his extremely fine hands—evidence of little manual labor—sits on a throne, smoking a cigarette with obvious pleasure.

Punishment for drunkenness

Drunkenness was considered to be a crime, and Aztec society often punished drunkards severely. Sahagún wrote, "If a youth appeared intoxicated in public, or if he was found bearing wine, or lying in the street, or in the company of other drunkards, if he was a *macehualli* (plebeian) he was punished by being beaten to death with a stick or garrotted before all the other youths assembled there; thus to serve as an example and to teach them to beware of drunkenness."

The laws of Netzahuacoytl established the death penalty for priests caught drunk, and also for dignitaries, civil servants or ambassadors found to be drunk in the palace. The harshness of these laws shows that drunkenness must have been considered a danger to society. In general, Fernando Alba agrees with Sahagún, but points out that if the drunkard was a plebeian, then the first time he was caught his head was shaved in the main square, the possessions taken from his house and the house demolished. "For, as the law says, whosoever loses his judgment is not worthy to have a house, but must live in the wild like a beast. And if he was caught a second time, he was punished with death. And if he was a noble, he was condemned to death in any case."

The only people who were allowed to drink *pulque* (fermented juice of the maguey) to the point of drunkenness were the old of both sexes, particularly at celebrations. The goddess of *pulque* was Mayahuel, who had 400 breasts and an equal number of children, of whom the most important was Ome Tochtli, the god of *pulque*.

---

grains and then spat them out into a jug where the enzymes contained in the saliva caused them to ferment. The resulting paste was put into a pitcher and buried so that the heat would speed up the process of fermentation. As the days passed, the percentage of alcohol increased. Depending on the state of intoxication desired, week-old, two-week-old or one-month-old *chicha* could be drunk. The figure of a drunkard being taken home by two friends may be seen on one example of Mochica pottery. Any special feast, any ritual of change—birth, puberty, marriage or death—and even any work done out of the ordinary was accompanied by heavy drinking sessions of *chicha*.

The Aztec got drunk on *octli* or *pulque*, made from fermented maguey juice. In spite of the severity of punishment, it seems that drunkenness was by no means uncommon. Nobles and high dignitaries paid for drunkenness with death. The only people entitled to drink as much as they wanted were the aged—both men and women. Fernando Alba Iztlixochitl tells us that "At nocturnal baptisms old men and women came together and drank *pulque* and became intoxicated. For this they set before them a pitcher full of *pulque*, and he who served poured it into goblets, giving one to each there present...And once intoxicated they would begin to sing...Others did not sing but chattered and jested and laughed uproariously at the jests of others."

The Maya drank *balche*, made by fermenting a mixture of honey and water and four pieces of bark from the *balche* tree (*lonchocarpus longistylis*) for a few days.

Tobacco was found all over America, but it was used mainly for medicinal, magical and religious purposes. It was chewed and also burnt, as the smoke expelled evil spirits. The Aztec, however, used it as a compliment to good food. Sahagún says that "After lunch Moctezuma II rose from the table, took in the smoke from one of those tubes, though but a little, and then fell asleep." Tobacco was smoked in richly decorated, cylindrical cane pipes in which a mixture of tobacco, charcoal and liquid amber was placed. It was considered *chic* to pass the pipe around.

In some regions the taking of stimulants was as common as smoking. The most popular stimulant was coca. The effects of coca, which is found over the whole of the Andean region, made it possible to work incessantly without feeling either hunger or weariness. Coca leaves and powdered lime were made into a ball (*mambe*), which was moved from one side of the mouth to the other. Tumaco and Mochica pottery have admirably depicted the coca taker with his small lump

---

Amerindians drank several types of alcoholic beverages in their celebrations. The Maya drank a kind of mead called *balche*. This figurine, from the Museum of the American Indian in New York, holds a double drinking cup in his left hand, while he makes a comical gesture with the right. Covering the upper part of his face is a mask of an old man's face, which is completely inconsistent with his youthful body. This extraordinary piece of pottery came from the island of Jaina, dating from the Late Classical period (700–900 A.D.).

of *mambe* in his mouth. The powdered lime was carried in a *poporo* and there are some beautiful representations of *poporos* on Quimbayan gold work in Colombia. The Inca brought vast amounts of coca from the eastern region and controlled its distribution, though the practice predated the empire. Moreover, it was also used in many small villages outside their territory. Another stimulant commonly found in South America, mainly in the Amazonian region (Siona, Kofán, Inga), was *yoco* (*paullinia yoco*), which was taken after long periods of ceremonial fasting, perhaps for its caffeine content.

Hallucinatory drugs were another matter. Some members of Spanish religious orders at first believed that these drugs were contained in the food eaten by the Amerindians. Hallucinatory drug-taking was widespread over the whole of South America. In the Amazon region and on the plains of Colombia and Venezuela, *nipoco* or *paricá* was used. This was a type of snuff extracted from the seeds of the mimosa plant. It was placed in the palm of the hand or on a ladle and inhaled through the nose by means of a complicated piece of equipment made of hollow bones, inserted into the nostrils. It was usually the shaman or sorcerer who took the drug to detect evil magic, cure illness and predict the future. The most powerful hallucinatory drug in the Amazonian region was *yagé*, also called *caapi* and *ayahuasca* (which means the dead). It was prepared with varieties of *banisteriopsis* (*caapi* and *rusbyana*), sometimes in combination.

Certain kinds of mushroom were also used both in North and South America as hallucinatory drugs. The Aztec called them *teonacatl*. With almost unbelievable naiveté, Father Sahagún got into the habit of eating these mushrooms, claiming that they were an *hors d'oeuvre* to the food at banquets. The Aztec took other hallucinatory drugs such as *tlapatl* grass (a solanum), *mixitl* grain and also *peyotl* (lophophora Williamsii) or peyote, a cactaceous plant originally from the north of Mexico, where it had been in use since 300 B.C. Several Nahuatl peoples, mainly the Chichimeca, used *peyotl*. Sahagún wrote, "Whoever eats it or drinks it sees fearsome or hilarious visions. The drunkenness persists for two or three

64

The most common Aztec alcoholic drink was octli *or* pulque, *which was made with fermented maguey juice. Its consumption was restricted to the agea, and laws against drunkenness were extremely harsh. Friar Bernardino de Sahagún recorded the penalty for a young man caught drunk: "If he was a* macehualli *he was punished by being beaten to death with a stick or garrotted before all the other youths assembled there . . . and if it was a noble, he was garrotted in secret." Nevertheless, drunkards were protected by* Centzon Totochtin, *the god of drink, and by* Mayahuel, *the goddess of the maguey. This illustration showing an Indian woman extracting maguey juice was painted on a screen. It dates from 17th-century colonial Mexico, and is now in the Museo de América in Madrid.*

Coca *(Erythroxylon coca) is usually associated with the Inca culture, although it is in fact pan-Andean and pre-Inca. Tombs of the coastal cultures of Peru frequently contain small coca bags, and little calabashes or* poporos *were used to keep lime in. The coca leaves were chewed with a little lime extracted from crushed shells to form the* mambe *or ball, which was passed slowly from one cheek to the other. Ceramic humanlike figures with the* mambe

lump have been found in some Formative cultures (5th–1st centuries B.C.) in Ecuador and Colombia. The Spaniards first encountered coca among the Indians of Paria (Venezuela) in 1499. The Inca may have received coca from the eastern rim of the Andes or from the adjacent plains in the region they called Antisuyu. A system of coca cultivation in the east using subject peoples has been attributed to Tupac Yupanqui (1471–1493). In the scenes below,

from the Museo de la Universidad in Cuzco, we see coca being collected in keros.

days and then disappears. For the Chichimeca it is like an entertainment that sustains them and gives them courage to fight and to not feel fear, nor thirst, nor hunger, and they say that it guards them from all danger."

Hallucinatory mushrooms: an unusual hors d'oeuvre

To Father Sahagún we owe a most interesting description of how hallucinatory mushrooms were eaten by the Aztec. He believed them to be the customary *hors d'oeuvre* before every great feast:

"The first thing to be eaten at the feast were small black mushrooms that they called *nanacatl* and that bring on drunkenness, hallucinations and even lechery; they ate these before the dawn…with honey; and when they began to feel the effects,

they began to dance, some sang and others wept, for they were already drunk on the mushrooms; and some who did not want to sing sat in their rooms lost in thought, and some had visions of themselves dying and they wept, others saw themselves eaten by wild beasts, some saw themselves taken captive in war, others saw that they were to be rich, some that they were to possess many slaves, others that they had committed adultery and so would have their heads crushed, some saw they were to steal and be killed for it, and many other visions they had. When the drunkenness of the mushrooms had passed, they

spoke with one another of the visions they had seen."

Without doubt, the priest here has told us about the taking of hallucinatory mushrooms, but not at a feast. Food would certainly have spoiled the effect. Sahagún's mistake probably derives from the translation of "the first thing," which should instead be "ancient" or "at the beginning." The *Madrid Codex* states: "It is an ancient custom for people to eat mushrooms and these they ate in a trice, as is said. They had had no food, except some cacao drunk the night before. They ate these mushrooms with honey."

Love and sex

Although the Amerindians followed their instincts regarding sexual matters, they still finally found themselves in situations very similar to those in Europe, as demonstrated in some of their love stories, which are full of romanticism. Love and sex were inextricably mixed together. Many marriages of convenience ended in love. Much sexual passion ended in tragedy. The eternal stories of men and women are told the world over.

Premarital sex education varied according to the customs of the people concerned. The Chamakoko Indians of El Chaco made men who wished to marry go through a type of initiation with older men and women, while the Inca considered sexual relations between young people to be the norm. Father Cobo wrote that virginity was considered a defect in women, as the Indian thought that virgins were women who could not be loved. Arriaga wrote that one Indian was opposed to his sister marrying a young person like herself because she had still not had sexual intercourse, which meant that it was not possible to know if the marriage would work.

But in most cases, men in Mesoamerica enjoyed a great deal of premarital sexual freedom. Women, on the other hand, did not. Concerned about social order, the high cultures forbade their women from engaging in premarital sexual intercourse and regulated the activity of the men.

Young Maya were allowed to take prostitutes to the homes where they were educated, whereupon Bishop Landa drew the remarkable conclusion that homosexuality was not practiced by the Maya. The bishop also said that "The poor prostitutes were exhausted after exercising their profession in the barracks, since so many young men went to them that they ended vexed or dead." Young Maya women were not allowed to have sexual relations with young men, and those who contravened the law were punished severely by their mothers. Landa states that "They beat them with cudgels and smear them elsewhere with pepper as a punishment and humiliation."

The Aztec also tolerated premarital sexual intercourse for men but recommended moderation. They told them, "Do not throw yourselves at a woman like a dog at its food. Do not act like a dog, eating and swallowing what you are given, giving yourselves to women before time. Though you have an appetite for women, resist, resist the dictates of your heart until you are perfect strong men." Young women were educated in the strictest celibacy until the very moment they were married.

The double standard within the sexual custom of other Mesoamerican cultures may be appreciated in two neighboring peoples—the Chorotega and the Nicarao. In the first society, the woman had to acquire sexual experience by giving herself to her suitors, from whom she received gifts in exchange, thus making up her dowry. The dowry proved her worth as a woman and made it possible for her to later choose the husband she wanted. To the Nicarao, on the other hand, the bride's virginity had to be proved when the marriage was consummated. Outside this geographical and cultural area, premarital sexual freedom must have been quite widespread. The chroniclers' reports often speak of the prostitution of women, since they took for granted that such relations were normal only for men. Thus, Fernández de Oviedo speaks of the prostitution of the Cueva Indian women of Panama and notes the same of the Araucanian women.

The sexual abstinence imposed on the young women of the Mesoamerican high cultures gave rise to the institution of the *alcahueta* or procuress and also to a great many difficulties in the

---

Mochica erotic art

It is not uncommon to find erotic art, and more particularly erotic pottery, in Amerindian cultures, since sex was a fact of everyday life. However, the Mochica, who lived on the coasts of Peru, developed their depictions of this particular aspect of life to an extremely high degree. Until only a few years ago, the Museo Nacional de Arqueología y Antropología in Lima had a special room displaying hundreds of erotic Mochica vessels, set apart from the eyes of children and impressionable adults. The erotic scenes were carved into the vessels, applied to them, or painted onto the surface, and they fall into five groups: vaginal intercourse in various positions, anal intercourse from the back and side, oral sex, masturbation, and phallic and vaginal images. The latter normally depict overdeveloped genitals and were usually found on vessels whose contents were drunk by placing the lips over orifices made in the phallus or vagina. There are marks on these particular parts of the pottery vessels that prove that they were indeed used in such a way. At right we see one such figure from the Lima museum, an Indian holding his unusually large member in his hand. It is curious that the effect of such pottery is usually more humorous than erotic.

The enormous size of the penis had its practical function, for in the vast majority of representations of this type on vessels, the end of the phallus is perforated so that the only way of drinking is through the orifice. The neck of the vessel—in this case the character's hat—has a series of openings in the form of a crown around the head, which make it impossible to drink from the vessel in any other way. Consequently, we see here an erotic representation associated with an object of practical usage, whose nature is unquestionable.

Copulation, whatever the position, was not the most common of motifs in Mochica erotic pottery. This, however, is one example, now in the Museo de Arqueología in Lima. Sometimes a woman is depicted copulating with a godlike figure (or a priest dressed in attributes of the god), which could have some connection with the supposedly divine origins of some of the great coastal families. At other times, the couple copulating are accompanied by more figures: a male, taking part in the sex-play, a couple standing impassively nearby (possibly the parents or in-laws) or children. A particularly common motif was a man copulating with a pregnant woman.

choice of a partner in marriage. The Aztec came up with the solution of punishing the procuresses, as Mendieta reported: "It having been discovered that they exercised that vile profession, they were taken out to the square and publicly shamed before all, their hair was singed with a firebrand until the scalp was burnt…and if the person who had procured was of high birth, more severe was the punishment, their lives even being taken. As did Netzahualpilli, the king of Texcoco, to a procuress who had brought a young lord from Tezoyuca, in love with one of the king's daughters, into the palace hidden in a trunk. The king discovered what was afoot and had them both hanged."

The selection of a partner in marriage was a decision for the families and not for the couple involved. The Maya devised one of the most complicated systems. The future bride could not be a relative of the future father-in-law, although she could be related to the future mother-in-law (she could even be a first cousin on the maternal side). She was also required to be of the same social class as the future groom, besides being virtuous enough to marry (women always appeared to denounce the vices of the future bride). After fulfilling these requirements, the worst was yet to come. This was to try and calculate under what star sign the young woman had been born, as she might be incompatible with her future husband. If the result was favorable, the marriage was approved and the services of a good matchmaker, or *Ah atanzab*, were sought. The matchmaker was entrusted with the delicate task of fixing a sort of dowry which the bride's parents would give to the groom's. Naturally there was much haggling before the amount was agreed on. Blankets, cacao, corn, cotton, feathers and precious stones made up the dowry, whose value represented the girl's worth and what the groom's parents could afford to pay. When all the obstacles had been cleared, a priest was sought. But the priest could spoil everything by saying that the couple had not been born under favorable or compatible star signs. Once everything was in order, a suitable date was scheduled.

With the Aztec a similar though even more difficult kind of marathon had to be run. As with the Maya, the services of a matchmaker had to be sought. She would likewise visit the future bride's parents to propose the engagement. Invariably she would return after the first visit with a refusal; a "yes" the first time was not well looked upon. The parents would then say that the girl was "silly" and that the matter should be discussed by the relatives. On the second visit, the matchmaker would receive a favorable answer, the whole family having by now assembled to discuss the matter. A priest was then consulted to see if the young people's signs were favorable and compatible and a date for the wedding fixed. The groom's teachers, the *calmecac* or *tepuchcalli*, also had to authorize the marriage. A great feast had to be given by the future groom's parents in the teachers' honor. At the end of the feast the old men of the family asked permission to take the future groom away. The teachers, pipe

The Maya marriage

The Maya wedding celebration was a grand affair. On the day chosen for the wedding, a group of men and elderly people went to take the girl to the groom. Then a priest, a *cacique* or simply an old man, depending on the social level of the wedding party, tied together the ends of the couple's blankets and performed the ceremony, giving blessings and exhorting the couple to lead a virtuous life. A great celebration followed, with all the relatives taking part.

The wedding night does not appear to have been very pleasant, since during the course of the night they were instructed on sex by two old women who would try to improve the couple's ignorance on the subject. Las Casas wrote, "At dusk, two old women of authority locked them in and gave them instruction on what they should do." Lamentably, the priest did not think it proper to give more details on this interesting subject. Much worse was what later awaited the groom, as he had to work for his father-in-law and live in his house until the price they had agreed on for the bride had been paid. Once it had been paid, the couple could set up a new home of their own or go to the house of the husband's parents, though in that way the couple would live under the guidance of both pairs of in-laws for a considerable time, which must have put their endurance greatly to the test. By contrast, there were tribes in California for whom it was forbidden to have any contact with the in-laws, even if they should meet by chance on the street.

Aztec weddings were performed in a religious ceremony—something not found in other cultures. The goddess of the enamored, seen here in this picture taken from the Bourbon Codex, was the protectress of those who were to be married. It was the task of the Aztec priests to consult the sacred calendar and verify that the couple's signs were favorable and compatible. After the wedding the couple was obliged to stay inside the nuptial chamber, praying and making offerings of copal to the gods, without consummating the marriage. On the fifth day, the priest came to bless them with water and declare them man and wife.

in hand, took advantage of the occasion to give a long-winded speech on the virtues of moral values, and all present were obliged to listen with resignation. The same rigmarole had to be repeated by the future bride's family, especially if she came from a good family, since in that case she would be attending the temple school. Needless to say, this moralizing long-winded speech was even longer and ended by recommending the future bride obey the gods and her husband and lead a virtuous life. Finally, it was necessary to work three days (and nights) preparing the great wedding banquet, to which all the relatives, friends, teachers and officials were invited, especially if the couple came from good families.

With the Inca the procedure was much simpler. There existed the so-called *servinacuy* or trial marriage, which solved innumerable problems. Two young people would live together for a certain period of time—which could be between a few days and a few years—enabling them to be sure whether or not they really wanted to be married. If there was discord between the two, the girl went back to live with her parents—even if she had had children during the trial period. She could try a second time, and if things went well she could make the decision to marry.

70

The wedding was usually a family affair. In fact it was more of a marriage between two families through the bride and groom. For this reason, the choice of partner was normally made by the groom's parents and not by the groom himself. The marriage also involved a series of compensations, especially regarding the price paid for the bride, which had to be fixed previously in lengthy negotiations between the two families. A low price paid for the bride could indicate low social standing, whereas a very high price could mean financial sacrifice on the part of the groom's family. Thus the arrangement was a very delicate matter. In this sheet from the Tudela Codex, we see a Yope Indian wedding in Mexico. Near the bride and groom, the two mothers talk excitedly, while below, the fathers make the final arrangements.

dios mayor de
las culebras.

los q aquy nacieron no
podian P aborreçidos d̃ nadie

Once an agreement had been reached between the parents regarding the marriage, diviners were consulted to see under which favorable signs the couple had been born. Such signs are depicted in this picture from the Bourbon Codex. *If compatibility or affinity was discovered, the wedding could proceed, but the diviners also had to fix the most favorable date.*

Marriage and divorce

Although marriages were normally monogamous it was not the case in all Amerindian societies. In fact even the fiercest supporters of monogamy allowed male aristocrats to have more than one wife. Some gatherer peoples were polyandrous, even though they were unfamiliar with the matrimonial systems that defined such a state. The hunters were monogamous through necessity, it being extremely difficult for a man to be able to feed more than one woman at a time.

Incestuous marriages or marriages between relatives, however, were forbidden in most societies. Even a man and woman who belonged to the same clan would be considered relatives, and this would prevent them from marrying. In some cultures this particular point was extremely complex. Father Juan Fochter wrote in 1544 that for the Michoacan Indians a marriage was not considered to be incestuous if a woman married a stepbrother fathered by her father or born to her mother, or if the marriage was between niece and uncle. However, a marriage between nephew and aunt was considered incestuous. The most peculiar thing of all, however, was that "Others say

The great ceramics tradition of Ecuador—it was in this area that the most ancient of all such traditions appeared 5,000 years ago—produced figurines of great beauty, like those from Jama Coaque, in the north of Manabí. These are hollow, large in size, and depict men and women both standing and seated. The figures wear only loincloths but are bedecked with feather-covered helmets, masks, nose pendants and earrings. Like this couple with the large hands, from the Museo del Banco Central in Quito, they usually perform typical everyday tasks, such as pounding food, here possibly yucca.

Married life imposed a certain rhythm of work on the couple, reflected here in this magnificent Chimú vessel depicting a large-handed man grinding food in a mortar and a woman pouring in what is possibly water from a small pitcher. Pottery vessels such as this one came in the most fanciful of shapes, with finely sculptured figures. Scenes usually depicted show aspects of war, everyday life and mythology. The expressiveness of the faces and realism of the figures make this one of the best examples of its kind on the South American continent. The vessel in the photograph is from the Museo de Arqueología y Antropología in Lima.

that a father-in-law may not marry his daughter-in-law nor the son-in-law his mother-in-law, though joining in fornication is tolerated."

To the Inca, the marriage of a man to his sister was not considered incestuous and was even necessary, because the sister was the only woman of the same solar rank. In the case of the Aztec, it would seem that there were ancient matrimonial restrictions regarding clans, but these had been lost at the end of pre-Columbian times when, apparently, incestuous prohibitions similar to those in the west prevailed. Dread of incest led the Onas to the practice of kidnaping their women from neighboring villages, causing themselves endless trouble. To the Chibcha and the Cueva, however, there was no such thing as incest, and marriage between blood relatives was allowed.

On the other hand, there were many levirate and sororate cultures, such as the Diaguita and the California, in which a widow was obliged to marry her dead husband's brother and a widower to marry his dead wife's sister. The Aztec, as Mendieta notes, also practiced leviration, "When one of the brothers died, it was the custom for another of the brothers to take the woman or women of his dead brother, even when the latter had had children, *quasi ad suscitandum semen fratris*, in the Jewish way."

It was not common practice to make wedding vows and even less common to ask priests or sorcerers to officiate. Cabeza de Vaca wrote that in Amerindia, there was no wedding ceremony. Furthermore, "They had the custom of leaving their wives when there was discord, and married again with whomsoever they desired to marry." This also happened frequently in the polar and subarctic regions. For the Aleut there was no such thing as wedding vows, in spite of lifelong partnerships. Cabeza de Vaca also added, "But those who have children remain with their wives and do not abandon them." Certain matrimonial rules regarding the price of the bride (money or working for the in-laws) set off certain defense mechanisms such as "kidnaping the bride." This was practiced by the Pampeano and Araucanian peoples, among many others. A ceremony was held in which the groom pretended to carry off the bride by force (everything had been arranged beforehand), thus saving himself the expense of having to pay for her. The Zapotec and Chinantec women put up fierce resistance to this procedure, perhaps because they thought that nonpayment cheapened them in the eyes of others.

The Maya and Aztec did have a wedding ceremony, with priests officiating. The Aztec ceremony was without doubt the most solemn. At midday on the day fixed for the wedding, a great meal was eaten at the bride's house. The married female guests brought gifts. In the evening the girl bathed, and she was "dressed" for the occasion. Her arms and legs were adorned with red feathers and her face painted yellow. In this attire she was then introduced to the groom's oldest relatives (having drunk as much *octli* as they could, they would by now be extremely boisterous), who made speeches welcoming her into the family, to which she replied with another, equally polite speech. At night a procession of relatives would take the bride to her fiancé's house and all would enter, singing and dancing.

The ceremony took place with bride and groom sitting together on mats. The bride's mother gave some new clothes to her future son-

73

The complex Aztec marriage, officiated by a priest or state representative, rarely took place elsewhere. Very few peoples, in fact, performed a civil, let alone a religious, ceremony. It was more common, on the other hand, for the family to play a part by either choosing the bride or fixing the price to be paid for her or the service the groom would have to give to his future in-laws. In these prints from Manners and Customs of the Peoples *(Paris, 1814), we see on the* *left a part of the Guayana Indian ceremony, in which arrows were shot between the couple; on the right is a scene from the ceremony of the Dakota Sioux.*

in-law, and the groom's mother would do the same with her future daughter-in-law. After exchanging clothes, the blanket and blouses of the couple were knotted, signifying that they were now man and wife. The first thing the newlywed couple did was to give each other a plate of *tamales*. The guests expressed their joy with singing and dancing, and then there would be a rush for the food, the old people reaching for their *octli*. The couple would enter the wedding chamber, where they were to remain for four days, in prayer and without consummating the marriage. During this time they were allowed to leave the chamber only at midday and to burn incense on the family altar. On the fifth day they bathed and a priest finally came to bless the couple. That night they were allowed to consummate the mar-

Punishment for adultery

Adultery could exist only in those pre-Columbian peoples for whom marriage was a deeply established institution, as was true of the peoples of Mesoamerica. In the case of the Zapotec and Chinantec, the only punishment was that the adultress was sent back to her parents. In the case of the Aztec, however, adultery was often punished with death. According to *Mendieta Codex*, "If a man and a woman were discovered committing adultery, or were strongly suspected, they were arrested and if they did not confess, were tortured, and after they had confessed to their crime, put to death.

"Sometimes they were killed by their hands and feet being bound, and, once lying on the ground, were struck on the temples with a heavy, round stone in such a way that, with a few blows dealt, their heads were flattened like a pancake. Others were strangled with an oak garrote. Other times they burnt the man and hanged the woman. Sometimes both were hanged, and if they were nobles, feathers would be put on their heads and then they would be burnt. Or the judges could have them stoned. They were taken to the main square, where many would gather, and

once in the center of the square, the man's hands were bound, and then they threw stones that fell on them like rain, and they did not suffer overmuch, for when they fell, they were soon dead, and covered with stones. Those who committed adultery while intoxicated with wine were not excused from death, for they died like the rest."

The chronicler Fernando Alba Ixtlichotitl wrote, "If the husband found a man committing adultery with his wife, both adulterers were put to death by stoning, and if the husband's suspicions were proven true, they were both hanged and then dragged to a temple outside the town, and all this even if the husband was not the accuser, but as punishment for scandal and for setting a bad example to the neighborhood. And the same for those that killed a third party. If the adulterers killed the husband, the man was roasted alive, and while this was going on, he was sprinkled with water and salt until he was dead, and the woman was hanged, and if they were lords or gentlefolk, they were garrotted and their bodies burnt, which was their manner of burial."

riage on a bed of matting on which were placed feathers and a piece of jade. At the weddings of rich people and nobles, this procedure was more complex.

To the Inca marriage was an exclusively civil event, religion playing no part whatsoever. The Inca state acted on the assumption that being single was an unnecessary luxury and that everyone should be married. A date was fixed for a great communal wedding, and on that day all the marriageable men and women stood in two long lines. Then the Inca emperor (in Cuzco) or his representatives in provincial towns asked each male which woman he had chosen (usually after a trial marriage). With no further ado, the woman was taken out of the line and given to the man. The only problems arose when a young man had not chosen a woman, but this was resolved easily by having him chose from whomever was left. If the young man was reluctant to choose, he was assigned a woman doing "a turn of duty."

Once married, the couple went to the bride's parents' house to tell them the good news. The father then proceeded to give away the bride symbolically to the groom, who accepted her and put the finishing touch to the ceremony by placing a sandal on his wife's right foot and giving presents to his in-laws. The couple then went to the village authorities, where they were given the newlyweds' trousseau—two sets of new clothes, one for working days and another for holidays. They were also given a house to live in, a pair of llamas and a plot of land to work.

In polygynous societies the wedding ceremony was performed only between the man and his principal wife, the one the Spaniards called "la legítima," and not the secondary ones. Aztec and Inca nobles were allowed to have more than one wife. Muñoz Camargo recorded that the "legitimate" wife gave orders to her husband's concubines and even adorned and groomed the woman he had chosen to sleep with him.

Divorce was rare, since it could only exist in societies in which marriage was completely binding, as it was among the Aztec. Divorce was granted when one of the spouses abandoned the home, when the woman was sterile or neglected her domestic duties, when the husband beat his wife or children or when he did not give the family enough to live on. All possessions were

divided equally between the two, and both were allowed to remarry. Spaniards belonging to religious orders caused tremendous confusion over the repudiation of secondary wives, which, in fact, probably never actually took place. What is clear, however, is that the Aztec could not divorce the principal wife. At least this is the conclusion drawn from the story of Moquihuixtli, *tlatoani* or king of Tlatelolco; his indifference toward his wife Chalchiuhnenetzin, sister to Axayacatl, brought about the destruction of Tlatelolco by the warriors of Tenochtitlan.

For the Inca, the institution of marriage represented not only a social tradition but a practical union as well. Both husband and wife worked the tapu *or plot together in order to obtain enough sustenance for their family. Here we see two agricultural scenes depicted on* keros *from the Leoncio Artega Collection in Peru. At top right, the man makes the holes in the ground with a* taclla, *bearing down with his foot, while the woman—the more fertile of the two, sup-* *posedly—drops in the seed. Above, the woman kneels on the ground, collecting the crop, which she gives to her husband, who then places it into a small basket.*

Homosexuality

Homosexuality was common all over the continent and possibly went back to ancient times. According to the Maya Chronicle *Chilam Balam* it was commonly practiced during the fourth age of the world. Sodomites abounded and this atrocious sin, committed by the "Flowers of Naxcit" with their fellows, was widespread. The Spaniards found it depicted on ceramic and gold figures. Lopez de Gómara recorded that in the port of San Antón (Mexico) they found among the trees a small golden idol and many more made of clay "of men riding some on top of others committing the abominable vice." Bernal Diáz del Castillo wrote that among the Yucatan Maya "There were many clay idols, some with faces of demons and others with faces of women and others of evil figures, so that it seems that some Indians were sodomizing others." As is well known, homosexual acts are often depicted on Mochica pottery.

The *conquistadores* encountered homosexuality in both hemispheres. Cortés branded all the Mexicans along the Atlantic coast as sodomites: "We have seen and also been informed that they are all sodomites and practice that abominable vice." Bernal Díaz says something very similar: "And also, all the rest of them were sodomites and especially those who lived on the coasts and in the hot lands. Boys dressed in women's clothes to earn their living from that abominable vice." Gómara recorded that homosexuality extended even as far as Pánuco, whose inhabitants, he said, "are great buggers who maintain public brothels in which they spend a thousand and one nights and more."

During his travels, Vasco Núñez de Balboa encountered homosexuality on the isthmus, persecuting and burning those who practiced it. He failed to understand that what he believed to be a sin was actually a social institution among the Cueva Indians, which obliged certain individuals to be raised to dress and act like women, and that this was the case in most of South America. Alvaro Núñez saw these *bardajes* (men who behaved socially like women) in La Florida: "And I saw a man married to another, and those are effeminate men, and impotent, who dress like women and do women's work and shoot arrows and are highly respected and among these we saw

many effeminate men, as I say, and they are stronger than other men, and taller and can bear heavy loads."

In South America *bardajes* were found all over the plains (Saliva, Piapoco, Guahibo among others), where this institution existed. It was noted by Fernández Piedrahita in his description of the Lache Indians of Colombia: "It was law that if a woman gave birth to five male children consecutively, without giving birth to a female, one of the males could feign to be a woman...And as they raised the child in that way, he was so perfect in the waist and in the rest of

the body that anyone who saw him would not distinguish him from a woman." Gómara said the same of some natives of Venezuela: "There are many sodomites who would be women were it not that they lack breasts and cannot bear children." Soarez de Souz recorded that the Tupinamba of Brazil "are very fond of the abominable sin, which among them is not outrageous; the one who takes the part of the male is held to be courageous and recounts this abomination as though it were an heroic feat...There are public houses for those who desire to act like public women."

Homosexuality was common all over the continent and was a source of scandal to the Spanish discoverers, who could not understand its institutional nature. This was the only manifestation that they were permitted to see, for homosexuality as a vice was practiced in secret. In some societies, male children were brought up as girls in order that they would later exercise a female function within society. As the chroniclers were able to witness for themselves, *some peoples—the Lache of Colombia, for example—held these males in great esteem. This figurine is in the Museo del Oro in Bogota.*

The subject of anal intercourse between men, as on this double vessel, one end of which has been dedicated exclusively to this motif, was not omitted from Mochica erotic pottery. For the Mochica, sex was an integral part of daily life that was expressed in their art, which even included scenes of intercourse between humans and animals. This vessel is in the Museo de Arte Precolombino in Chile.

Among the Aztec, however, homosexuality was severely punished. Mendieta recorded that "both of those who committed the abominable sin would die for it. And from time to time they were sought out and an inquisition performed in order to expose them and put an end to them, for it was well known that such an abominable act is against nature." He added, "He who dressed himself as a woman, and she who dressed herself as a man, were both sentenced to death." Fernando Alba Ixtlixochitl confirmed the seriousness of this crime and tells us more regarding the punishment: "The abominable act was punished with great severity, for the agent, tied to a stake, was covered with ash by all the boys of the town, until he was buried in it, and his partner's entrails were extracted through his sex, and he was likewise buried in ash."

The Inca also considered homosexuality a crime. Garcilaso de la Vega says that when the Inca conquered the Uiña, Camana and Carauli valleys, "The Inca ordered that with great diligence inquiry be made concerning sodomites, and in the public square those who were discovered were burnt alive, and not only those found

These Xochipala warriors, with their earflares, necklaces and headdresses, demonstrate their contempt for the strict moral customs in Mesoamerica by exposing their backsides. This piece of pottery is from the Museo R. Tamayo in Oaxaca, Mexico.

guilty but also those accused, however weak the accusation, and that their houses be burnt and covered over with earth and the trees of their heirs burnt, their maize uprooted, so that in no manner would there remain the memory of such an abominable thing."

Celibacy was required of the priests, and this gave rise to homosexuality in the priesthood. Bernal recorded that in Cipalcingo (Mexico), "Those *papas* (priests) were sons of nobles and did not have wives, but practiced the cursed vice of sodomy." Something similar occurred in Peru. Cieza de León was told by Father Domingo de Santo Tomás of homosexual education in the temples of the Yungas, where, "Depending on the idol they worship, they have a man or two or more who are dressed in woman's clothes from the time of their childhood, and they speak like women and in their ways and clothes and all the rest imitate women. With these on holy and important days they have, as if in holy and religious ways, lewd carnal intercourse, especially the nobles."

"Till death us do part"

We would not wish to end this chapter without first telling some of the beautiful love stories that delighted the Indians in 1492, as they do even now in modern times.

The story of Tupa Amaru is one of the most beautiful. The chroniclers tell of how this Inca was the brother of the famous Tupac Inca Yupanqui and was so favored by the sovereign that at times he was allowed to govern the empire when his brother embarked on conquests. It happened that Tupa Amaru fell in love with Cusi Chimpo, a beautiful *ñusta* (noblewoman), who did not return his love, though with affectionate imprudence she uncovered her beautiful breasts and at times, laughing, allowed him to touch them. Tupa Amaru wandered disconsolately in the country until he came to a spring, to which he told his troubles. A spider—a sign of good fortune—appeared, followed by two courting snakes, playing on the water. The female evaded the male until he finally cut a flower and touched her with it. It was then that she agreed to copulate. Tupa Amaru understood that that particular flower had extraordinary qualities and took one. He touched Cusi Chimpo with it and she fell at his feet in surrender.

The story of Acoitapia and Chuquillanto is that of a forbidden love. Acoitapia was a humble shepherd who looked after sacred llamas, and Chuquillanto one of the Inca emperor's chosen women. The story begins with a trip into the country, taken by Chuquillanto and a friend. She set eyes on the shepherd and took a liking to him in his attractive cap with a picture of a heart and

two *papa* worms on it. It goes without saying that the shepherd also fell in love with her and his spirits fell when he discovered there was no way he could marry her. He was so affected that he fell seriously ill and his mother—a sorceress who had practiced her arts at the famous Pachacamac sanctuary—had to look after him. Having cured her son, she told him not to worry and made him up a brew of magic nettles. While all this was taking place in the humble shepherd's hut, the love-stricken lady was in the *akllawasi* or palace of the chosen women.

One night, Chuquillanto had a dream in which there appeared a bird who knew all about her troubles and advised her to go to the courtyard and sing to the four fountains. If they accompanied her in her singing, it would be proof that her love was returned. The girl did what she had been advised and received a favorable omen. So she decided to go to the shepherd's hut in search of her loved one. There she met the mother, who gave her some magic nettles and a stick. She returned to the palace of the chosen women, where, according to custom, she was searched

Sexual attraction and love were well represented in Mochica ceramics, which typically depict aspects of everyday life. At top right, this double vessel with a stirrup handle depicts a wife's fidelity. The woman holds the member of her dead husband, to whom she remains loyal in spite of her widowhood. A similar vessel, above, extols the virtues of carnal love in a scene of sexual intercourse, which is far from erotic.

The two pieces are from the huge collection of Mochica erotic art belonging to the Museo Nacional de Arqueología y Antropología in Lima.

thoroughly by the guards. They did not find anything out of the ordinary on her. At nightfall the spell took effect. Acoitapia appeared miraculously out of the stick and was finally able to lie with his love. At dawn, he went back into the stick. Chuquillanto felt happy and went out for a walk in the village. Believing herself to be safe, she asked the shepherd to take on human form again. He did so, but their luck had run out and he was seen by one of the temple guards, who had followed Chuquillanto. The guard denounced her, and the lovers fled and were forced to wander afar until they came to the Calca mountains, where they were changed into two hills, Suauciray and Pitusiray, which stand together. And now, no one can separate them.

The best-known Inca love story is the tragedy of Ollantay, written in the colonial period, which we will see later in the discussion on the theater.

The Aztec also had romantic stories, especially from the times of *tlatoani* Netzahualpilli, the king of Texcoco, whose daughter had a forbidden love for a young man whom the procuresses sent to her wrapped in a carpet. As far as the king himself was concerned, he lived only for his favorite, the lady Tula, who lived with great pomp in a palace where she wrote poetry. This state of affairs disturbed the king's first son and heir, who wrote a satire on the lady Tula. The lady defended herself by accusing the young man of treason, and the whole affair ended in tragedy with the death of the prince. The story is easier to understand if we take into account that Netzahualpilli, in spite of his 2,000 wives, loved the lady Tula tenderly.

Let us finish this chapter with a story of jealousy whose main character is also Netzahualpilli. Among his many wives there was one who was King Axayacatl's daughter. Although young, she was completely promiscuous. The chronicler Fernando Alba Ixtlilxochitl relates: "She took to any handsome young gentleman who appealed to her tastes and inclinations, gave him secret orders to take advantage of her, and having satisfied her desires, she had him killed and a statue of him made or a portrait painted." Things reached such an extreme that, according to the same chronicler, there were finally so many statues of those she had had killed

that they lined the walls all around the room. Her husband was a man who lived with his head in the clouds, though he was rather surprised that the number of statues kept growing. One day, however, he went to look for his wife and instead found a statue in her bed. He kept searching and finally found her engaged in an orgy with three high-born men. Full of jealousy—as you might expect of a man with 2,000 wives—he had the four killed. It seems that the affair rather spoiled the hitherto good political relations between Texcoco and Tenochtitlan.

79

The death of the cacique was the despair of his wives, who expressed their grief with theatrical gestures, as seen in this 18th-century print from the Biblioteca Nacional in Madrid. This scene depicts an unknown Orinoco tribe in which polygyny existed. The widows were often ordered to cut their hair or break their teeth (and sometimes to die) in order to express their grief. In other cultures, the brother of the dead husband was obliged to marry all his wives.

Life in the cities

Urban life developed in Mesoamerica around 1200 B.C. with the appearance of the Olmec culture, and later reached its height in the 15th century. The figure of the Maya ballgame player (New Orleans Museum of Art), on the previous page, and the construction of an Aztec house (from the Florentine Codex), seen above, contrast work and leisure in the city.

The great cities

Urban centers went back in Mesoamerica to Olmec times and in South America to Chavín times, but particularly to the Classic period. At the end of the 15th century and before the arrival of the Spaniards, there were many cities, grand and full of life. Others were in decline and there were even completely deserted ghost towns, like Copan, Uaxactún, Tikal, Teotihuacan and Tiahuanaco. All that remained of some, such as the legendary Tula, were a few stumps of stone.

The most outstanding cities in Mesoamerica were those in the valleys of Mexico (Texcoco, Culhuacan, Cuautitlan, Azcapotzalco): Cholula, the holy city, full of temples; the Tarasca cities (now forming part of the Michoacan and Jalisco regions) of Patzcuaro and Ihuatzio, with its T-shaped temples; the Mixtec (Oaxaca) cities of Mitla and Yagul, with their beautiful palaces; and ancient Monte Albán of the Zapotecs (now occupied by the Mixtec), with one of the greatest stone ceremonial centers in the whole of America. On the Atlantic coast were the Totonac cities, the greatest being Cempoala. Farther south, in Yucatán, were the Maya ghost towns.

Similar centers existed in the Andean region. Quito had been a magnificent Inca city and Tomebamba (now Cuenca), built by the Inca Huayna Capac, rivaled Cuzco itself. When the Spaniards discovered Tumbes they were astonished, as they were with Huánuco, Jauja, Huaytara, Vilcashuaman with its stone pyramid, and Cajamarca with its thermal baths. On the coast, powerful cities like Chan Chan, Ica and Nazca still flourished.

The most important cities were, of course, the capitals of the two empires—Tenochtitlan and Cuzco, which deserve very special attention, as it was there that the quintessential development of urban life took place, with its two most characteristic expressions: work and leisure.

Though food production was still very important in the Aztec and Inca capitals, it was less so than it had been in the past, and even then they could hardly have produced a fraction of the food consumed in the empire. Tribute paid as a result of conquest freed the citizens from the task of food production, therefore enabling them to engage in the activities that contributed to the quality of life in the cities.

The Indians' fondness for leisure was continually criticized by the Spaniards of the 16th century, in spite of the fact that they themselves firmly believed in leisure as a way of life, contrary to the ideal of hard work observed by many other European nations of the time. To the Amerindians, work had to be reduced to the minimum necessary for living, and at times they gave it a festive air, as in the Andean region, to make life more bearable.

The Tenochtitlan of 1492 was not one city but two—Tenochtitlan and Tlatelolco, separated by an arm of the lake and connected by a bridge. The two cities had been built on islets and were joined to the shore by means of three great causeways stretching out to Coyohuacan, Tlacopan and Tepeyacac. In this coastal environment were the other great cities such as Azcapotzalco and Tlacopan to the west, Iztapalapan to the south and Tenayucan to the north.

The two cities expanded by means of *chinampas*, artificial islands made of reed anchored to the bottom of the lake, on which were thrown earth and fertilizer (excellent for agriculture). Many of these islands connected with others, and resembled beautiful orchards and gardens. Like all lake cities, their main streets were canals, on which canoes, the only form of transport, circulated. There were also some dirt roads, which the Indians used when carrying loads on their shoulders, and there were even combinations of the two—canals with pavements for pedestrians.

In the city centers there were great temples, palaces and residential areas with their stone houses and terraced roofs, while on the outskirts, near the *chinampas*, were the shacks. In each district there were ceremonial centers and, on a smaller scale, civic centers. Several things impressed the Spaniards when they first saw the city: its enormous proportions, its great temples, its strategic position and its market—probably the same things that would catch the eye today.

They were able to appreciate its proportions from the high vantage point in the great temple of Tlatelolco, where Moctezuma took them to show his domain and thus discourage any hope of conquest. Bernal Díaz was extraordinarily expressive in his description of this episode: "And

In the southern region of Peten lies the origin of Classic Maya urban culture, associated in particular with the city of Tikal, whose ruins are pictured here. The oldest known stele—from 292 A.D. came from Tikal. An immense platform was constructed here around 100 A.D. at a time when the construction of funeral temples began. It was also in Tikal where the fashion of pictorial glyphs developed as a symbol of political unity, later appearing in

Uaxactum, and possibly related to political alliances. Maya history began in Tikal with its monarch Jaguar-Claw occupying the throne in 330 A.D. He was succeeded by Fluted Nose, who was in turn succeeded by Stormy Sky, on whose death in 455 the age of Maya splendor in Tikal came to an end.

The Andean region also underwent a long process of urbanization, which culminated in the Inca culture and the constructions that so amazed the European conquerors. The cities were built on steep terrain surrounded by terraced farmland and were made up of veritable swarms of houses blending in with temples and palaces, as may be seen in this view of Pisac.

Tlatelolco market, the veritable belly of the immense city of Tenochtitlan, was recreated in this mural painting in the Palacio del Gobierno in Mexico by the imagination of the brilliant Diego Rivera. It was one of the two great plazas of the city formed by Tenochtitlan and Tlatelolco, the other plaza being the location of the great temple in the religious center. The market was built over a shining tiled floor and framed within arches. One of its ends led onto a dock connected to the canal, which ran along the northern causeway. Canoes were moored at the dock and products and merchandise transferred to land. Specific products were sold in specific places, making purchasing easier. In order to buy vegetables, blankets, rugs, crockery, obsidian knives, feathers, etc., it was only necessary to go to the respective area of the market. The vendors, who were usually women, placed their merchandise on mats and haggled with their customers. The market was a hive of activity, with none of the din that is so typical of European markets. The Aztec bought and sold carefully but with enthusiasm. Warriors walked among the crowds of people, ready to intervene in the occasional inevitable argument.

then he [Moctezuma] took him by the hand [Cortés] and told him to look at his great city and all the other cities within the waters, and many other towns on land, around the same lake…and thus we were gazing, for that great, cursed temple was so tall that it dwarfed all things; and from there did we see the three causeways that enter Mexico…and we saw the fresh water that came from Chapultepec, from which the city took its supply, and on those three causeways the bridges placed at regular intervals where the water came in and went out of the lake; and we saw in that great lake such a number of canoes, some carrying provisions and others with loads and merchandise; and we saw that for to pass from every house of that great city and of all the other cities that were populated on the waters there were drawbridges made of wood, and if not then they passed in canoes…The human throng living there must be impressive, and it is calculated that the city, the cities, have more than 250,000 inhabitants, though many claim the number reaches half a million."

Monuments filled Tenochtitlan and Tlatelolco's two main *plazas*, where the temples stood. The first, situated where the Zócalo is today, was rectangular in shape, 525 by 590 ft. (160 m. by 180 m.), and surrounded by a canal, the shining new palace of Moctezuma II, the two-story houses of the civil servants and the great *cu* or temple, completed in 1487, in all its splendor. Here were the twin pyramid temples of Huitzilopochtli, the god of war, and Tlaloc, the god of the rain, accessed by majestic stairways. At the top were the altars and the figures of the deities. The temple's macabre companion was the *tzompantli*, where the skulls of sacrificial victims were set out in rows. Also in this *plaza* was the great stone used for the sacrifices as well as the sun wheel or Aztec calendar.

The most remarkable aspect of Tenochtitlan must have been its people, swarming everywhere, dressed in white and adorned with beautiful feathers showing their rank as artisans, warriors, merchants, etc. Apart from the temples, the main meeting place was the market, especially Tlatelolco market, where everyone went to buy and sell a variety of commodities.

That immense city of thousands of houses with its orchards and gardens, palaces and zoological parks, countless schools and temples, ball courts, steam baths and an infinite number of features we cannot even imagine also had a magnificent system for carrying sewage to the lakes, one thousand street cleaners who kept the city spotlessly clean, a large number of public latrines (with cane blinds), the cool weather of the *altiplano*, and the rains sent generously by the god Tlaloc.

85

The lake city of Tenochtitlan, a veritable American Venice, seen here in the imagination of the brilliant Mexican painter Diego Rivera. It was a source of amazement to the Europeans. Bernal Díaz, who was one of the few to see it before its destruction, commented that it did not seem real but "like the things of enchantment that are recounted in the book of Amadís." He described the city in these words: "And from there (from the great temple), did we see the three causeways that enter Mexico . . . and we saw the fresh water that came from Chapultepec, from which the city took its supply, and on those three causeways, the bridges placed at regular intervals. . . and we saw on that great lake such a number of canoes, some carrying provisions and others with loads of merchandise and others that returned with loads and merchandise, and we saw that for to pass from every house of that great city and all the other cities that were populated on the waters there were drawbridges made of wood, and if not then they passed in canoes . . . and we saw in those cities cues or places of worship with towers and in the form of fortresses, and all was white, which was a cause for admiration."

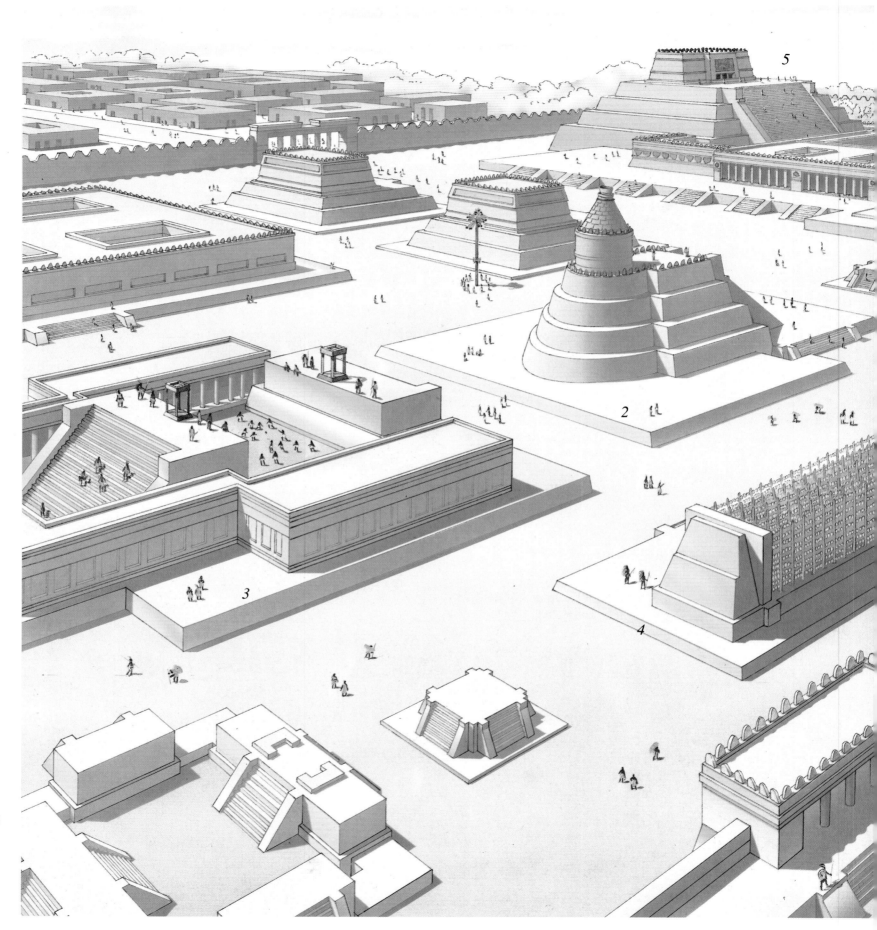

1

6

The Aztec citadel was truly monumental. The most important site was the sacred compound, at the center of the city, where the Iztapalapa, Tacuba and Tepeyac causeways intersected. It occupied a rectangular area of some 1,148 ft. by 984 ft. (350 m. by 300 m.). The main building was the great temple (1), which was rebuilt over a period of almost 200 years and completed shortly before the arrival of the Spaniards. Facing west, it consisted of a great pyramid formed by four or five levels 98 ft. (30 m.) high with a base of 328 ft. by 263 ft. (100 m. by 80 m.). At the top of its 114 steps was a square area supporting the temples of the gods Tlaloc (god of the north) and Huitzilopochtli (god of the south). Opposite the great temple was a round temple dedicated to Quetzalcoatl (2), whose entrance, according to the *conquistadores*, resembled a monster with two great fangs, what would be in the Western world the mouth of hell. Behind this, to the west, was a ballcourt (3) surrounded by atlantes and a sculpture of Xochipilli. Nearby was the *tzompantli* or altar of the skulls (4), with a base of decorated stone, where poles were placed to hold the skulls of sacrificial victims. On either side of the great temple were two other temples; the one to the south was dedicated to Tezcatlipoca (5), 66 ft. (20 m.) in height, with a stairway of 80 steps. Flanking both sides of the stairway were four more temples: The southernmost contained the gods of conquered peoples; the others were dedicated to the goddesses Cihuacoatl, Chicomecoatl and Xochiquetzal. To the north of the ballcourt was the *calmecac* (school), and south, past the *tzompantli*, was the temple of Xipe Totec, the stone used in the gladiatorial sacrifices, and the temple of the sun (6). Behind the *tzompantli* was a sacred spring.

Tenochtitlan

The three views on this page, taken from the Florentine Codex, *illustrate the skill of Aztec artisans.
Feather tapestries and mosaics were made with me-
ticulous care by tying the down to a weft of cloth during the weaving process. In this way the craftsmen
made capes, shields and tapestries with beautiful,
colorful patterns depicting animals, plants and simple geometrical motifs of enormous decorative value.*

The typical day of a male citizen of Tenochtitlan began at sunrise, signaled by the temple
trumpets and shell horns (the women got up a
little earlier to do the household tasks). He would
throw off the blanket and leave it on the mat on
which he had slept. Then he would stretch, go to
the *temazcalli* or bathroom, which was an adjoin-
ing room, and then return to the bedroom to dress.
This was a simple operation, as he slept in his loin
cloth, so all he had to do was put on his blanket
and sandals. He rinsed out his mouth, washed his
face, and picked up some *itacatl* to eat later. Then
he went off to work. The women normally stayed
at home, looking after the children, cooking,
feeding the animals and cleaning the house.

Houses varied from the modest hut to great
palaces, but the commonest type of dwelling was
the stucco house with its garden, the yard with its
hearth, a bedroom for the whole family, another
small room and the bathroom. Furniture consisted of the sleeping mats. The mat would be
placed on a dirt or wooden platform that also
served as a seat, even in the law courts. An *icpalli*,

another kind of refined seat used by men of high
rank, was made of reeds or wood with a backrest
(but no legs). The rest of the furniture was made
up of cushions and a few cases for keeping household goods. In Moctezuma's palace there were
some small tables and screens, but these were
considered luxuries.

Aztec clothing for normal, day-to-day life
consisted of two pieces, the *maxtlatl* and the
tilmatli. The first was the typical loin cloth; this
was the only item worn when doing hard work
such as lifting heavy objects or working on the
land. It was tied around the waist, passed between
the legs and knotted at the front. The model worn
by the upper classes was embroidered and edged.
The other item of clothing was the maguey blanket or cape. The dignitaries wore *tilmatlis* made
of cotton and even of woven feathers and rabbit
fur. The cotton version was usually decorated
with attractive, colorful patterns. Some are illustrated in the *Magliabecchi Codex*. Women's
clothing was made up of the *cueitl*, a skirt reaching down to the calves and held at the waist by an

*One of the many crafts in Tenochtitlan was that of
the featherworker, depicted here. This craftsman
made crests, crowns, shields, insignia, etc., using the
feathers of tropical birds brought by the* pochteca *or
merchants from the tropical regions.*

*Aztec goldsmithery was only in its beginning stages
at the time of the arrival of the Spaniards. The technique had been developed in South America, particularly in the north Andean countries, many ornaments finally reaching Mesoamerica. Mixtec goldsmithery was of a high standard, and the Aztec were
beginning to develop this craft using copper as well
as gold.*

Clothes worn by Aztec women of the aristocracy were essentially the same as those worn by the poorer classes but were easily distinguished by the beautiful embroidery decorating them, especially on the neckline of the huipilli. *However, unusual fashions using loud colors and a diamond-shaped cape arrived from the Atlantic coast and were adopted by those who wished to be considered elegant.*

embroidered girdle, and the *huipilli*, a blouse with an embroidered neck that hung over the top of the skirt. Women from poor families went about bare-breasted. The clothing of the women of the aristocracy was the most ostentatious, with elaborate embroidery and patterns. The *quemitlo*, a short cape originating on the Atlantic coast, was occasionally worn. Footwear consisted of *cactli* or sandals with soles and heels made of vegetable fiber or leather. They were tied around the foot with straps. It was not unusual, however, for the men to walk barefoot.

As regards personal hygiene, several points are worthy of mention. The Aztec was very clean and liked to bathe at least once every two days in the waters of the lake or canals. He also took frequent steam baths in the *temazcalli*. Soap was made from the fruit of the *copalxocotl*, which the Spaniards called the soap tree or American root. The women were also very clean. In the advice given by a father to his daughter: "Wash your face, wash your hands, wash out your mouth…so that your husband shall not hate you, dress tidily,

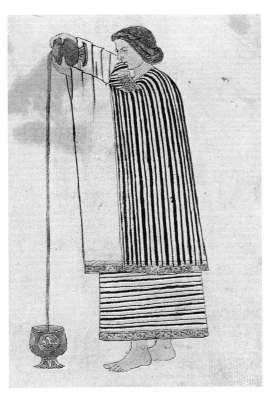

The usual form of dress of the Aztec woman was a long skirt that came down to the calves and sometimes to the ankles, held at the waist by an embroidered belt, and the huipilli *or voluminous blouse, which went from the shoulders to the knees. Poorer Aztec women went barefoot. This picture from the* Tudela Codex *shows an Aztec woman at work.*

wash yourself and your clothes." They often washed their hair, as we can see in the *Florentine Codex*. They wore their hair smoothed down or styled into two small horns. The women of the aristocracy used cosmetics, painting their faces with a yellow pigment, though this was not recommended by fathers to their daughters: "Let it never occur to you to paint your face and use colors on it in order to adorn yourself, for this is a sign of the mundane, carnal woman…Shameless women use it." It was not considered shameless, however, to adorn the ears or to wear necklaces or armlets, provided they were worn with care, since such items indicated the social level of those who wore them and for that reason were restricted.

Having washed and dressed, the Aztec went off to work. A crowd of people would jostle him and give him hardly enough room to walk along the narrow streets. The streets seethed with noise and smells and a sea of white blankets, some of them embroidered in the typical style of the east. The city was coming to life. Old men in sober

blankets and elegant goatee beards would mix with priests in black tunics with hair short at the sides and combed into a crest on top and with warriors dressed in quilted clothing and beautiful plumes.

Work continued without interruption until ten o'clock in the morning, when the shell horns and drums sounded again. It was time for the first meal of the day. The worker could eat food brought from home or purchased from the women street vendors, who exhorted the passersby to buy their cups of *atole*, pancakes and *tamales*.

After this break, work continued until midday, which was announced by another sound of the shell horn and drums. It was now lunchtime and most people went back to their homes to eat. After lunch they went back to work (some took a brief nap), which would continue uninterrupted until night, at which time the people went back home, had supper, chatted with the family, and finally went to sleep on their mats in readiness for the next day.

Aztec men's clothing was made up of two garments: the maxtlatl *or loincloth and the* tilmatli, *which was a kind of cape made of cotton, maguey fiber and even rabbit fur interwoven with feathers. The nobles, like this lord of Texcoco depicted in the* Florentine Codex, *also wore other garments, such as the short skirt.* Cactli *or sandals with soles made of leather or vegetable fiber were worn on the feet.*

There was an extremely wide variety of jobs and professions in the city. Some people still farmed and fished, but they were virtually relics from the past. More common were those who served the public as woodmen, watersellers, street cleaners, painters and builders. On the Chapultepec aqueduct, for example, a gang of men worked on cleaning and maintenance. Craftsmen were very important, but the highest-paid professions were those of the administrator, the merchant, the warrior and the priest, who usually came from the nobility. Aztec expansion had given rise to an enormous bureaucracy—ambassadors, tax collectors, military leaders, and others.

A merchant held enormous prestige. By definition, the word "merchant," or *pochteca*, meant one who traded with the outside—not the small shopkeeper. He dealt in valuable goods, which he took from coast to coast in canoes and caravans with *tlameme* porters. These carried loads weighing up to 50 pounds (23 kg.) on wooden frames resting on their backs and strapped to their heads. From the valley the merchants took cotton cloth, gold jewelry, earmuffs, obsidian knives and a host of other goods. They brought back jade, emeralds, sea snails, feathers, sea turtle shells, jaguar skins and amber, among other things. They lived in the most exclusive areas in the cities, always keeping in touch with their fellow merchants from other cities.

Merchants' corporations existed in some 10 cities in central Mexico. The business was handed down from father to son within a very close-knit group. The apprentice merchant had to be accepted by the merchants' guild and was also required to accompany his master on at least one trip. If he returned successful from the trip, he was considered capable enough to travel with a caravan with his own merchandise. After completing several business trips he was expected to offer a sumptuous feast, after which he was authorized to lead or guide caravans. This amounted to recognition as a full-fledged merchant. The merchants were powerful not only for financial reasons but also because of their knowledge of the Mesoamerican world. They were therefore used by the Aztec authorities as spies in finding out which peoples were worth con-

90

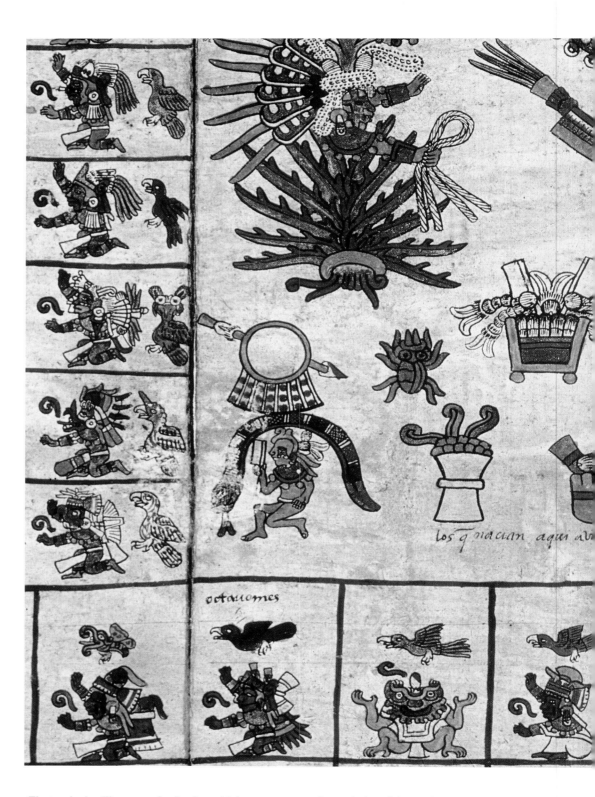

The tonalpohualli *or sacred calendar, which was recorded in the* Tonalamatl *or book of predictions, ruled the destiny of the Aztec and had to be consulted on all the important occasions in a person's life or when one was about to embark on an important undertaking. It was made up of 260 days or 20 months of 13 days, which ran without interruption over the months, thus forming complicated combinations of a magical nature. A deity governed each 13-day period, and the combinations of the different periods resulted in a favorable or unfavorable sign for each person. Even if the prediction were negative, there was always a method of finding a favorable combination by consulting the* tonalpouhqui *or reader of destinies. Here, on a page from the* tonalamatl *from the* Bourbon Codex *(Bourbon Palace, Paris), the protector of* octli *or pulque drinkers is depicted emerging from a giant maguey, sur-*

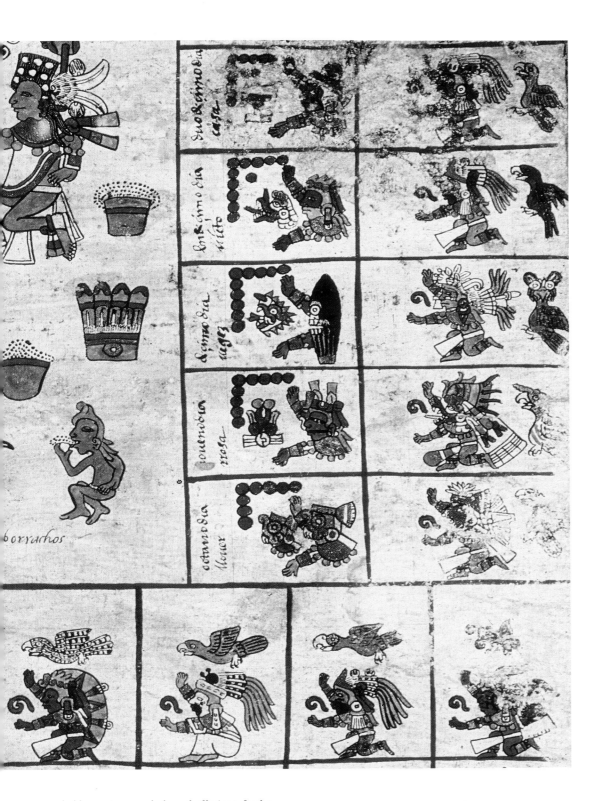

borrachos

rounded by various symbols and offerings. In the smaller paintings are the days of the month from 1 to 13, with their respective gods. The other sections depict the gods of the hours of the day. In the center is the legend "those who are born here shall be drunkards," and in the lateral sections are the "first," "second" days, etc. In order to avert one's fate, it was possible to appeal to the same gods as those who had determined it.

Night life

The second time the shell horns and drums were sounded in the temples (the first was at nightfall) was at around 9 p.m. It signaled bedtime for the vast majority of Tenochtitlan's citizens. For others, however, it announced the beginning of another night's fun and entertainment.

In the houses of some of the rich, magnificent banquets were given as a prelude to the long lively nights of singing and dancing that would go on until dawn. In others a birth or wedding might be celebrated, in which the old people would drink and drink while they told jokes and laughed.

The *telpochcalli* students would begin their frenetic dances, which, according to Sahagún, "Lasted until midnight had passed. And then no one covered his body. Thus they danced, all wrapped in *ayates* (thin blankets) from Chalcas. In truth it was as if all went naked. The singing concluded, they all dispersed. The next day will be thus, and the next day once again. They go together to each *tlazillcalli* and there they sleep in the dormitories of the *telpochcalli*, and the grown ones, those who already know of earthly things, sleep with their lovers." Night time was also the time of the *auianime* or courtesans, those ladies associated with the *quachictin* (warriors), who went to the *cuicatalli* to dance with them. These ladies wore cosmetics and jewelry.

Thus the evening was spent until midnight, when the priests were called to get up for prayer and penitence. At the next watch, at around 3 a.m. the boys in the schools were awoken to bathe in the rivers, and the girls, who were educated in the temples, to begin sweeping. Also awoken at this time were merchants who had far to travel.

Thus the night had its own rhythm—as in any other city in the world—with its banquets, drinking sessions, dancing, work and prayer.

In January 1932, in Monte Albán, archaeologists discovered tomb number 7, which contained the biggest and best treasure trove of pre-Columbian Mexican goldwork ever found. Among the various objects were 10 breastplates made of gold and decorated with renderings of deities and mythological characters. The most common shape was of a head with a large filigree headdress and two square plates forming the body, as in this example. All the figures wore earrings and various ornaments. Monte Albán was an ancient Zapotec settlement occupied later by the Mixtec. Also found were gold objects from South America, thus demonstrating the transpacific contact between Mesoamerica and the southern hemisphere. The ritual mask in the photograph is in the Museo de Oaxaca.

quering and the kind of tribute they were capable of offering. It was a dangerous profession, and each time a merchant was to set out on a new expedition he gave a banquet to his fellow merchants in exchange for useful advice.

After this prestigious profession came that of the craftsman, whose members have given us the most precious examples of pre-Columbian American art. It has been said that the Aztec artisans inherited a legacy of craftsmanship that enabled them to reach such a degree of perfection, but this is not exactly true. The Aztec obtained the most valuable pieces from the conquered peoples, and the origin of the Aztec society—including the artisans—is still a mystery. It should not be forgotten that they became civilized at a very late stage, thus being able to assimilate the advanced crafts of the Classic cultures. Perhaps that is why the Aztec artisans were called Toltecs—undoubtedly an allusion to their origin. It is possible that when Tula was destroyed, some of its most brilliant citizens went to the villages in the Valley of Mexico, where they worked and passed on the artistic traditions that the Aztec inherited through their conquests.

The craftsmen lived in special areas within the city and had their own gods and even their own religious ceremonies. Apparently, Moctezuma II had them incorporated into the state machinery, and this is why there were so many craftsmen working within the palace. According to Berna, "He had masters, and of these there were a great many, of all the crafts there were among them." This large number of specialized workers was apparent in the markets, called *tianquiztli*, where many of their products were sold.

The artistry of the Aztec craftsmen

One of the most highly respected artisans in Aztec society was the precious-stone engraver, who worked mainly with turquoise, of which the best examples come from Azcapotzalco. There were also great masters of stone carving, who combined elements of fantasy and realism in their work, the best of which can be seen in the Museo de Antropología in Mexico. The most popular is the solar calendar wheel, carved at the time of Moctezuma and discovered at the end of the 18th century. It is almost 12 ft. (4 m.) wide and represents the fifth sun, surrounded by its four predecessors. The statue of the goddess Coatlicue is also famous. Over 10 ft. (3 m.) in height, hands and feet resembling claws, she wears a skirt of snakes and a necklace of human hands and hearts. No less impressive is the goddess Coyolxauhqui, of the same size, the top part of her body dismembered and the blood flowing from her severed joints. Also worthy of mention are the *cuauhxicalli*, the jaguar-shaped vases where the hearts of human sacrifices were collected, and the stone of Tizoc, which depicts the *tlatoani* of the same name.

There were great masters of featherwork in the capital, though these did not reach the perfection of the Totonaca artisans, whose work was imported. They made colorful mosaics, headdresses, crests and insignia for the dignitaries. The feather artisans lived in Amantlan, where the shrine of their patron god Coyotlinahuatl, or "he who is dressed as a coyote," stood. The ceramists were masterful in their coiling technique and made ceramics for everyday use as well as for ceremonial occasions. Aztec ceramics was of good quality, but the best, as used by the *tlatoani* of Mexico at mealtimes, came from Cholula, where at least two kinds were made, "one red and one dark," according to Bernal Díaz.

Weaving was mainly done by women. The Aztec demanded enormous tribute in cotton as well as blankets from the peoples of the tropical regions. The goldsmiths and silversmiths seem to have come from the Pacific coast. Metal-working reached Mesoamerica from South America relatively late, about 900 A.D. The jewels, sheets and little tiles of gold made by the goldsmiths were highly treasured by the Aztec and were part of the treasure of Axayacatl, which Moctezuma kept hidden (behind a false wall) in his father's palace, where he very naïvely lodged the Spaniards.

Finally, we should also mention the painters and wood carvers. Of these, Bernal Díaz wrote that in Mexico there were three who were so skilled that, "had they been contemporaries in ancient times of the renowned Apeles, or of Michaelangelo or Berruguete in our times, these three would have been placed among them." Mural painting was used extensively in architecture. Excavation work in the great temple of Tenochtitlan has shown that the reliefs and friezes were painted, which demonstrates the fine sense of town-planning and aesthetics achieved in the capital of the Aztec empire. The city possessed a large number of monuments painted by the *tlahavilo*—the mural painters—men endowed with a special religious and aesthetic sense that enabled them to interpret the will of the gods through the symbolism associated with the different colors used in their excellent work.

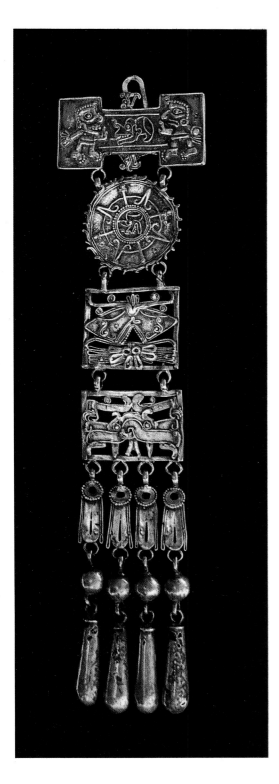

The best pre-Columbian works of gold in Mexico were made by the Mixtec. This was made possible by the coincidence of gold deposits in the area and the influence of metallurgy from the south. This beautiful breastplate is a fine example of how several sections were joined. The design, stylization of the figures and economy in the use of precious metals were typical characteristics of this craft.

Cuzco, the way to the clouds

In the beautiful Andean valley where the Huatanay and Tullumayo rivers meet, encompassed by a circle of mountains rising to 11,500 ft. (3,400 m.) above sea level—among them Huanacauri, where, according to legend, Manco Capac sank his golden staff, where the clouds descending from the Andes linger lazily—lies the city of Cuzco, the capital of the empire whose god was the sun. Cuscu or Cuzco probably does not mean "navel," as some have suggested, but in any case it was considered the navel of the Inca world. Perhaps for this reason it had the rare privilege of being built on arable land, something the Inca usually avoided; good land was too valuable and scarce to be wasted by building houses on it. Cuzco was not ancient, and although its origins went back to 1100 A.D., the truth of the matter is that it was virtually rebuilt by Pachacutec around the middle of the 15th century. It is thought that to build a better city a model in clay was first made. It is also said that 30,000 men worked on the construction. Near the city, toward the mountains, Tupac Yupanqui built the imposing Sacsahuaman fortress. The

Beyond the clouds, on the road to the sun, where the Andes touch the sky with lofty snow-capped peaks such as Nevado del Cuzco, was the capital of the Inca empire. It was a gigantic city of probably 100,000 and perhaps even 200,000 inhabitants. Cuscu or Cuzco was and still is in a beautiful valley, 9,900 ft. (3,000 m.) above sea level, irrigated by the rivers Huatanay and Tullumayo, one of the few cities built by the Inca on arable land. It has a clear sky and a reddish light, a fresh climate and an aura of silence and mystery peculiar to all the Andean cities. Its legendary origin goes back to the year 1100 A.D., but in fact it owes its greatness to Pachacutec, who made the city what it was only 80 years before the arrival of the Spaniards. It is claimed that 30,000 Indians worked on its construction, and it is possible that work was carried out according to a model made in clay. Like the two Mexicos, there

were two Cuzcos: Huanan Cuzco, the upper,
and Hurin Cuzco, the lower. According to tradition,
the first was made by those whom the son of the sun
civilized, and the second by those civilized by his
wife and sister, the coya.

structure had three successive walls made of enormous blocks of stone forming salients and entrances.

There were two Cuzcos, Huanan Cuzco or Cuzco the High, and Hurin Cuzco, Cuzco the Low. According to legend, these were the places settled by the people civilized by the son of the sun and his sister and wife. It was also divided into four parts, each one corresponding to one of the *Tahuantinsuyu* or Four Corners of the World.

In the center of Cuzco was the *collcampata*, the main area, where the Inca king, his relatives and descendants of other emperors lived. People from other parts of the empire built their houses in areas surrounding the center, and each area had its own particular inhabitants. By knowing where they lived, it is possible to calculate how long each group had resided in each district in Cuzco and also where in the empire they had migrated from.

The layout of the city was like a chessboard, with two main squares forming the centers. These two squares were joined in times of celebration to make it even more magnificent. Garcilaso wrote, "The square that they call Cusipoata is a place of joy and happiness. In the times of the Inca, those two squares were made one; all the stream was covered with thick beams and on top of them were placed great slabs of stone to serve as a floor, for there gathered so many lords and vassals at the main festivals which they held to honor the sun they did not all fit in the square that we call the principal square. For this reason they widened the space with another square no less great than the first." Cuzco was equally amazing to the Spaniards. Sancho de la Hoz wrote of Cuzco, "It is full of stately palaces, and we saw no sign of poor people. Each lord built his house, although he did not necessarily reside permanently in it. Most of these residences are of stone and the others possess half of the façade of this same material. There are also many houses made of brick and they are set out in perfect order along the length of the narrow streets, all of which are paved and have a groove making a stone channel in the middle." The stone channel, flanked on both sides with pavement, was used to keep the streets clean.

The most important buildings were beside the main square. They were made of stone, each block fitting perfectly into the others. They usually had a large yard inside, decorated with vases full of flowers and overlooked by all the rooms. There were no doors, the openings being covered with beautiful tapestries. Animal skins were laid out on the floor. As the distance from the center of the city increased, the height and quality of the houses decreased, so that on the outskirts the houses were made of straw.

The building that stood out among all the others was the Coricancha or great temple of the sun, situated in front of a great square where, according to Garcilaso, "there arrived those who

This print, which accompanied the publication of the work Civitas Orbis Terrarum *in 1595, depicts an idealized Cuzco in no way similar to the real one. Although its layout was like a chessboard, as in the print, its main plaza was in the center and not at the side. In the center, too, was the main district or col-lcampata, where the Inca emperor, his family and the descendants of previous kings resided. At its four cardinal points peoples who had been civilized through conquest subsequently came to live. There is no trace in this fictional recreation of Cuzco's most characteristic architecture, with its polygonal stones and trapezoidal doors and windows.*

Characteristic of Cuzco was its cosmopolitanism, for people from all over the empire could be seen there wearing regional dress and headgear. This was not, however, due to any fashion but because it was compulsory for each person to wear the particular type of clothing worn in his place of origin so as to be more easily identified. High functionaries, warriors, priests and merchants walked the streets of Cuzco alongside countless herds of llamas. The most

eminent pedestrians were the nobles or orejones, who wore symbols of their high social standing and sometimes traveled in litters. In this 18th-century colonial painting from the Museo Pedro de Osma in Lima, we see two Inca nobles still wearing clothes typical of their social class.

were not Inca with the offerings they had brought, for they could not enter into the house." Pedro De Cieza De Leon says that it was a rectangular compound with a perimeter of 400 paces, constructed of stones placed together without mortar. Halfway up, there was a cornice made of gold, four handbreadths wide. Its doors, covered in gold, led to a garden where there was a representation of a maize field and a small flock of 20 llamas. Everything was made of gold—the corn ears, the leaves and the life-size llamas.

Inside the garden were four sanctuaries whose walls were also covered with gold. In the largest of these sanctuaries was the solar deity, an enormous golden disk emitting rays of light. It was, according to Garcilaso, "so great that it covered all the space of the temple from wall to wall." On the other side of the temple was a cloister in which the moon (Quilla) was worshiped. Quilla was represented by a great silver (or possibly platinum) disk on which was etched the face of a woman. The chapel and its doors were covered in sheets of silver. In the other chapels the gods of lightning (Illapa), and of the rainbow (Amarru) were worshiped. Not far from the Coricancha were the temples housing the mummies of the previous Inca kings, seated on golden thrones.

Inca constructions are characterized by rectilinear, rather than curvilinear shapes, walls wider at the base to better withstand the effect of earthquakes, the use of trapezoidal wall openings with monolithic lintels and perfectly fitting blocks of stone in which the joints were frequently beveled, giving a quilted effect to the wall.

Although estimates vary, more than 100,000 or possibly 200,000 people lived in Cuzco. As with Tenochtitlan, the most impressive of all were the inhabitants dressed in *uncus* or blankets, wearing caps whose varied colors indicated their place of origin. High officials, warriors, priests and merchants walked its streets, at times alongside herds of llamas. In general, the city was clean, partly due to the cold, dry climate. Garcilaso attributed the absence of flies—"Nor mosquitos of that type which bites"—to the climate, and also the fact that it was possible to dehydrate the *papa* to make *tasajo*, or beef jerky.

Cuzco was not only the capital of the empire but an architectural showpiece as well. Some-

times the design was reproduced on a smaller scale when, for example, it was necessary to set up a large military camp, as happened when the forces of Chiquimancu were attacked. Pachacutec had a "mini-Cuzco" built at the entrance to the Canete Valley. Coyor and Chuquilin

were also reminiscent of the capital. The imperial city began to lose importance at the beginning of the 16th Century when Huayna Capac insisted on building Tomebamba (modern Cuenca, Ecuador). The double capital was then ruled by Atahualpa and Huasca

A Cuzcoan's typical day

Unlike Tenochtitlan, daily life in Cuzco was not regulated by the sound of the shell horn and the drum. Nevertheless, time was perfectly ordered and planned. The citizen awoke to the infernal din of his wife beating the corn in the *metate*, a rhythmic banging which at times echoed through the floor like an earthquake. The woman got up half an hour to an hour before her husband.

The man got unhurriedly out of bed, which consisted of a llama skin draped on the floor and folded in the middle. The lower half acted as a mattress and the upper as the blanket. People from the higher classes placed mattresses of straw or dried grass underneath, making their beds warmer and more comfortable.

When he got out of bed, he dressed in one of his two llama wool suits, the choice depending on whether it was a holiday or a normal working day. Both sets of clothes had been provided from public or government stores on his wedding day, and he looked after them with great care. If, for any reason, they were torn, his wife would sew them for him, darning the area affected until it

had been restored. When the Indians saw the rough patching up that the Spaniards did to their clothes they were greatly amused.

The Inca man usually wore three items of clothing. The size and color of all clothing was uniform, and so each person adapted the clothing to his measurements. The first item was the *huarca* or loin cloth, the second the *uncu* or sleeveless blouse with three openings—one for the head and two for the arms—and the third was the *yacolla*, a narrow rectangular cape placed over the shoulders and tied around the chest. Finally he dressed his hair with finger-wide head bands made of llama wool (*llautu*), winding them around his head several times. (It was the Colla Indians who wore the woollen cap with earflaps, which is nowadays believed to be typical of the Inca.) Women's clothing was also very simple. It consisted of a tunic reaching down to the calves or possibly the feet, with a slit up the side to make walking easier, and a gray cape (*lliclla*), similar to the man's, held at the chest with a broad-headed pin (*topu*). The tunic was usually gathered at the waist with some kind of embroidered

belt. The footware was unisex and consisted of *usuta* or sandals made of llama leather. The sole came from the neck of the llama skin, this being the thickest part. The sandal was tied at the ankle and instep with a strip of brightly colored wool. The unusual feature of the *usuta* was that it was smaller than the foot, so that the toes protruded, allowing them to be used when necessary, as, for example, in walking down steep slopes.

Washed and clothed, the Cuzcoan had a light breakfast, eaten in a squatting position. If he was a farmer, the house would be a hut with pressed earth walls. It would be made of stone if he belonged to a higher social class (on the coast the walls were made with adobe). Houses were given to newly married couples and were built by the local community. They consisted of a single windowless room with a small opening over which a mat was placed to serve as a door. The area was divided up into two parts by a central wall, giving the hut an area for cooking, eating and living in one part, and a bedroom, in which all the members of the family slept, in the other. In the living area were the hearth, the mortar for

98

Though the Inca married couple shared the work, it was the woman who endured the larger share. As well as looking after the house and the children, she had to reap and sow, along with her husband, and had to tend the pair of llamas they had received from the state upon their marriage. The wife always ate after the husband, and she was also responsible for transporting food and dishes when they were to eat outside the home (usually in some communal cel-

ebration). According to Pedro Pizarro, she even followed the man to war, carrying his chicha *(beer) and weapons. Depicted on the possibly colonial* kero *on the right, from the Museo de la Universidad in Cuzco, an Inca woman looks after a pair of llamas, with the aid of her* boleadoras. *On the* kero *on the left, belonging to the Leoncio Artega Collection in Lima, we see an Inca couple working together on the land.*

grinding, plates and utensils. Clothes were hung from pegs on the wall or kept in clay containers. In one corner was a box made of woven reeds where the woman kept her personal effects and homemaking tools, such as spindles, wooden needles, wool, pins, a mirror and a few trinkets. The house was dark and badly ventilated, but it served as a shelter from the cold Andean nights. In any case, it was not used frequently as a place for the family to gather, except during the rainy season in January, when the family sat around the oven telling stories, jokes or things of interest that had happened in the city. They also took advantage of this time of the year to cut each other's hair, darn torn clothing and make small repairs to household utensils. The custom in Cuzco was to wear the hair short, contrasting with the custom of the Colla and Rucana Indians, who wore it long.

While the husband ate his breakfast his wife would make the beds, feed the couple of llamas they had been given on getting married and perform other household tasks. If she was young she would spend some time on her appearance. She

99

The plain, functional ceramics of the Inca do not provide any information about their everyday life, as was also the case with artifacts of other peoples from the coast of Peru. Inca wood keros, however, sometimes do depict common scenes, such as those pictured here. The main disadvantage is that the vast majority of those that have survived are from the colonial period, very few being pre-Columbian. At right, we see a kero *from the Museo de América in Madrid depicting a farmer working the land with a short hoe, which, along with the* taclla *or digging stick, was one of the pre-Hispanic agricultural tools. The Inca used llama dung, fish and guano as fertilizer. On the left, we see an Inca noble—an* orejon— *in his cape and feather headdress, armed with a lance and shield. From the Museo de la Universidad in Cuzco.*

would wash her clothes and rub them with *cabuya* leaves, use urine to wash the grease from her hair, wash and comb it with a cactus-spine comb, and even depiliate parts of her body. If she was no longer young, she would be more disheveled and dirty, giving the excuse that the housework left her no time for looking after herself. And she had reason to complain; she had to gather firewood, cook, weave, darn, look after the children, the animals and the garden, help her husband work the land, go to the market to barter and in the evening delouse the family.

As the Cuzcoan made his way to work, the streets would be full of other people, usually walking in silence. As it was the law for each man to wear clothing denoting his place of origin, the streets would be filled with a whole range of different, readily identifiable races and customs. Here would be a Huanca from the north with his black turban, there a Colla from Titicaca with his typical woollen cap, and over there a Cañari wearing his wooden crown, or a Cajamarca Indian with a fine cord in his hair. Watersellers with their *aribalos* on their backs would come and go, *amautas* or teachers, the children of leaders from far-off lands who were obliged to send their sons to Cuzco to be educated, women carrying bundles of firewood, and even important lords. Sometimes there were traffic jams, especially when a *cacique* in his litter coincided in the street with a flock of llamas. Naturally the llamas had priority.

It was the Inca who invented the complete working day. Work went on uninterrupted from eight or nine in the morning until five in the evening. If a worker felt tired or hungry, he would chew a few coca leaves and soon recover his strength. When work finished he would go home and eat his main meal, which was prepared between five and six in the evening, often accompanied with *chicha*, a corn beer. Then everyone would go off to bed to recover their strength for the hard work of the next day, when the same process would be repeated.

A great tradition in textiles

The Inca inherited the greatest textile tradition, going back more than 3,500 years, in all of America.

One of the cultures to excel in this particular tradition was the Paraca, which flourished between the sixth century B.C. and the first century A.D. The discovery of its existence in 1925 was one of the most spectacular in the history of archaeology, for it made possible the further discovery of a cemetery in the Paracas desert, where the funeral urns of important personages buried over a period of 400 years were found virtually intact. The oldest section is called the *Caverna* (caverns) and the most recent the Necropolis, so named from the shape of the graves. The latter accommodates 429 mummified bodies wrapped in cloth and accompanied by funeral urns. Some of the graves contained as many as 16 blankets embroidered with figures, 48 garments (among them *llautos* or headbands, skirts and *uncus* [blouses], used later by the Inca) and 31 pieces of rough cloth, as well as other objects (slings, a stone club, 30 gold ornaments, a pyrite mirror, a shell necklace, among others).

The basic materials used were both cotton and wool, which was dyed after it was spun (there were as many as 190 different shades of color). It was woven on vertical looms using a variety of techniques. The material was decorated using framing techniques as it was made (two-colored tapestries with lines and geometric designs following the weft and warp) or embroidered with the back-stitch and loop process (in which case the motifs were polychrome), or painted onto the cloth. Themes depicted were naturalistic (animals, severed human heads, natural objects) or fantastic (exotic creatures based on real animals). Another popular theme involved imaginary animals and creatures that were a combination of animal and man.

Decoration on the cloth was used to create a harmonic effect, using a symmetrical design and regular patterning of figures. The Paracas cloths show not only a perfection in the art of textile making but also a tremendous degree of specialization, partly due to the large number of master spinners, weavers, dyers, embroiderers, etc., all of whose techniques were used in Peru.

In the Valley of Nazca, in southern Peru, lived a pre-Inca culture whose art blended the style of Tiahuanaco with its own particular style. Its ceramics were thin, polished and brilliant, decorated with the most beautifully vivid colors, making it one of the most exceptional types in pre-Columbian America. In this example a bottle depicts a young woman whose body is out of all proportion and imitates the shape of a type of food. Her dress is printed with steplike geometric designs typical of Tiahuanaco. Her hair is plaited, her face decorated with dots, and she is wearing a headdress. On the right side of the mouth the small bulge of the mambe *or ball of coca leaves and lime is clearly visible. The ball was moved from one side of the mouth to the other and was a popular stimulant. The piece is on display in the Museo de Arqueología y Antropología in Lima.*

The craftsmen of the Andes

As in Tenochtitlan, civil servants and craftsmen were numerous in Inca cities. The difference between the Aztec and the Inca was that there were probably more civil servants and fewer craftsmen among the Aztec, as more man-hours were required for working the land than for any other activity. Even the Cuzcoans, who had risen in status with their conquests, were still primarily farmers.

Administrative posts were numerous: governors, inspectors, regional and local chiefs, large- and small-scale shepherds, stewards, judges, etc. As regards other professions, it seems that there was no distinction between high and low levels,

as was the case with the Aztec. Working on construction were stonecutters, engravers and masons, and here the workers were true artists. Great blocks of stone had to be cut, worked with bronze chisels and polished with wet sand until they would fit perfectly together. A hollow wooden ruler with small round stones inside was used as a level, and vertical positioning was gauged using a primitive plumb line consisting of a small metal bar tied to a thread. Stonemasons are portrayed on some vessels from Puno and Santiago de Chao; some are seen carrying bags of materials on their heads, others placing stones in salients, and others leveling the ground.

Inca artisans excelled in feather decorations, ceramics, weaving, tanning and goldsmithing. Parrot, macaw and toucan feathers were brought from the east, kept in the royal warehouses and given out to the craftsmen, who made the most remarkable tapestries and headdresses from them. Inca ceramic artists inherited the Tiahuanaco and Chimú traditions. Tupac Yupanqui even had craftsmen from the coastal region brought to Cuzco to set up a school of ceramics. Inca ceramic work was functional, with bowls and vessels in the Tiahuanaco tradition and a very commonly found receptacle that was later called the *aribalo*, reminiscent of the shape of the char-

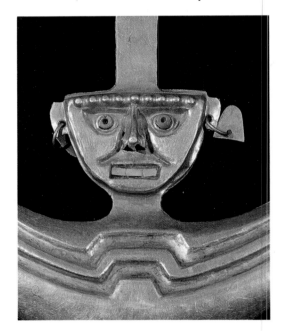

In the Inca empire, precious metals were state property and used only in the making of religious objects, funeral urns, ornaments for the nobles and tableware for the Inca emperor. Typical of the Cuzco area were gold and silver figurines of men and animals like this llama made with layers of 14-carat gold fused together. In these figures, moderately stylized forms and the static position of the animals

stand out. The piece pictured here is in the Museo de Arqueología y Antropología in Lima.

One of the greatest collections of pre-Columbian works in gold—the Brüning Collection—is in the Museo de Lambayeque in Peru. Shown here from this collection are two pieces. The first is part of a pair of tweezers encrusted with turquoise, and below it is a funeral mask with lapis lazuli eyes.

The tumis *or semicircular axes that were so characteristic of the Chimú and Mochica were later made in large quantities by the Inca, who usually carved a figure such as the head of a llama or of a person on the handle. On this breastplate there are two mythological human-looking creatures, one of which is holding a* tumi *in its hand. The piece is made of gold.*

acteristic cylindrical Greek vessel. With its high neck and its truncated-cone shape, it could be moved easily. Two low-placed handles made it easy to use and even to carry on the back when strung with a rope. The Inca decorated these receptacles with black and white geometrical patterns on a red background.

Textiles were made mainly by the women. In the convents of the sun virgins and chosen women of the Inca emperor, enormous amounts were made to meet the demands of the cult, the emperor and the royal warehouses. Llama wool was mainly used, cotton being imported from the coast. Women could be seen spinning wherever they went, often while they carried their young children on their backs and a heavy object on their heads. The looms they used were rudimentary, the most common being the vertical loom with two sticks driven into the ground, or the belt type, where one of the ends hung from a branch or from a beam and the other was a belt that the woman adjusted around her hips to move the weft

of cloth gently backwards and forwards. Another two sticks made it possible to move the warp, between which a wooden needle with the thread was passed. The cloth was not dyed when finished because the yarns were pre-dyed. Inca textiles were mainly functional but were decorated with great elegance, with the finest examples coming from the warmer regions.

The tanners worked with Andean hides, which came mainly from the llama. These were dried and kept in containers filled with urine, then beaten smooth and used to make sandals and wine skins.

The goldsmiths were supreme artisans. The best work in America came out of the Andean area between Panama and Peru, where metallurgy had originated in the Formative period. The smiths worked with gold, silver and copper, though tin and arsenic residues have been found in many pieces. Only one pre-Columbian mine, in Cerro Blanco, Peru, has been discovered. Here were found triangular hammer heads most probably used as tools. Not far from the mine, *metates* and smelting ovens comprised of holes in the ground have been found. In these hollows the fuel (firewood or coal) was placed, then the mineral,

103

Erotic realism in Mochica goldwork is clearly visible in this gold figurine from the Brüning Collection, impudently showing off his member. The figurine is practically identical to the one on the left, except in the size of the earrings and the hands. It weighs 28 grams and is 3 in. (7.5 cm.) tall.

A funeral statuette of a human figure made of two metals. Though the piece is of gold and enamel and similar in size to that on the left, the earrings, belt and breastplates are of iron. Like the other pieces pictured on this page, it belongs to the Brüning Collection in the Museo de Lambayeque.

and finally stones or clay to cover them, leaving slits for the air to enter through. The metal was refined in crucibles. The process is depicted on some Mochica vessels.

Gold and copper alloys were used commonly to reduce the melting point and to save on fuel and gold, which was always rare. Pre-Columbian goldsmiths used wax, hammering and soldering techniques. The Inca had excellent pieces made in gold, but many actually came from other regions like Quito, where the great piece of "white gold" representing the moon may have been found by the Spaniards. This was kept in the temple of the moon in Cuzco and was most likely platinum.

Although no Inca painting has survived, painting must have been important, for Garcilaso speaks of a mural from the times of Viracocha Inca commemorating his victory over the Chanca, and Sarmiento de Gamboa states that Pachacutec had ancient myths painted for the temple of the sun. We also know that the viceroy of Toledo employed native painters to depict Inca costume, armies and religious life on cloth. These paintings were sent to Madrid, where they were unfortunately lost.

The profession of merchant in did not exist as such in Inca society, perhaps due to the fairness with which everything was shared. Some Indian women traded on a small scale in the local markets. The woman would place her goods on mats on the ground and await a buyer. The buyer would place an item next to another article that he considered to be of equivalent worth. If the woman picked it up, this meant that she accepted the barter, and if she did not move, it meant that she did not consider the exchange to be fair.

The profession held in highest esteem by the Inca was that of the farmer. The best farmers in pre-Columbian America were Inca, perhaps because they had reaped the benefits of long experience in the cultivation of the arid Andean land. They would terrace the mountainsides, making stone platforms on which they threw good-quality soil and fertilizer, usually guano (nitrogenous excrement from certain birds found in large numbers on the coast) or rotten fish. The terraces were irrigated by means of canals. The whole family worked the land, the man digging with a long

104

In their pottery the Mochica so faithfully represented scenes from the world around them and from daily life that Hork-Heimer quite rightly called it the "illustrated dictionary" of Mochica culture. And it is true that the information and illustrations on Mochica pottery give us a good if not a better idea than the chroniclers gave us of the Inca. From the impressive gallery of huacos *portraits, whose vessels include veritable sculptures of Mochica men and* women, comes this man's face bedecked with a headdress made up of two birds. In the eyes of the birds are the classic stains that would later appear as tears on Mochica depiction of human faces. The huaca portrait *belongs to the Museo de Arqueología y Antropología in Lima.*

Another extraordinary Mochica sculpture is this fisherman rowing a strange totora *boat, which is in fact a gigantic fish with a huge mouth and feline fangs. Mythological symbolism confirms the degree of intellectual creativity achieved by this people. The vessel is in the Museo de Arqueología y Antropología in Lima.*

pointed wooden stick (*taclla*), which had a cross-piece at the bottom for the foot to rest on and to push the point into the ground. The women and children came behind him, picking up stones and breaking up clods. Sowing was done with a sharpened stick, men making the holes, and women dropping the tubers into them and then covering them over. The hut in which they lived was kept free of weeds with a stone hoe, and animals and birds were frightened away. In his work, Guaman Poma depicted an Inca scarecrow, covered with an animal skin.

There were some strange professions in Inca society, too, and these arose as a result of the Inca philosophy that no one should remain idle. Cripples, for example, had to gather straw and delouse themselves, taking the vermin to a civil servant to prove that they had really been doing their job. The duty of the blind was to clean cotton from the stalks and to shuck the corn.

Entertainment and amusement

The Aztec had innumerable ways of filling their time: eating, drinking, dancing, hunting for sport, theater and many others. When the *tlatoani* of Mexico was bored, he would go to the *mixcoacalli* to be entertained for a while by the singers and dancers. According to Sahagún, "There was (in the *cuicalli*) another hall called the *mixcoacalli*. In this place did gather all of the minstrels of Mexico and Tlateilolco, awaiting the pleasure of their lord, to dance or to sing songs of new composition, and they had at hand all their instruments, drums large and small with sticks for playing them, and rattles...If the lord ordered the minstrels of Uexotzincayotl or Anahuacayotl to sing, and if the lord ordered that the masters who sing and dance perform the piece that is called *Cuextecayotl*, they took up the instruments necessary for the piece and put on painted masks with pierced noses and red wigs...And the minstrels had many and diverse costumes to use for the songs and dances." The Aztec lords held long poetry readings, attended performances of plays or devoted their free time to gardening, and, as Sahagún added, "For their recreation (they themselves) planted flower gardens and pleasant places where they had all manner of trees and flowers."

But it was not only the great lords who had a good time in the cities. So, too, did the common people. The young people of Tenochtitlan, for example, held balls which Father Durán described as "characteristic of dishonest women and lewd young men. There were others of less gravity and more lively, being songs and dances of pleasure, which they called bachelor dances, in which they sang songs of flirtation. There was also a dance so frivolous and dishonest that it almost compares with the saraband that our people dance with so much frivolous movement, gestures and grimacing and is easily recognized as being of dishonest women and lewd men. They call it *cuecuechcuicatl* which means 'ticklish dance.' "

Some Aztec preferred to go to the theater for their entertainment. The theater in the Cholula temple was a very good one, according to the *Ramírez Codex*: "After eating, all the people gathered and the actors came out and making interludes, feigned deafness, to have colds, rheums, to be lame, blind, and one-armed, coming to beg good health of the idol, the deaf talking nonsense, and those feigning to have colds coughing and blowing their noses, and the lame limping told of their misfortunes and complaints which made the people laugh heartily." If all this happened in a theater in the provinces, imagine what took place in performances in the city. The theater was also good in Cuzco, where performances were staged in the *aranwa*, with a gardenlike center (*wallki*) full of artificial plants.

And then there were the official holidays, which were always partly religious or offical ceremonies, giving way later to entertainment. The city with the largest number of holidays was undoubtedly Cuzco, where, it is said, there were 158 each year. In the Inca world there was an average of three holidays a month, and in some of these ritual could be used as a pretext to enjoy oneself a little. Thus the ritual to celebrate the planting of the *papas* was accompanied by popular dances. In the first dance, each person danced with his hoe in his hand and in the second the women danced while they held their capes in their hands, imitating the work they had done during the planting. But the real merrymaking began afterward, at the great banquet, where an abundance of food was washed down with *chicha*. Each guest sat on the ground with his food and drink, the high-born and the low squatting opposite each other, the Inca emperor or his representative presiding over the party at the end of this line. There was dancing, singing and storytelling, and those present offered each other drinks. The alcohol loosened their tongues and they told jokes or exchanged gossip.

A fundamental aspect of leisure was sport, although it was not an activity exclusive to town

The most popular Aztec game of chance was patolli, *which was similar to the famous Hindu game of* parcheesi. *It was played by two people or two pairs using a mat or blanket on which a cross made up of 52 squares was painted, as in this copy taken from the* Tudela Codex. *Small stones were moved forward from square to square on the board toward the middle of the cross, depending on the number obtained by throwing kidney beans with painted spots. There were four beans or dice and twelve stones or counters, which had to reach the middle of the board. This game had its origins in religion, but it became a vice for many Aztec, who lost all their possessions playing.*

dwellers. Hockey is based on an Iroquois ballgame using a racket, and the *volador*, in which men swing on ropes round the top of a high pole, was practiced all over Mesoamerica and even by the Nicarao. It was more prevalent in these towns, perhaps because the population had more free time once they did not have to worry about food production.

According to Landa, the Maya "Had a great white house, open on all sides, in which the boys gathered for amusement. There they played ball and a boardgame as is used in games of dice and many others." It is likely that the young men had more than one of these houses for their education. The second game cited here by Landa is probably the Aztec game *patolli*, which we shall discuss below. The Inca also held sports competitions such as races, wrestling, mock combat and ring-throwing. The most popular pre-Columbian sport, however, was the ballgame.

The Mesoamerican ballgame originated with the Olmec, a court having been discovered in La Venta. Later it was played by a great many Classic peoples, mainly the Maya, and finally by the Post-Classic cultures. Much has been said about the ritual nature of this game, and there is no doubt that this was the case. In one bas-relief of the many extant in Rajín, near the famous niche pyramid (circa 850 A.D.), we may see a player sacrificed by another with the help of a third, while a fourth player watches from the court. In another bas-relief in Chichén Itzá (which may date from 1200 A.D.), we see a ceremony in which a player is being decapitated. In both of these sites headless figures with seven snakes coming out of the necks represent the calendar name of the corn goddess or of the seven serpents. The ballgame seems to have been connected in some way with the rhythm of the sun, the fertilizing of the maize plant and the life given by the shedding of blood. This would explain why the Spanish priests forbade the game. Friar Diego Durán wrote, "Some players did do a thousand ceremonial and superstitious things…and they do invent omens and idolatries."

The secular, sporting and festive nature of the ballgame, however, is as evident as the religious, at least among the Aztec, where the great lords even had courts within their palaces. Durán states

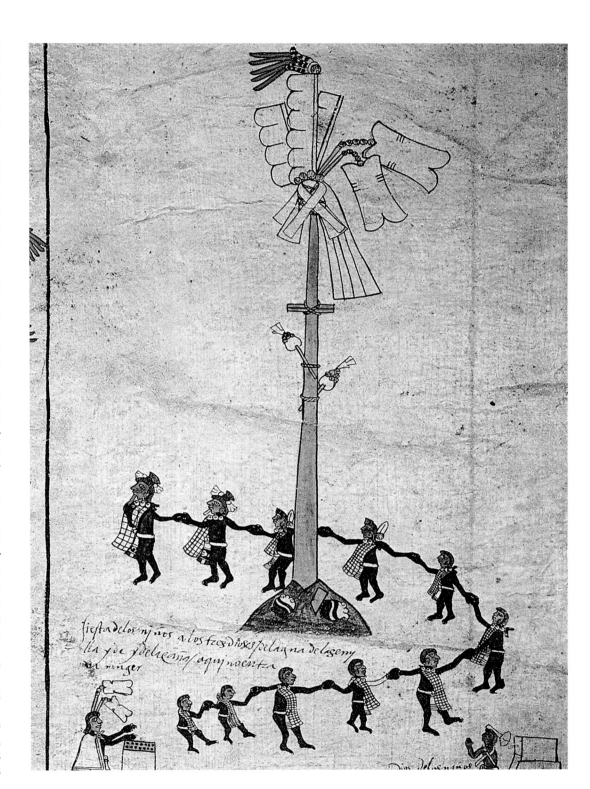

107

Religious festivals were very common in the high pre-Columbian cultures, for they were also an excuse for enjoying oneself by taking part in the singing and dancing. In this picture from the Bourbon Codex, *a festival dedicated to the goddess of water and the sowing season is depicted. In this festival Aztec children decorated with feathers danced, accompanied by an adult on a drum, around a post on which were placed the symbols of the gods. Because of legend, women did not take part in this particular festival, which is extraordinary, since in all pre-Columbian cultures the fertility of the female was always associated with water and sowing time.*

There is no doubt that the ballgame was a sport and even a game of chance for the Aztec. It was called tlachtli and was played with a rubber ball on an H-shaped court divided into two fields, as shown here in the Bourbon Codex. Durán wrote that the Aztec wagered valuable objects: "What they wagered were jewels, slaves, precious stones, fine blankets, ornaments of warfare, clothing and women's ornaments. Others wagered concubines, which has to be understood, as I say, among very important people such as lords and captains and men of valor and esteem." He added that for some it was a veritable vice: "As gamblers having no other occupation, they neither ate nor had any other interests."

The ballgame in pre-Columbian America

Juan Bautista Pomar described the ballgame as follows: "There were two groups of players who faced each other on opposite sides of the court, and they served the ball with the hand…and bouncing, (the ball) reached the players on the opposite side, where the player at the head came out to receive the ball, never passing over the line with his feet, nor yet with his hands nor yet reaching it, and the player hit the ball with his haunch or thigh. And the other players followed in turn until certain faults were committed that were counted and borne in mind. And the ones who reached first the lines they counted for winning won all the jewels and valuable objects that they wagered." Durán watched many ball games and wrote: "They play using their knees and buttocks, and considered it a fault to touch the ball with hands or any other part of the body except the two aforesaid parts, the knees and buttocks." He confirmed the importance of the bounce out of the court and that the stone rings or hoops at the sides of the court were for sending the ball through: "And so that we may know what these stones were for, the stone on one side was for the one team to pass the ball through the hole in the stone, and the stone on the other was for the other group to pass the ball through, and whichsoever of them was the first to do so, won the prize.

"Those stones also served them as a guide, for running parallel below them, on the ground, was a black or green line made with a certain grass, for through being of that particular kind or grass, and no other, it was not lacking in superstition.

"To win, the ball had always to cross this line, for though the ball came rolling along the ground, as it had been hit with knees or buttocks, if it crossed only by two fingers over the line it was not a fault, though it if did not cross then it was a fault."

An infinite number of attempts have been made to get the ball through these rings using the thighs and hips, yet up to now no modern-day sportsman has succeeded, which says a great deal in favor of the pre-Columbian ballplayers. It seems that they won the game by scoring points or by sending the ball through the holes in the stone rings.

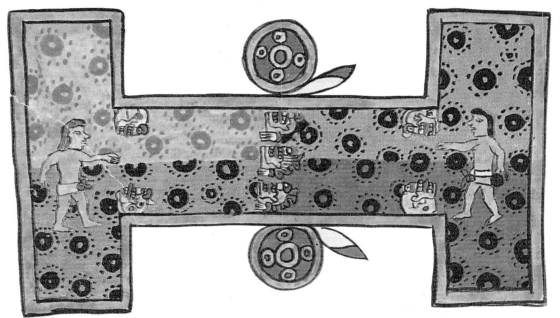

that valuable objects were at stake: "What they wagered were jewels, slaves, precious stones, fine blankets, ornaments of warfare, clothing and women's ornaments. Others wagered concubines, which has to be understood, as I say, among very important people such as lords and captains and men of valor and esteem." He adds that for some it was a veritable vice: "As gamblers having no other occupation, they neither ate nor had any other interests." The chronicler Juan Bautista Pomar confirmed this: "For there were rich and important persons who did wager precious stones and jewels and gold and plumage, slaves, all manner of blankets and arms and trappings of war, and there were many gamblers watching one team or another." Thus it would seem that the ballgame was a great show, where spectators made heavy bets on the winner.

The ballcourt was T-shaped or I-shaped, with terraces for the spectators all along the sides and lines around the edges. Pomar describes this in the Relación de Texcoco (report from Texcoco): "[the ballgame] took place in the public square, and in the middle was the field itself, and somewhat raised, of thirty feet in width and ninety long, enclosed by high walls, with four corners very bright through the sunlight that fell within, the floor itself unwhitewashed but very clean, a line made down the middle of the width of the court."

The game was played with a rubber ball, which Pomar describes as "being the size of a medium-sized human head, very round, made of the liquid from a tree, which to solidify they cooked to a certain degree, at which it turned black, and weighs about four pounds." Durán states that the ball was "similar to the kind used in Spain to play bowls but made of olli, which tells us that it is a resin from a special tree, that once cooked becomes elastic…It has a property to bounce and recoil upward and jumps hither and thither, wearying those who run after it."

The purpose of the game was to send the ball into the other side of the court without it bouncing on one's own side, and this could only be done with a part of the body other than the hands and feet. This required the use of deerskin pads on the most vulnerable parts of the body, such as the hips, the knees, the hands and at times the head. The contest would be rather reminiscent of rugby.

The Aztec were true masters of this game, which they called tlachtli. Durán states, "There were some who played with such skill and expertise that in one hour the ball did not stop on one side or the other and no other (ball) was needed."

108

He adds, "Some shone so bright in playing this game and did such things that it was wondrous to behold, especially one thing I shall recount, which I saw done many times by Indians, and this was to use a curious bounce, and seeing that the ball was high, they were so skillful that when it neared the ground did arrive and with the knee or buttocks make the ball return with a curious velocity."

The most famous game was that between the *tlatoanis* of Tenochtitlan and Texcoco, Moctezuma II and Xocoyotzin (Netzahualpilli), played to annul a prediction. The priests of Texcoco had predicted that Moctezuma would lose his kingdom, which the priests of Tenochtitlan denied. Netzahualpilli supported his priests and wagered his status as a lord against some turkeys put up by Moctezuma. Moctezuma won the first two games but lost the next three.

Another Mesoamerican game that called for great skill, and had religious connotations, was the famous *volador*, practiced by the Totonac, the Huastec and even by the Maya. In this game, which was interpreted as a sun dance, four men adorned with eagle feathers were tied by ropes to a tall post and slowly lowered from the top. Offerings were placed at the bottom of the post.

Games of chance were a passion for the pre-Columbian peoples, especially for the Aztec. Durán wrote, "Of which games there was no lack in this Mexican people, for they had games and ways of losing their possessions and even themselves, for having lost all they wagered themselves and became slaves for life, and usually lost their lives at the same time, for it is well-known that, once slaves, they end by being sacrificed to their gods." Among the games he mentions are *alterque* or draughts: "Imitating our game of chess, one piece taking another, with stones for pieces, one set black and the other white. Another was played on a white surface with small hollows serving as a board, and one player taking 10 stones and the other also, and one placed his stones on one side and the other on the other side, opposite, and threw small cane sticks with grooves in the middle up into the air, and the stones were moved forward the same number of hollows as the number of sticks that fell with the groove facing upward, and when a stone caught another, it was removed until no stones were left, yet it sometimes happened that a player had lost five or six pieces but with the four that remained…he won the game."

According to Bernal Díaz a royal game was *tololoque*, which, he reported, Moctezuma liked to play. So much, in fact, that when he was being held prisoner by the Spanish, he taught the *conquistadores* Hernán Cortés and Pedro de Alvarado how to play, although he did not like playing with the latter, as he always cheated. According to the chronicler, "It was a game using small, very smooth clay pellets, which Moctezuma had of gold for that game, and they threw the pellets some distance at some tiles, which were also of gold, and at five lines. They won and lost certain pieces and rich jewels which they wagered."

The most important game of all was *patolli*, which was depicted in three Aztec codices: the Florentine, the Mendoza and the Magliabecchi.

The ball game is Mesoamerican and not Olmec in origin, for a court was discovered at La Venta. Several Classic cultures, mainly the Maya, also played the game, which continued to be played well into the Post-Classic period. In this picture made up from scenes depicted on a Maya vase from the Late period (between 600 and 800 A.D.), whose original—possibly from Calakmal in Campeche—is in the Dallas Museum of Art, there are four Maya players.

The object of the game was to send the ball into the opponents' side of the court without it bouncing on one's own side. The ball could be touched with any part of the body except the hands and feet, which led the players to adopt very difficult positions, sometimes crawling on the floor. In order to avoid bodily harm, protectors made of deer leather or wooden pads were worn on the hips, knees, hands and sometimes on the head, as may be seen in this picture.

According to Durán, some people were addicted to the game: "Carrying the mat around with them under their arms and the dice tied up in a piece of cloth, rather like some modern-day card sharp with the playing cards in his hose." This is his description of the game: "On this mat was painted a large cross stretching from corner to corner. Within the hollow of this cross were lines drawn across it which served as squares, the cross and lines being marked in melted *olli*, which has been described before. For these squares there were twelve small stones, six red and six blue, shared out between those who played. If two played, as was usual, one took six and the other also, and though many played, one did throw for all, and all depended on the luck of that one, as with the Spanish the game of *albures* is played, each hoping for the best luck. Thus they depended most on he who best shook the dice, which were black beans, five or ten, depending on how much they wished to win or lose, each having small white holes, on which was painted the number of spaces they advanced, and if they had five painted it was ten, and ten twenty, and one was one, and two two, and three three and four four, but five was ten and ten twenty, and those white marks were the luck and number of the lines that, from one space to another, were to be moved."

Unfortunately, except for this description, no more is known about this game. It seems to have been played by two people or by two couples using a mat or blanket on which was painted a cross with 52 squares, as described in Durán's *Atlas*, although the *Florentine Codex* mentions 56 and the *Magliabecchi Codex* 58. The stones were moved from one space to the next toward the middle of the cross, according to the points scored by throwing the painted beans. Sahagún speaks of four beans, and Durán, as we have seen, of from five to 10. The codices are more in agreement with Sahagún, since in the *Magliabecchi Codex* we may see four beans in the middle of the cross and in the *Florentine Codex* there are also four, though not on the mat. There is agreement, however, as to the 12 playing pieces.

Patolli is reminiscent of the popular Hindu game of *parcheesi*, known as *parchís* in Spain, *parqués* in Colombia, and *parkasséen* in Mexico.

Apart from being just a sport, the Mesoamerican ballgame was without doubt a ritual. In the bas-relief above, a ballplayer is being sacrificed by another, assisted by a third, while a fourth player looks on from the court. In another bas-relief in Chichén Itzá depicting the game (possibly 1200 A.D.), a player is being decapitated. It seems that the contest was related to the rhythm of the sun, the fertilization of the maize and the new life given through the shedding of blood. In this relief we see one of the players in a feline mask, which once again demonstrates the religious aspect of the game.

The Copán archaeological site in Honduras (below) is one of the most important in helping us to understand the complex world of the Maya cities. This picture shows a ballcourt whose most noticeable feature is its easily identified H- or T-shape. The stands are crowned by a stele with the effigy of the god to whom the games held in this particular court were dedicated. During the game the Maya priests played out the drama where they emerged victorious over death and also ensured cosmic order through their union with the sun, the great dictator of the vital rhythm of the world.

Its religious significance would seem to be related to a divining ritual. The cross would represent the cardinal points and the 52 spaces the cycle of years of the Aztec calendar. Thus, Sahagún is accurate in his description: "This game has been abandoned for it is suspected of harboring certain idolatrous superstitions." There is no doubt whatsoever that it was extremely popular. Durán wrote that some Aztec had an absolute passion for the game of *patolli*: "These players were always very short of money. They wagered their jewels, their stones, slaves, blankets, trusses, houses, their wives' trinkets. They wagered their lands, their cultivated fields, barns full of grain, maguey plantations, trees and orchards, and when they had no more to wager, they wagered themselves at any price, on condition that if within a certain time they were unable to pay, they would for life be the slave of he who had won."

The Inca also played many games of chance. One of the most popular was *wayruque*, played by moving small stones or beans along holes according to the number obtained at the throw of the dice. The dice were made of bone and had the numbers 1, 2, 3, 4, 5 and 20 marked on them. The name of the game was derived from one of Tupac Yupanqui's concubines: The Inca emperor, who was very fond of the game, was playing it in his country house in Yucay, when he attributed his good fortune to the presence of the lady in question. He gave her the valuable jewel he had wagered and ordered that from then on the game would bear her name.

There were numerous other games using dice, beans and holes. *Chuncaraera* was also played with dice, and different-colored beans moved up a line with five holes, each of which increased in value by 10. Thus the value of the first was 10, the second 20, and so on up to 50 in the fifth position. Whoever reached the top first was the winner. *Apaytalla* is said to have been invented by the wife of Pachacutec. The player stood in the middle of several concentric circles and popped broad beans out of their pods. The person to send them farthest and with the most noise was the winner. *Apaytalla* is depicted on some Chimú vessels, suggesting that the Inca took the game from the Chimú.

Society and
power

The importance of social class became more and
more developed in agricultural societies, reaching a
degree of extreme complexity by the Classic period.
This Maya bas-relief at left from Yaxchilán, from the
late Classic period, depicts the majesty of the monarch and great warrior Jaguar-Bird with a captive.
Above, a print from the History of America by Belloc (1849), depicts a sovereign from Florida with his
cortège.

Painful childbirth

From the fisherman who worked in his humble *totora* boat to the mighty Inca king who sat on a chair of gold, all the men in the empire underwent a series of rituals that marked the important moments in their lives. This was what distinguished them as Inca and made them different from the Araucanians, the Tehuelche, the Pasto or the Chibcha peoples, who in turn had other rituals of their own. These rituals of change, these milestones in their lives, were common in everyday life and were the most important aspect of the social behavior of pre-Columbian peoples.

The important moments in their lives were like a cultural mantle, a shield protecting the collective memory and guarding it against others. Every man had to run the long race of life alone, but in the most important moments his people came to his aid, showing him the best way to face up to these challenges: what to do when a girl had her first period, how the young should marry, how to have a child and integrate it in society, and what to do in case of illness or death. Each tribe had the inherited experience of its elders, passed down from one generation to the next. Perhaps this was what made each nation different from the others. The privileged few who held power felt compelled to form a class or group apart from the common man, to whom they denied access to their social level. The everyday life of the powerful compared little to that of the common man, for they bore the marks of distinction. If rituals of change organized American societies across the social spectrum, power did so from the top downward.

Usually, giving birth was the concern of only two people—the mother and child. The Indian woman would have her baby on her own, managing somehow to sever the umbilical cord, bury the placenta and lay her baby in a cradle. Western society erroneously believes that it was easy for the Indian woman to give birth, but in reality it must have been extremely difficult for her to deliver her own child by herself, as she was expected to do in most Amerindian societies. Garcilaso tells us that the Inca woman "gave birth without a midwife, nor were there any among them, and if one served as such, it was more a witch doctor than a midwife." Only Aztec women, Maya women and some from a very few

Except when food was short, pregnancy was normally welcomed by the Amerindian peoples. Moreoever, it was a common belief in the high cultures that childless couples were ravaged by sin. Once pregnant, the woman was not allowed to eat certain foods and in many cases was told to avoid sexual contact. Depicted on this Mochica vessel from the Museo de Arqueología y Antropología in Lima is a woman in an advanced stage of pregnancy.

The degree of refinement of the coastal cultures of Peru is depicted on this Mochica vessel from the Museo de Arqueología y Antropología in Lima. While Inca women of the mountains gave birth virtually on their own, Mochica women were aided by two women, the midwife and a relative. The former helped to deliver the child while the latter, sitting behind, helped by pressing down with her hands on the mother's belly. Surprisingly, modern gynecology considers this way of giving birth more suitable than the mother lying on her back.

North American and coastal cultures of Perú (Chimú) were aided by midwives. The Crow women were helped by midwives, both women and men, who put pressure on the mother's abdomen while she knelt, holding onto two sticks driven into the ground. Cheyenne women did not have midwives either, but they at least had the consolation of knowing that a witch doctor who received his powers from the otter was working with the spirits for the baby to be delivered as easily as the otter slides in the mud. His magic was rarely successful, however. Another way was to ask for the help of an older woman who had already had children, as did the Iroquois, or from one's own mother, as did the Hopi. Curiously, with this people, the mother left the daughter alone at the actual moment of birth—for reasons of modesty. The daughter was left kneeling on the sand at the crucial moment, although her mother did come back afterward to sever the umbilical cord and attend to the child.

After the delivery, the Inca woman would sever the umbilical cord with a shard of pottery or a piece of hemp and keep it safe to give to the child to chew should it later fall ill. Then she looked for a nearby stream and washed both herself and the baby. Finally, she wrapped the child in a blanket and laid it in a cradle. Then she went back to the work that had been interrupted by the birth pains. With few variations, this was the manner in which women gave birth in most of America. The Witoto women gave birth in the jungle, severed and tied the cord with vegetable fiber, and after bathing the baby, wrapped it in latex from the rubber plant.

The Aztec woman was an exception. A midwife would massage her abdomen and, if she foresaw difficulties, give her a concoction of *cihuapalt* (*montana tormentosa*) to drink in order to induce strong contractions. In extreme cases, the patient was given a piece of the tail of a *tlaquatzin* (opossum) to chew, which was supposed to miraculously bring on childbirth. The midwife also severed the umbilical cord, lifted the child in her arms and gave him the first of the many speeches the Aztec would have to listen to all through his life, a greeting and a welcome to this life. The happy event was immediately announced to the rest of the family, and soon afterward the older members of the family would arrive and make a second speech to the child, this time praising its virtues. The baby would be showered with presents, and then the father would send for a diviner who, on payment of turkeys and cloth, would read the sign of the child in the *Tonalamatl* (Book of Days) and fix a favorable date on which the child would be named.

The Maya woman's experience was similar. According to Father Landa, she was assisted by a woman sorceress who invoked the protection of Ixchel, the goddess of fertility. All the objects used during the birth, including the hot stone placed on the mother's belly, were thrown into a river or stream, where offerings had previously been made. The child was then purified with water and the priests chose a favorable date for severing the rest of the umbilical cord, which was done with a knife over a corn cob. The knife was thrown into the same river or stream and the ear kept until sowing season, when the kernels were planted in the child's name. When these seeds bore fruit, a portion was given to the priest and the rest used to make *atole* to feed the infant, and

in this way, "He ate not only from the sweat of his brow, but from his own blood." This was done as a reminder that man was made of the maize.

The killing of deformed children was a common practice among Amerindians, including the Araucanians. Another practice was to abandon them in the wild, as was done by the Witoto. The Araucanians also killed twins, whom they considered to be a sign of bad luck, while the Witoto killed the second child. It was also common practice, among the Iroquois for example, to abandon children whose mothers had died in childbirth or while breast-feeding, unless there was someone available to look after them.

While there was never any doubt as to the identity of the mother, it was not always the same in the case of the father. The practice of couvade—in which the father mimicked the pangs of childbirth—was the solution to this problem.

The newborn child received special care. The Algonquians, for example, put moccasins full of holes on the baby's feet to prevent it from returning to the world of the spirits, from which it had come. The Inca bathed the baby every day so as to "harden" it. In the case of other peoples, such

Couvade: the solution to the problem of paternity

Couvade was common throughout pre-Columbian America and even in North America. It was more commonly practiced along the great arc formed by the plains of Colombia and Venezuela, eastern Brazil and El Chaco. This custom shocked the Europeans (though probably not the Basques, among whom it was also a common practice).

The father would lie in a hammock and complain of a difficult delivery and receive gifts from relatives and friends, while the mother went on working as if nothing had happened. In reality, this was a way of making it known publicly who the father of the newborn child was. The father's responsibilities also imposed certain limitations so that he would not harm his child. This was the case with, for example, the Abipon, in El Chaco, who had many taboos particularly related to food, or the Shoshoni, where the father would remain in his hut for five days without eating meat or drinking soup until the baby's umbilical cord fell off. Witoto fathers also had to rest until the umbilical cord healed and could not eat game or touch their weapons, while the Bororo father of Brazil would make his lungs bleed using a twig and then sprinkle the blood on his body to simulate the birth.

The practice of couvade was particularly hard on the would-be father of the Caribbean peoples of Guayana, as he was obliged to fast over a period of six months before the birth, after which he was scratched and beaten by his neighbors, who continued until they thought him to be in a physical condition similar to a woman giving birth.

What is particularly surprising about couvade is that it was practiced by cultures separated both in time and space and thus unable to influence or be influenced by each other. It was a practice held in common by European peoples, Polynesian tribes and the Amerindians. The conclusion is that its origin is associated with the imitative and sympathetic magic that attempts to drive away evil spirits wishing to harm a new-born child.

116

Virtually all of the rituals built around the important moments in a person's life, especially birth and marriage, were only performed after a diviner had been consulted. It was the diviner who was able to interpret the good or bad signs concerning the event. In this picture from the Tudela Codex, *we see an Aztec patient consulting his specialist, who throws black beans and grains of corn to discover the cause of the problem.*

as the Chinook from British Columbia, the Colla from Upper Peru, the Chorotega from Central America, the natives of Tierra del Fuego and most of those who spoke the Maya and Karib tongues, the child was submitted to the torture of cranial deformation. The only reason for this custom would seem to have been one of aesthetics, and the result was a head of remarkable shape. Splints were tied to the front and back of the head with string or straps, forcing the skull to grow upward (more complicated shapes also ex-

The tenth month of the Aztec sacred calendar was dedicated to the goddess of childbirth. During this period pregnant women consulted the diviners regarding the omens for the birth of their children. The diviner cast spells and burnt copal, *as may be observed in this picture taken from the* Borgia Codex.

isted). According to the Maya, this practice had been advised by the gods themselves, so that men would look more noble. Father Landa tells us that this was done four or five days after birth: "They laid it [the baby] on a small bed made of twigs, and there, face down, did place the head between two boards of wood, one on the back of the head and the other on the brow, and pressed them exceeding hard, and there did keep it in suffering until, after some days, the head was flat and molded as is their custom."

117

Child care and education

Child-rearing was not excessively complicated. It was limited to breastfeeding, washing, and making sure babies did not get used to being picked up all the time. Inca mothers would even lean over the cradles to breastfeed their babies and so avoid having to pick them up. Maya women kept their babies in cradles made of twigs and grass for only the first few days after birth. Soon after, they were carried on the mother's back or astride her hips while she worked. The most common way of carrying babies in South America was on the back, tied with strips of cloth (*chumbes*). In North America, they used large leather bags (as did the Crow) or baby-carrier baskets, which they used like backpacks. These baskets resembled a wooden trough (in the North they were made of fur and in the South of birch bark), sometimes shaped like a ladder.

As breastfeeding continued until relatively late, it was common to see the Indian mother carrying her baby everywhere on her back. In this 19th-century print from the work Prints of Popular Types in America, in the Museo Naval in Madrid, we see a young mother from colonial Quito with her baby.

Weaning varied from one place to another, but breastfeeding usually continued until quite late. Inca children breastfed until they were two, while according to Cabeza de Vaca, in the tribes of southeast North America, "They breastfeed until they are twelve years of age, for by then they know how to find food for themselves. When we asked them why they raise them thus, they answered that it was because of the famine that there was in the land." Landa states that Maya children were breastfed for almost four years: "They breastfed them much, for, as long as they were able, they did never stop feeding them milk, though they were three or four years of age, and that is why there were so many strong people among them." However, while they were breastfeeding, they began to introduce other food, such as *atole*, *tortilla* and porridge. As they were weaned, Aztec children first ate half a *tortilla*, then a whole one, and finally one and a half.

Naming a child meant recognizing him as a person and a member of the community. Some peoples did this soon after the birth, but others waited until the child was 10 years of age. It was a common custom to give the child two names, one at birth and one at puberty, as the Iroquois

and the Maya did. With the Maya, the first name was related to the favorable birth sign and was chosen by the priest. If the child was a boy, he would wear a small tassel on the head and, if a girl, a shell covering her sex, thus showing that the child had received its first "baptism." Iroquois women had to choose the name from a list given by the clan leaders, taking care not to choose one already belonging to a person still living. The Inca named their children when they were between five and 12 in a great ceremony before the entire family, where the child's hair and nails were cut. Usually, it was an uncle who carried out the ceremony, using a silex knife. The hair and nail parings were safely kept so that they could not be used for evil against the child. Afterward, they gave him presents and the name was announced to all. The name had two parts, one

Childcare did not give excessive work to the mother, who confined herself to breastfeeding, washing her baby and ensuring that it did not get used to resting in her arms. Even when the child was still at an early age, the mother carried her child on her back or hips while she did her housework, as may be seen in this 19th-century lithographic print from the Biblioteca Nacional in Caracas.

Yndios Apaches. 16

One of the sights most astonishing to Europeans was that of the Indian woman carrying her children on her back. Carrying the child was common practice from Canada to Patagonia, wherever the woman was obliged to take her smallest children with her to work. The baby-carrying basket was invented of necessity, and it was used from the Great North to the Great Basin. The basket was a kind of wooden bowl hung over the back, sometimes, as in the case of the Shoshoni, in the form of a ladder. In the Arctic Circle it was made of skin or of birch wood, and in the south of fiber or tree bark. In South America the problem of carrying the child was solved by using chumbes or strips of material made from llama wool or cotton, which held the child to the mother's back; it was decorated with fine embroidery to express the mother's love for her child. In this 18th-century painting by Vicente Alban, from the Museo de América in Madrid, we see an Apache couple, with the woman carrying her two young children on her back.

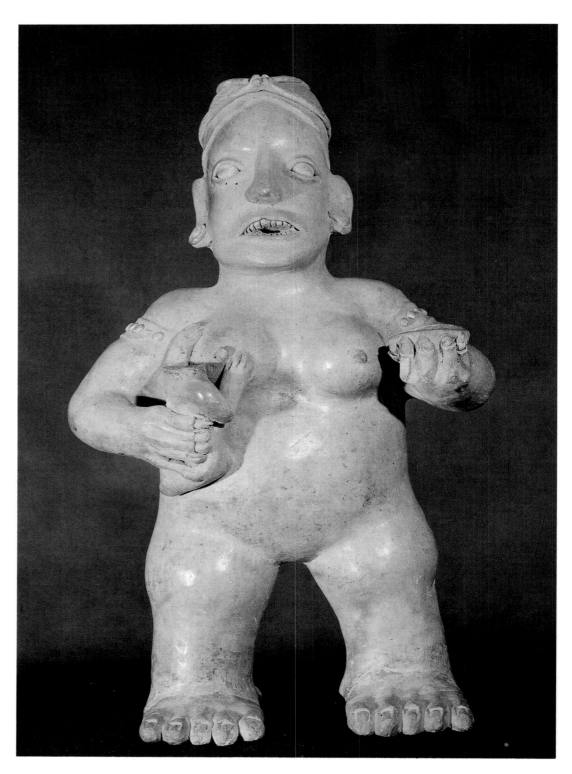

Breastfeeding

Amerindian women continued to breastfeed their children for a prolonged period, for the mother's milk helped to make up for what was basically a deficient diet.

It was common for children to breastfeed until the age of two and a half, as was the case with the Inca, though at times this period was extended. Maya women, for example, breastfed their children up to the age of four, and it was to this that Father Landa attributed the hardiness of the Maya children, "where there were so many strong people among them."

Extremely long periods of breastfeeding were recorded in the tribes of southeastern North America, where, according to Cabeza de Vaca, "They breastfeed until they are twelve years of age, for by then they know how to find food for themselves. When we asked them why they raise them thus, they answered that it was because of the famine in the land." During this period, however, the diet was not limited to mother's milk exclusively and was supplemented with vegetables. When the time came to break what had become a deep dependence on breastfeeding, the women applied bitter-tasting substances extracted from plants to their nipples and even physically mistreated their children when they asked to be breastfed.

Many Amerindian peoples, principally those who spoke Mata and Karib, practiced deformation of the cranium a few days after the birth of a baby. The frontal and occipital parts were placed between wooden planks, as seen in this ceramic figure of an unweaned baby with its Bahía Indian (Ecuador) mother. The piece is from the Museo de Arte Precolombino in Chile.

The care of the child up to the age of four or five was usually the task of the mother. The child was not considered a member of the group or even to be a person until it had undergone the ceremony held at puberty. This piece comes from the Bahía culture and is in the Museo de Arte Precolombino in Chile.

meet the baby and welcome it to the community. The moccasin with the holes was taken off and a real pair put on its feet.

It was the Aztec who named their children with the most ceremony, and the Spanish priests compared the Aztec baptism to the Christian, as it was, in fact, similar. The night before, friends and relatives gathered in the house where the event was to take place. At dawn, the midwife addressed the child, holding a jug of water in her hand and telling it of Chalchihuitlicue, the water goddess. At the same time she sprinkled a few drops of water on its lips with her fingers. Then she touched the child's chest with her wet fingers, sprinkled a few more drops on the head, and finally washed all its body while chanting a prayer to purify all ills with water. After this, she presented the child to the sun four times and also to all the heavenly divinities and to the earth. She then took some arrows and called upon the gods to make the child a fierce warrior (if a girl, she would use a spindle and shuttle). Finally, she solemnly announced the name of the new member of the family, and afterward a great celebration was held, with a feast for the guests. In this

corresponding to the *huaca* (we shall call it sanctuary) and to *ayllu* (clan), and the other of a private nature. Finally, a great feast was held with singing, dancing and heavy drinking.

In North America the child was often named a few days after birth. The Hopi Indians named their children 20 days after birth, when the confinement of mother and child had ended. Relatives from both the father's and mother's sides of the family began to look for a suitable name, and at dawn the child was presented to the sun with his real name. The Shoshoni kept mother and child in confinement for 40 days, the Omaha only eight. At the end of this period, the priest went to

Children were also depicted in the portraiture of the Mochica culture. Here we see a child with certain signs of obesity, carved on a pitcher. The piece is in the Museo de Arqueología y Antropología in Lima.

way the child could be introduced to the community.

It was common for children to help with the work and so learn to be useful. The boys helped to hunt and work the land while the girls helped with the housework. If they were naughty, they were punished. Maya girls were pinched or pepper was rubbed into their eyes, and the boys were whipped with *chichicastle* branches, which produced a skin rash.

121

Becoming a man, becoming a woman

Reaching puberty was an important moment for the individual and was usually connected with his or her future life as a member of the community into which he or she would soon be able to marry. The girl who reached puberty was usually confined to a small house where she would remain for some time, abstaining from certain kinds of food. This process ended with purification and celebration. This was the custom at least in South America. With the Guahivo and other tribes of the plains (the Saliva, the Piapoco), the young woman would leave her home and go to the nearby "house of menstruation," a little hut where from now on she would always go for the duration of her period. She would remain there, eating only the permitted food, until it had finished. Then she had to be purified by the exorcisms of a shaman or sorcerer. After having a bath, she was expected to resume her usual duties with renewed "frenzy," since it was believed that otherwise she would be "slow" for the rest of her days.

Curiously, the Shoshoni in North America shared the same belief and customs. Among the Californian tribes, the women were forbidden to eat meat, drink cold water or scratch themselves with their fingers—this could only be done with a twig. In the case of some of the tribes in El Chaco, the women went to meet the girl at the "house of menstruation" and there danced in a ring, holding sticks with deer-hoof rattles in their hands. They then carefully wrapped up her body so that she could not be entered and made pregnant by evil spirits and later give birth to deformed children. The Teuelches, from the Pampa, placed the girl in a tent, from where she would watch a dance performed by men in white paint, adorned with nandu feathers and wearing belts with rattles (to frighten off evil spirits).

For the natives of Tierra del Fuego (the Ona, the Alacaluf), puberty in men and women was marked by great fasts and frequent bathing as well as the traditional "tests of puberty." Similar tests were imposed on the youths of the North American prairies, although this occurred in a more recent historical period and not at the end of the 15th century, when the prairies were almost deserted. The Iroquois celebrated puberty in males (in females there was little variation from the general pattern) by locking the boy up in a hut where he was looked after by an old man or woman for an entire year.

The Aztec seem not to have performed any puberty rites in particular, apart from sending the young man to the schools of the *calmecac* (for nobles) or *tepochcalli* (for tradesmen). The Maya, on the other hand, held great celebrations, of which records still exist. These were such formal occasions that many believe they were reserved for nobles, but they must have been basically the same for the common people. The aim was to integrate the youth into society. First, the young people put aside their childhood names and took those of their fathers. Then there was a community celebration, each young person arriving accompanied by an old woman or by his or her school tutor. The ritual area was marked with four ropes, held by old people. The space was purified by each boy putting corn and nopal into a burner. Then *kopo* leaves were sprinkled inside and mats laid down. The old men covered the youths with white cloths and asked them if they had sinned. If so, they confessed. After blessing them with a kind of sprinkler, they rubbed pure water on different parts of the young people's

The transition from girlhood to womanhood was celebrated in virtually all of the Amerindian peoples' ceremonies dedicated to puberty. Above, right, and opposite page-left, we see how this milestone in life was celebrated in different ways. The representation of the female form, as seen above in the enormous thighs and arms and wide shoulders (in contrast to the small breast, whose outline is hardly distinguishable), is a very different ideal from that of the Western world. This Venus from the Chorrera culture is in the Metropolitan Museum in New York. Above is a young girl from Tajin (Mexico) that may be seen in the Museo de Arte Precolombino in Chile. The girl on the right with her body painted is from the Nicoya culture and is currently in the Museo de Antropología in San José de Costa Rica. The naked figure on the opposite page (left), from the same museum, reveals accentuated sexual characteristics.

bodies. Then they removed the white cloths, gave them flowers to smell, some food and a glass of *balche* or mead to drink. Then an offering was made to the gods. The ritual ended with the removal of the childhood symbols: the seashell covering the sex of the women and the small tassel from the men.

For the Inca, too, puberty rites meant the integration of the individual into the community or *ayllu*. On her first period, the girl would fast for 48 hours, eating a little uncooked corn on the third day, and on the fourth she took a bath to purify herself. She was then given a new dress, a pair of sandals and, most important of all, her final name. The males, on reaching puberty, were given their first male attire, their weapons and their new names.

123

Obesity and a seated position were two esthetic characteristics celebrated in Mesoamerican art. This emphasis went back to the time of the Olmec, from which Maya art developed. In this statue from the island of Jaina, the immense Olmec cemetery of the late Classic period (700–900 A.D.), two characteristics give this young woman—possibly a courtesan—an oriental look. She is wearing an enormous turban, and the remarkable contrast between the powerful abdomen and the conical breasts is a distinctive feature of Asiatic art. The piece is in the Art Museum at Princeton University.

Procreation

The Maya believed that those who did not have children were ravaged by sin and ought to purify themselves by bleeding themselves and sacrificing birds. If after this they were still unable to have children, they consulted the priest. The priest always confirmed that the reason was sin and ordered the couple to sleep apart for 40 or 50 days, not to eat salt or bread, but only corn, and to live in a cave; all this was intended to win the sympathy of the gods, who would then grant them children.

This method was considered infallible, but if after all this the couple still did not have children, their sins were thought to be so terrible that they were not worthy of forgiveness. The couple's endurance must have had a limit, for after a time they preferred to admit to grave sin rather than go on living in the cave.

Children were equally desired by the Inca and Aztec. For the Aztec, the news of a pregnancy was received with great happiness by the whole family, who then organized a feast in celebration. At the end of the feast, at pipe-smoking time, an old man gave a speech for the occasion. The mother-to-be was from that moment under the protection of Teteoinnan, mother of the gods, and of Ayopechtli, who watched over births.

For the inhabitants of Tierra del Fuego, news of pregnancy was not always well received, perhaps because their territory was often stricken by famine. Consequently, abortion was a common practice. The young women of the Cueva Indians preferred to abort rather than have children, though this may be attributed to coquetry, since they were happy to become mothers once they were more mature.

A common practice during pregnancy was to forbid the mother-to-be to have sexual relations and to eat certain kinds of food. Cabeza de Vaca states that in the tribes of southeast North America, "All the Indians that we have seen up until now have the custom of couples not sleeping together from the moment the woman feels she is pregnant until two years after, when she has raised her child."

The Inca imposed certain restrictions on the food eaten by pregnant women, and an Aztec midwife decided on the best therapy for the mother by examining the fetus with her hands.

The recommendation was often to stop eating certain kinds of food and to avoid looking at anything red, which would result in a difficult birth.

The female ideal in Maya society is seen here in this beautiful Venus, a fine example of the type of ceramics made on the island of Jaina. The delicacy of the features is typical of the late Classic period. The piece is in the Art Museum at Princeton University. On the facing page, in contrast, is the masculine character of the posture and clothing in this ceramic piece from the Kimbell Art Museum, depicting a great Maya lord dressed in aristocratic finery to celebrate his having reached adulthood.

Death and funeral customs

All of the Indian peoples attributed illness to two causes, sin or witchcraft, each to a greater or lesser degree depending on the tribe in question. A person could be washed clean of sin through expiation. The Inca, Aztec and some Chibcha tribes (the Kougis and the Ijka) first confessed and then did penance. Witchcraft was countered by the shamans or sorcerers.

When the afflicted individual was past hope, whether through the seriousness of his sin or the potency of the witchcraft used against him, he was left to his fate so as not to infect the rest of the group. Some tribes, such as those of El Chaco, buried him alive. The Omaguaca simply placed him within a ring of arrows stuck into the ground, thus isolating him from the community. In the case of the hunting-gathering communities, who

needed to be constantly on the move, the person was simply abandoned by the group. Cabeza de Vaca wrote that in southeast North America, "If any fall ill, and they are not children, they leave them to die, and all the others, if they cannot go with the rest, remain; but to take a child or brother, they carry them on their backs."

The belief that the spirit of the dead person did not leave the vicinity of death was the reason for the special rites being performed, particularly by the relatives, to appease the spirit. The relatives of the tribes of El Chaco, for example the Omaguaca, held great feasts lasting several days to honor the deceased, at the end of which he was buried along with his possessions and his house burnt. The relatives of the dead Charrua cut off one of their fingers to the first joint, the sons

pierced their arms with slivers of wood or were buried up to the chest for one night. The women of the Dene or Beaver Indians of North America also cut off finger joints, while those of the sub-arctic tribes cut off their hair and painted their faces black.

In the case of the Araucanians, the eldest son was obliged to marry all the wives of his dead father, with the exception of his mother. The widows of the Californian Indians underwent a ritual similar to the one experienced at the onset of menstruation: they could not eat meat, drink cold water or scratch themselves with their hands. Moreover, they had to paint their faces black and wear a special collar during the period of mourning. The Inca from the central region kept watch over the body for a night. The women cut their

Burying the dead twice

The belief that the spirit of the dead remained in the house in which it had lived, upsetting the members of the family, gave rise to the tradition of a second burial. When a person died, he was buried "provisionally" until the spirit showed signs of continuing on its journey. It was then that the spirit went round and round its old house, startling the wife, children and relatives. When it was tired of going round and round, it signaled that it was ready to move on to the world of the dead. The Guahivo knew that this time had arrived when someone's foot sank into the ground, which was the sign to dig up the bones (decomposition had usually ended by then), and a party was held by virtually all the members of the community. The remains were then buried again, this time permanently. The second burial was common both in North and South America. The custom among the Chechehet and Puelche of Patagonia was to send an old woman out to where the body had been buried the first time to dig it up. She then cleaned the remains and painted the bones red (a magical color), and only then was it possible to hold the final burial in a burial hut. In Brazil, the second burial was common among the Bororo and the Cayapo and, on the plains of

Colombia and Venezuela, the Saliva, the Guahivo, the Piaroa and the Piapoco. In North America it was practiced by the peoples of the southeast, who buried the body on a mound and, when it had decomposed, took away the bones and placed them in wooden boxes. The Hurons used the same system, holding a great celebration every 12 years in honor of the dead, at the end of which they threw all the bones into a common grave made for all of those who had died within that period. The Sioux and Pani placed the bodies on provisional platforms, and the final burial was made in funeral mounds.

The bodies of Aztec children were not incinerated, since for the peoples of Mexico the death of a child was not final, and those who had died before reaching an age at which they were capable of reasoning when to the *chichihuaquauhco*, the "place of the wet nurse tree," where they were fed milk through its branches until they returned to Earth as an unborn fetus inside another pregnant woman. The legend of the god-civilizer Quetzalcoatl was also associated with temporary death, and the Aztec believed that he would return from the land of the dead to rule once more over the world of the living.

It was a custom of the Karib-speaking peoples to bury the bones of the dead in large, roughly made funeral urns with stoppers depicting human faces, like the one above from the downriver region of Magdalena, now in the Museo Nacional de Colombia. Evidently, this was used in a second burial.

hair, placed their capes over their heads and, weeping and groaning, sang the praises of the deceased. Food and drink were offered in honor of the deceased and special dances performed.

A belief in the temporary survival of the spirit of the deceased gave rise to the practice of the second burial, though a single burial was more common. There were, however, numerous ways of burying the dead. The Patagonians placed the body in a seated position on a hill, covering it with stones until a round mound was formed. The Aleut also placed the body under a mound of stones, first wrapping it in skins and then leaving it on the tundra, the grave surrounded by a circle of stones. The Californian Indians burned the body, while the remaining peoples of the northwest, including the Shoshoni, buried it. The Kaingang Indians of Santa Catalina (in the south of Brazil) also burned the body. In Colombia, the Chibcha first mummified the corpses of their chiefs and then buried them wrapped in blankets in their "houses of the dead." The Cueva of Panama did the same, leaving the remains of the

common people outside, exposed to the elements.

The Aztec burned the bodies of those who had died from natural causes, whereas those who had died as a result of accident or disease were buried. The Maya burned the bodies of persons of high standing, putting the ashes in effigy vessels made of clay or in statues made of wood. In Guatemala, the ashes were buried in funeral urns, as was typical of the Karib. The Inca had several forms of burial, depending on the region. In the central region, the body was buried in its normal clothing and placed in the fetal position (as man is born, so shall he be laid to rest). In the coastal region, bodies were wrapped in llama skins and buried in coffins. In El Collao, bodies were buried in mausoleums, while in Paracas they were buried in bottle-shaped tombs.

Burial was carried out in accordance with the importance of the deceased: If he had been powerful in life, he would continue to be so after death. The peoples of the North American southeast, for example, buried plebeians without ceremony, whereas *caciques* and persons of high standing received a second burial in the temples. This was also done by the natives of Tierradentro in Colombia, who were possibly Karib, where underground chambers with funeral vessels containing bones of *caciques* have been found. The Dene usually abandoned the corpses of those who had not been of high rank socially, while the

Algonquians did the same with the bodies of children.

The Tarascans wrapped the ashes of their kings as if they were mummies and buried them at the foot of their pyramids. The Aztec buried their high dignitaries in underground chambers and killed their servants (as did the Tarasco and the Chibcha) so that they could accompany their master on the journey to *Mictlan*, the land of the dead. On the coast of Peru, the internal organs of important persons were extracted and the bodies mummified. In Cuzco, all the emperors were mummified and kept in a place near the temple of the sun, from where they were removed on certain important occasions and borne in procession through the streets of the city to preside over the ceremonies.

The Maya were deeply religious, especially concerning the moment of death, when man was taken in by Yum Tzek, the lord of death, who was represented as a human skeleton. The Maya also buried their dead in very beautiful funeral urns, like the one pictured here from the Museo Popol Vuh in Guatemala.

The Mochica were familiar with death, and this was often shown in their ceramics, with paintings of skull-men from beyond the grave having intercourse with skull-women and with sculptures like this one of a dead man playing the drum with obvious great pleasure. The piece is from the Museo de Arqueología y Antropología in Lima.

The social classes

Most of the Amerindian peoples did not have sufficient food resources to sustain a class whose primary task was governing and the administration of justice, warfare and religion. Normally it was one group—called *caciques* in the Caribbean—who did all of these things. It was the Spaniards who extended the term to include all those who performed similar functions. Male and even female *caciques* existed in the hunting-gathering societies, though they had a minor function since they lived in small communities, usually in bands, and resources were scarce. In those groups practicing extensive farming, food surpluses existed, though these were not enough to sustain privileged classes, with the Natchez of the lower Mississippi being, perhaps, one exception.

The intensive agriculture practiced in the Mesoamerican and central Andean areas, on the other hand, gave rise to a food surplus large enough to maintain social stratification. Moreover, war led to a disparity between victor and vanquished, which in turn emphasized the differ-

Maya nobility was hereditary, being passed down both on the father's and mother's side. The nobles occupied all the political and religious positions in the empire. Maya art, from the end of the Classic period, depicted the power of the nobles and their ceremonies. Individuals could be identified by the type of clothing. Masks, like the one pictured at top left from the Museo de Popul Vuh in Guatemala, were also frequently worn. The nobles were expected to serve

as an example to others, and this is well illustrated in the piece on the right, in which a noble inflicts a wound on his penis in a supreme sacrifice. Above, court ceremony is seen here on a polychrome vessel from the Kimbell Art Museum in Fort Worth, with a lord surrounded by his courtiers. In the final years of the Classic Maya culture, the nobility had reached the height of its power. Their clothes and ornaments were of the utmost sophistication, as seen

on the facing page. The lord is seated on a bench and holds a heavy stone mask, which is worn over the head. The piece is from the Kimbell Art Museum, Fort Worth.

At the bottom of the great class system of the high cultures came the slaves, whose status was, in fact, very different from that of the slave in Western society. In Aztec society slaves were prisoners of war, criminals or people who had to work in order to pay a debt. In many cases, the slave was able to keep his own belongings, was free to marry and could even have servants of his own. A common fate for slaves, especially those who had been taken as prisoners of war, was to be sacrificed to the gods. In this scene from the Tudela Codex, *a musician playing a shell horn walks before a litter bearing a slave, who is being honored by all and is on his way to be sacrificed in celebration of the seventh month of the Aztec sacred calendar (our June).*

ence between one class and another regarding entitlement to goods produced and access to power. There appeared a clear structure in which privileged groups at the top benefited from the work of those below. Curiously, however, at the end of the pre-Columbian period, each of the three great empires was dealing with the problems of their social organization in quite different ways. The fall of the Maya in the middle of the 15th century put an end to the oligarchy, with the result that what remained of Maya society were small groups of peasants spread out over the Yucatán Peninsula. In the case of the Aztec, a class-based society was taking shape, reminiscent of those in the ancient Mediterranean. In the *Tahuantinsuyu*, the privileged class had been the dominant ethnic Inca group. Their prerogatives, however, were now spreading to the dominated sectors, as a greater equality in distribution limited the control the aristocracy had previously had over goods.

The Aztec are the best example of a rapidly formed class-based society. Around 1300 A.D. theirs was a classless society, whereas at the beginning of the 15th century a feudal aristocracy—with its hierarchy of royalty, nobility, freemen, plebeians, a landless proletariat and slaves—was developing to replace the socialism of the old clan. This formation of a class-based society probably dates from 1428, with the war

The supernatural powers of the chiefs

Though much younger than the Eurasian cultures, the Amerindians had nevertheless formed a strong leadership structure related to magical or religious powers. Thus it was the task of many of the chiefs to ensure the fertility of the soil or to control natural phenomena. An Inca chief, for example, would pierce the ground at the beginning of each year with his golden staff (the symbol of magical power) in order to make the soil fertile once again. He would also be charged with banishing the rains. On one occasion, Pachacutec himself had to extinguish an erupting volcano in Arequipa using small clay balls soaked in llama blood, which he shot into the volcano with a sling. In cultures of less social complexity, such as those in North America, the magical and religious attributes of the leaders were emphasized. In this print by Henry Schoolcraft, made in Philadelphia in 1853 and taken from *An Album of Information on the History and Ways of Life of the Indian Tribes of the United States of America*, we see a ceremony to acknowledge the new chief of the Mandan Indians, whose language was Sioux, as well as the ritual to fertilize the earth, represented by the corn.

Due to military expansion, in little more than 200 years Aztec society had changed from a classless to a class-based society, in which there was even an incipient hereditary nobility. The process was accelerated due to the war against Azcapotzalco, in which the power of the nobles or pilli was reinforced. Motecuhzoma Ilhuicamina completed the process when he conceded an ideological foundation to the dominant class, which was henceforth considered to *be semidivine. In this print from the* History of New Spain, *by Bernardino de Sahagún, published in the 16th century, we see the great variety of Aztec social groups as well as the work done by each.*

against Azcapotzalco, in which the leaders and those who followed them agreed on the conditions for taking part in the campaign. If they won the victory, as did in fact occur, the people would obey them and work for them in the future. If they lost, they promised to give their own flesh as food. The first dramatic restructuring of society occurred as a consequence of the military campaigns of expansion. The vanquished were placed at the bottom of the social scale; however, they remained classified as payers of tribute. Later, Motecuhzoma I ruled that the *pilli* or nobles belonged to a semidivine class and were therefore to be obeyed by the *macehuales* or "men of the people." He built district schools or *telpochcalli* which taught this doctrine to the new generations. Finally, Motecuhzoma II (Moctezuma) declared his authority divine.

The Inca society had similar origins. Military conquest enabled them to absorb other peoples, whose social structures they left intact. In the reign of Pachacutec, however, a decisive change was brought about in the unification of the empire when the existing hierarchy was combined with the entire Tahuantinsuyu population to form a system of production and consumption of goods. Pachacutec made all the *caciques* of the neighboring peoples and the heads of the Inca *ayllus* (clans) into civil servants, giving them the task of administering goods in accordance with his orders. Thus a society was formed composed of an aristocratic class and a people who could not be exploited by this class—a people who were even respected by this class. The social hierarchy was

thus composed of royalty, the nobles, the *curacas*, the people and the *yanaconas* or serfs.

Of the Maya, we may finally add that at the height of the empire there was a social organization based on lineage, with a social hierarchy composed of nobles, plebeians and slaves.

131

Above we see a group of Aztec warriors wearing distinguishing signs and carrying arms. The picture, from the Mendoza Codex, *enables us to appreciate the predominance of the warrior in society over the civilian.*

The rich and powerful

The difference between the privileged classes—made up of the great leaders, the nobles and the *caciques* or *curacas* —and the rest of the people was appreciated from the very start by the Spaniards, who married the women of the Inca and Aztec aristocracy, whom they considered to be their social equals. They had virtually no contact with the women of the lower social levels, rarely even taking them as concubines.

For the Europeans, Moctezuma and Atahualpa personified the height of power, magnificence and refinement. The luxury at court, the special education given to the emperors, and their enormous wealth were discussed at great length in all of the chronicles, which is why we know so much about these particular aspects of Amerindian life.

The so-called emperor of Mexico was in fact the *tlatoani* (orator) of Tenochtitlan. And it is true that he talked a great deal—more than the average Aztec, who himself was never at a loss for words. Every large city had a *tlatoani*, the one in the capital being the greatest of all. For this reason he was called *huey tlatoani* or "great orator," as well as *tlacatecuhtli* or "leader of the warriors of the Aztec confederation."

The *huey tlatoani* was elected from a lineage that claimed to have ties to the old Toltec but that in fact went back to the plebeian lords of Culhuacan. No particular relative of the previous ruler was elected, though his brother was preferred whenever possible, but the person chosen had to be of the royal blood and considered most suitable for the position. Self-possession and discretion were qualities greatly appreciated in the ruler, as Sahagún tells us: "No arrogant man, nor haughty, nor presumptuous, nor boisterous has ever been chosen as lord; no discourteous man, nor bad-mannered, nor foul-mouthed, nor one reckless in speech, nor one who speaks the first thing to come into his mind has been placed on the dais or on the royal throne." The choice was made by a council of 13 supreme dignitaries, district public officials and active and retired military leaders and priests.

The *tlatoani* chosen thanked the gods for the decision; it was believed that the council had only executed their wishes. He then did penance, exchanged speeches with officials and addressed

Inca society also became divided into classes, in this case through militarism. In addition to the nobles were the curacas, *the plebeians, and the* yanaconas *or serfs, who were the result of military conquest and also rebel peoples in a position of perpetual servitude. Much has been said about Inca "yanaconage" as far as its relation to slavery is concerned. It is known that after the war with the Chimú, many young Chimú women worked as ser-* *vants of the Inca, neither receiving remuneration for their services nor paying tribute. The picture at top, from the Chávez Ballón Collection in Lima, shows a warrior leading several women prisoners whose hands are tied with ropes. Below, from the same collection, we see a herd of llamas (possibly belonging to the Inca emperor or to the sun) being caught for shearing.*

Few societies were more complex than the Inca, for the social hierarchy was combined with the equal distribution of goods. Pachacutec brought about this explosive symbiosis by attempting to unify the empire and preserve the existing social systems at one and the same time. The result was a population made up of an aristocratic class and a hard-working, obedient people, though distribution of goods by the state was fair for all. The Quechua people were raised to the ranks of the privileged and put in charge of the army, whose leaders became the elite of the privileged. In the painting on this kero from the Museo de América in Madrid, we see a privileged Inca warrior with his wife.

The orejones, thus called by the Spaniards because of their custom of wearing large earflares, were Inca nobles descended from the previous emperors. They were educated for four years in special schools and enjoyed the privilege of being able to wear their hair short, like the Inca himself. In this kero from the Museo de la Universidad de Cuzco is an orejon with an enormous feather crest.

In this kero from the Universidad de Cuzco Collection, we see an Inca warrior with his distinguishing marks, holding his lance and shield. All of the officers in the Inca army were Quechuan and it was they who were responsible for conquest and maintaining law and order in the empire.

the people, exhorting them to keep to the code of morality. Then he reappeared wearing the symbols of his rank: a triangular crown made of gold and turquoise, a green cape, green jewels and a sceptor in the shape of a snake. The *tlatoani* of Tenochtitlan lived in great luxury.

Moctezuma increased the majesty of the figure of the emperor, as we have seen. He left his father Axayacatl's palace to the Spaniards, and had a new one built with outbuildings, gardens, a zoological park and other structures. He expelled all those serving him who were not nobles and finally devised a new order for the palace, more in accordance with his absolutist ideas, which included secretaries, carpets, litters and complex ritual. Hernán Cortés wrote that whoever appeared before him had to do so barefoot: "With the head and eyes lowered, kneeling, and when speaking do so with great obeisance and reverence, and not look him in the face…Whenever Moctezuma left the palace, which was but rarely, all those who went with him and those who chanced to be in the street turned their faces away, in no way looking at him, and all the rest

These 18th-century pictures, which illustrate Diego Panés y Abellán's manuscript The Theater in New Spain *in the Biblioteca Nacional in Mexico, depict some of the splendor of the* tlatoani *or king of Texcoco. On the left, the king receives settlers who have arrived in new territory under his jurisdiction. On the right is Netzahuacoyotl, the famous intellectual, musician, poet and ball player, who had a tem- ple built to the god of creation. Countless stories are told of his feats as a king and lover.*

prostrated themselves until he had passed. He had always before him a lord of those with three thin long staffs, which I believe they did so that it would be known that he was passing."

Bernal Díaz also left detailed information on the character of the *tlatoani*, who, in his opinion, "was very polished and clean, bathing once each day, in the evening; he had many women as friends, daughters of lords, and two great cacicas as his legitimate wives who, when he was with one, it was with so much secrecy that none but those who served him knew with which he was. He was clean, the garments that he wore on one day were worn again only after four days; he had some 200 men in his guard…and when they had to speak with him, they took off their fine clothing and dressed in poor, which, moreover, had to be clean, and they had to enter barefoot, with their eyes lowered, looking at the ground, and not look him in the face, and with three bows, saying with each, 'Lord, my Lord, my Great Lord' before they reached him; and then they told him their business and he sent them away with few words; on withdrawing they did not turn their backs, but with their heads and eyes cast down to the ground where he stood, not turning their backs until they had left the hall."

The figure of the Inca king was also perceived by the Spaniards as representing the height of power and magnificence. He was considered by   135

Self-possession and discretion were the main qualities of the tlatoani *or Aztec king. Sahagún wrote, "No arrogant man, nor haughty, nor presumptuous, nor boisterous has ever been chosen as lord; no discourteous man, nor bad-mannered, nor foulmouthed, nor one reckless in speech, nor one who speaks the first thing to come into his mind has been placed on the dais or on the royal throne." The* tlatoani *was elected by a council represented by members of the armies of each city, the* huey tlatoani *or great king being chosen to rule the Aztec confederation by 13 dignitaries, district functionaries, active and retired military leaders and priests. In these pictures that illustrate Diego Panés y Abellán's manuscript, we see, top left, a* tlatoani *Maxtla on his throne receiving reports from one of his lords; on the right, Tezozomoc,* tlatoani *of Azcapotzalco, speaks with his colleagues, the* tlatoanis *of Mexico and Tlatelolco; above, the burial of Huitzilihuitl, the priest and leader of the Aztec people.*

Inca princes with the symbols of their rank in a detail from a painting of the Colonial school of Cuzco, attributed to Marcos Zapata (18th century, Cuzco, Church of the Jesuits). At the height of their political power, as privileged members of the imperial family, the princes followed one after another in a complex network of endogamous marriages.

his people to be the incarnation of the sun god, and he lived in a wonderful palace made of stone, the walls covered with gold, and walked in a garden whose plants and animals were of gold and silver. He sat on a low chair made of wood and covered with fine material, or on a throne of solid gold. When he moved from one place to another, he was carried in a litter supported by 25 *araucanas* from Cuzco, and with such care that the bearers never stumbled (apparently this was true, since to fall meant to be condemned to death). He ate from gold and silver plates, slept with sheets and blankets of the finest vicuña wool and bathed, according to Garcilaso, "In great tubs of gold and silver... and where there were fountains of natural hot water he also had baths made with great majesty and riches." In his presence one had to go barefoot, with the eyes lowered and a bundle on the head, as a sign of submission.

The Inca emperor wore the same type of clothing as the other men in the empire, but his of course was of the very finest quality. He wore the traditional *uncu*, the tunic which came down to the knees, and the *yacolla* or square blanket. Large amounts of clothing were made and embroidered for him by the virgins of the sun with the finest vicuña wool, for the king never wore the same clothing twice. He also carried a *chuspa*, a small bag for coca leaves, which he wore crosswise from his left shoulder to his right side, under the armpit. His symbols of authority were the *mascapaicha* or multicolored tress, wound four or five times around his head, and the *llautu*, a red fringe with red tassels from which hung small gold tubes.

The greatest ceremony in the Inca empire was the investiture of the new emperor. It was carried out in Cuzco's main *plaza*, in the presence of ambassadors from the provinces and the mummies of previous emperors. On the same day, in the temple of the sun, the Inca married his sister, the *colla*, the true symbol of female refinement. She wore a tunic of soft colors and sandals of white vicuña wool. Her eyebrows were plucked, her face rouged with arnotto and her hair dyed a deep black. According to the Spaniards, only the *colla* could bear the heir to the throne, though the emperor did have other children by his numerous concubines. The emperor was tireless. He di-

This gallery of oil paintings of Inca emperors is from the 18th century and in the tradition of the Cuzco school. It is kept in the Museo Pedro de Osma in Lima. It fits in perfectly with the Spanish idea of tracing the genealogy of the Inca kings through "legitimate" and "illegitimate" lines. This attempt ended in total confusion, as the position of king in Inca society was not a hereditary one. On the death of each Inca king, civil war broke out among his sons, brothers and nephews, which evoked the state

of chaos that had existed until Manco Capac brought civilization and order to the world (the "world" was the Inca territories). The victor thus became the restorer of civilization and was revered and respected for this feat. In these portraits we see what is claimed to be the 14 Inca kings from Manco Capac to Atahualpa. The latter was called "the usurper," for furthering the interests of Francisco Pizarro.

The Spanish conquistadores invented stories of the fabulous wealth of the Inca, though this wealth was, in fact, not so great. Precious metals were not in circulation among the general population, which in any case lived austerely. Only the Inca and his nobles were allowed to wear ornaments made of gold and silver, objects made of these metals usually being kept in the temples and the convents of the chosen women and of the Inca's wives. When Atahualpa paid his ransom to the Spaniards he had the gold brought from the sacred places, so that most of the objects given to Pizarro were, in fact, Chimú. In this picture we see a beautiful gold feline head, typical of the Frías style. It is now in the Brüning Collection in the Museo de Lambayeque in Peru.

rected the government and sometimes the wars, ordered cities built and officiated at weddings. He also went hunting, the traditional pastime of royalty, in special areas, such as Huamachuco, reserved exclusively for his use.

The Inca in power at the time of the arrival of the Spaniard was no more than the product of a cultural evolution—a complete enigma to Europeans. It was impossible to trace the emperor's family tree through the "legitimate" and "illegitimate" lines, since the Inca did not follow a hereditary line of succession. Each time an emperor died, civil war broke out among factions led by the sons of the dead man, his brothers and nephews. The winner was proclaimed emperor and his first duty was to restore order to the empire. In this way they commemorated the origins of the Inca when Manco Capac had established civilization for the first time. Each new Inca, therefore, began his reign with a pilgrimage to Mount Huanacauri, where the golden staff of Manco Capac had been sunk into the ground. In order to avoid this type of civil war, some emperors (Viracocha, Pachacutec and Tupac Yupanqui) appointed their successors while still on the throne, but to no avail. In any case the struggle for power on the death of the Inca had become an institution of Inca politics, nor was it uncommon while the Inca was still alive. The emperors were obliged to give themselves up to governing, which meant leaving the army in the hands of those who could use it to lead a *coup d'état.* Thus, the emperors often tried to choose one of their sons to control the army, the outcome of which was not, however, always favorable. Viracocha was the victim of an attempted *coup* by his son Pachacutec (who had led the great campaign against the Chanca), who in turn fell victim to that led by his son, Tupac Yupanqui.

The traditional marriage of the emperor to his sister, the *colla,* began after the reign of Tupac Yupanqui. Previously, the Inca had married the daughter of a neighboring *curaca,* thus enabling him to form key military alliances within the empire. In fact, there is evidence that Huayna Capac was the only emperor to marry his sister. Tupac Yupanqui, on the other hand, married his aunt on his father's side.

In order to assume the supernatural powers he would use to benefit the community, the emperor first had to be invested by the high priest in the sun temple. Then, at the beginning of each new year, it was the emperor's duty to plunge his golden staff into the earth, so restoring fertility to the fields and sweeping away sickness in the rainy season. During his reign, Pachacutec was obliged to go in person to an erupting volcano in Arequipa to extinguish it with small clay pellets soaked in llama blood, which he shot from a sling. Gradually the Inca emperors assumed greater authority in the sun cult. Tupac Yupanqui abolished the position of high priest, while Huayna assumed the position himself. It was, in fact, he who claimed that the emperor was the reincarnation of the sun.

As regards the court ceremony that so amazed the Spaniards, it would also seem that this was of recent origin. Tupac Yupanqui took it mainly from Chan Chan, as he did the rite of acknowledgment of the Inca by the *curacas.* Huayna Capac took many of his rites from the Chimú. While traveling in his litter, his subjects bent their heads to the ground in order not to look on him, and when he died, 4,000 people from among his wives and servants were sacrificed to accompany him.

The Maya had had no great leader since 1100, the year in which Mayapan was destroyed. Each Maya city had its own leader, called the *halach huinic,* "the true man." The position was hereditary through the existing lines (the Cocom in Mayapán, the Xiu in Uxmal, the Itza in Chichén Itzá and the Chel in Tecon), and one of the hereditary duties was to have the public servants examined to see if they were in full possession of their faculties. Fortunately for them, the examination took place only once every 20 years. They were tested on a wide range of subjects, some of which related to esoteric knowledge, which has led some experts to believe that these leaders exercised some religious power and used it to increase the prestige of leadership.

139

The best works of gold in Peru were Chimú. Gold objects and even goldsmiths were brought to Cuzco, with the result that many pieces that are even now believed to be Inca are, in fact, Chimú. Above are two such examples: a necklace made with soldered sheets of beaten gold and a repoussée goblet with a false bottom (which rattled when used), possibly made over a wooden mold. The best collection of Chimú goldwork was brought together at the begin- *ning of this century by the German Enrique Brüning and may be seen in the Museo de Lambayeque in Peru. With the archaeological discoveries made in the area over the last 50 years, the number of Chimú gold objects has increased considerably.*

In the shadow of those in power

Dwelling in the shadow of those in power was a veritable host of nobles and civil servants, most of whom belonged to the ruling ethnic group, though some came from those dominated nations that had adapted to their new masters in order to maintain their privileges.

In Aztec society, after the *huey tlatoani* came a series of civil servants who shared the task of governing with their king. First came *cihuacoatl*, or "the snake woman," who was not, in fact, a female but most probably the high priest of the Aztec religion. The king trusted him totally, and in practice his position would have been that of a kind of viceroy, placed in charge of the government whenever the king had to leave Tenochtitlan on some military campaign or some other business. His symbol of office was a black and white cape, ranking second only to the green of the *huey tlatoani*. Below him came the four great military dignitaries who advised the king on matters of war and were normally relatives. Moctezuma had himself held this office during the reign of his father, Ahuitzotl. Then came the *tlalocan*, or supreme council of the city, which dealt with important matters and was the center of the electoral council. In ancient times they must have been the representatives of the *calpulli*, or clans, but were later appointed by the *huey tlatoani*.

The higher nobility of the empire were the *tlatoque* (the plural form of *tlatoani*) of the largest cities. They were normally in contact with

those in Mexico. The title was hereditary, but each new *tlatoani* had to be approved by the *huey tlatoani*. He received tribute and submission in his domain. After these came the *tetecuhtin* or lords, who may be called nobles by merit. These were persons who had excelled in the army, in the civil service, in espionage or in religion. They were allowed to dress and adorn themselves in a

special way, though never like the nobles by birth. They lived in great mansions in Tenochtitlan, away from their colleagues in the *calpulli*, and owned lands and serfs in conquered territories. Back in the old classless Aztec past, when these nobles had died, their lands had been distributed among deserving individuals. In the new class-based society, however, the son of the noble usually considered himself to be entitled to the lands. Thus, noble status followed hereditary lines in the era of Moctezuma.

The word *pilli* was synonymous with noble and these were in fact the descendants of the *tlatoque* and the *tetecuhtin*. The *pipiltin* (the plural of *pilli*) owned land and occupied posts as administrators, ambassadors, judges and tribute collectors. Their number was unlimited, whereas the number of *tlatoque* was restricted. The *tetecuhtin* were also very few. The *pipiltin* were polygamous, educated in special schools, had their own law courts and wore clothes exclusive to their position.

The Inca aristocracy was made up of the *orejones* and the *curacas*. The former (*orejon* means long-eared after the large earflares they wore, which enlarged their ear lobes) were descendants of the previous emperors. Each new emperor meant the beginning of a new line of descendants or *panaca*, whose members were bound by family ties. For four years the *orejones* were educated in special schools where they learned Quechua (the official language of the

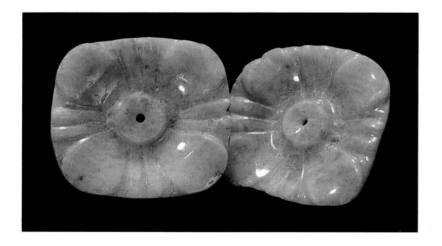

Jade typified the high standing of the Maya nobility. At the top of the page is a jade mask from a very early period, possibly between 50 and 300 A.D. and most probably from a tomb, as it would by no means be an object of everyday use. It is now in the British Museum in London. Above, left, are typical jade earrings as worn by the nobles. These were made by cutting a sphere and boring a hole through the middle to hold a pin, at the end of which was a small circle to keep the sphere in place. They belong to the late Classic period (600 to 800 A.D.) and are kept in the Denver Art Museum. Above, right, are some curious green jade ornaments in the shape of a four-petaled flower. There is a hole through the middle for attaching them to a headdress or to clothing. Without doubt they belonged to a Maya lord of the late Classic period. They are on display in the Museum of the American Indian in New York.

This extraordinary portrait on a jade breastplate is a mystery of Mesoamerican cultures. It was originally made by an Olmec mason in the mid-Pre-Classic period between 1000 and 600 B.C., but the inscription is Maya from the beginning of the Classic period, which would be between 50 and 250 A.D. The piece is perfectly polished, as was typical of the work of the Olmec artists, and depicts a young lord wearing disk-shaped earrings. The mouth with the corners facing down is typically Olmec. Without doubt such an exquisite piece was highly valued by the later Maya lord, who used it as a breastplate. This gives rise to the question of whether the later lord did this through love of an antique or because the Olmec esthetic model had not changed with the passing of time.

Rulers

To the Spaniards, Motecuhzoma II Xocoyotzin or "the Lord who becomes angry" (1502–1520), whom they called Moctezuma, was the symbol of the power and wealth of the Amerindian sovereigns. In fact he was not a king but the head of the Aztec confederation, itself made up by the alliance of various cities, each of which had its own tlatoani. As he was the tlatoani of Tenochtitlan, Moctezuma was the huey tlatoani, or "great orator." He was elected by a council and could therefore also be deposed—some-

thing Cortés did not know. The pomp and ostentation of the Aztec court was introduced by Moctezuma with the aim of elevating himself in the eyes of his subjects—which must have met with opposition from the nobility. In the print at the top of the page, taken from the Durán Codex, we see Moctezuma sailing on the canal in his palace. Above, we see the tlatoani ordering the construction of the Mexico-Xochimilco road.

Inca, which is still spoken today), religion, the use of the *quipu* and history, as well as some geometry, geography and astronomy, under the *amautas* or sages.

On completing their studies, they "graduated" in a solemn ceremony in which they demonstrated their knowledge in examinations. They dressed in white and assembled in the great square in Cuzco. All the graduates had had their hair cut and wore around their heads a black *llautu* with feathers of the same color. After a prayer to the sun, the moon and the thunder deities they ascended the nearby hill of Huanacauri, where they fasted and held ceremonies and dances. Afterward, they took part in a series of competitions, including a race to the top of Huanacauri, archery and slingshot contests, after which they went before the Inca emperor, who presented them with a pair of tight trousers, a crown of feathers and a metal breastplate. Finally, the emperor himself pierced their ears with a gold needle so that they could begin to wear the symbol of their class—the earflares. The *orejones* had numerous privileges; they were entitled to own land and possess several wives. They often received gifts from the king, such as women, llamas, valuable objects, permission to be carried on a litter, or use of a throne. The *orejones* filled the civil service posts of the empire.

The *curacas* and *ayllu* leaders derived personal benefits as supervisors of the system of local distribution. They were in charge of groups of workers who also cultivated the *curacas'* lands and looked after their animals. In return, the *curacas* would provide food, housing and even some payment (with cloth and animal skins). The *curacas* were the local nobility, some of their ancestors being more ancient than the Inca themselves, but they had agreed to become part of the imperial structure in exchange for the right to keep some of their privileges. Any threat to the empire that they might represent was neutralized by each new *curaca* who took control of his area being obliged to demonstrate his loyalty to the Inca by sending his son and successor to be educated in Cuzco, where he would learn the language, religion and customs of the state. The *curacas* would often offer a daughter or sister to

the Inca as a secondary wife, and the Inca would send women and dependents in return. Each year the *curacas* had to go to Cuzco to offer to the Inca a part of what had been produced. When the Lupaca revolted, Tupac Yupanqui subdued them, had their *curaca* brought to Cuzco and obliged them to choose another leader.

Another privileged sector of Inca society (though not a social class, since office was held only for life) was filled by the administrators, who normally came from the *orejon* class, though there were also others from Cuzcoan *ayllus* of humble origin. First came the four *apu*, or administrators, from the four quarters of the *Tahuantinsuyu*, who advised the emperor personally. Beneath these were the *tucricue*, or governors of provinces, who lived in the provincial capitals and were periodically inspected. The *tucricue*

142

were assisted by the *quipucamayoc*, or accountants, whom we shall speak more of later. Their job was to supervise the incoming and outgoing goods of the state warehouses, the demography of their provinces and special events. The administrators received a *yana*, or secondary wife, from the house of the chosen women of the Inca, and they usually possessed lands around Cuzco, though never in the areas in which they were administrators. The system of distribution itself prevented them from becoming a landowning bureaucracy.

Territorial conquest had demonstrated the danger of placing the administration of the empire in the hands of one single ethnic group, and in the times of Huayna Capac northern peoples who had been slightly "Incanized" began to occupy administrative posts. The ethnic group made up of Cuzcoan Inca began to feel threatened, therefore creating an air of tension, which made itself felt when the military leaders left the Quito front to return to Cuzco with their troops.

The death of Huayna Capac almost certainly interrupted a sociopolitical evolution.

Women in Inca society were regarded as another commodity of the distributive economy. They were classified into two groups by the state: the *acllacunas*, or chosen women, and the *huasipascunas*, or discarded women. This latter group was fated to be the wives of plebeians. The *acllacunas* were taken to the convents of the Inca, where they remained for four years, receiving training in religion and practical matters (they were taught to spin, weave, cook, etc.). When they reached puberty, the most skilled were selected as secondary wives for the emperor and those *orejones* on whom the Inca wished to confer distinction, while the rest stayed on in the convents leading chaste lives filled with hard work, such as weaving the wool of the llamas of the sun.

143

This print from the Durán Codex *(top) is titled "where it is suspected that the Indians of these Indies and the islands of terra firma are from" and alludes to the legend of the seven caves from which the Aztec embarked on their long wanderings. Although a mythical place, it was interpreted by the Spanish priests as a sort of earthly paradise from which all the Indian races had come. The highest lords of any Aztec city, seen above in an interpretation from the* Durán Codex, *were distinguished by the use of special clothes and jewels. They were polygamous and lived in palaces maintained by the subjects of their cities. They were also landowners and received money and food supplies from the* huey tlatoani.

The proletariat and slaves

The Maya nobles were called *almehenob*, meaning "those who have fathers and mothers," naturally an allusion to known fathers and mothers, or to those whose ancestry was known on both sides. Thus, theirs was a nobility through blood. They possessed their own lands and occupied high political, military and religious positions. They were also the great merchants. In reality the Maya oligarchy was of Mexican origin, and when an official was to occupy a high position in the administration, he had to undergo a test on the content of an occult catechism called the *Zuyua Tongue*.

Even the lowest social level was not made up of one class, for low-born people belonging to the dominant ethnic groups, such as the Aztec or Inca, were in a relatively privileged position compared to the dominated peoples within the empire, especially in Mesoamerica, where a great deal of tribute was exacted from the vanquished. As we have seen, in the Andes, the dominant ethnic group was that group in charge of administration, the army and the priesthood.

The *macehualli* were Aztec free men or plebeians who made up the greater part of the pop-

ulation. They belonged to *calpulli*, kindred organizations that the Spaniards called "barrios," districts or town areas. They were most likely true clans in ancient times before the the formation of the empire. At the beginning of the 15th century any Aztec could marry a woman from his own or any other *calpulli*. He was even entitled to change *calpullis* if he wished to.

Inca free men usually lived in *ayllus*, similar to the Aztec *calpulli*. The *ayllu* was a localized structure of kinship, though not a clan nor a direct line of descendants. It tended to be endogamous with parallel patrilineal and matrilineal descent (the men descended from the father and the women from the mother). The *ayllu* gave land to the *cacique*, to its members, to the sun and to the Inca emperor. Its social unit was the family (made up of the couple and its unmarried children), who formed the unit of production and consumption, the work being shared among its members. The peasant received common pasture land and a plot of land (*tupu*) from the *ayllu*. The amount of land given would vary in size according to soil quality, and he might be given several plots at different thermal levels.

With the land he was given he was able to maintain his wife and family. He helped his neighbors with the sowing and harvest and received the same help in return. He was also expected to play his part in tilling the land of widows, the sick and old, and in the building of houses for new couples. With the other members of the group, he was also expected to look after the land and animals of the *curaca* and those of the *huaca* of the *ayllu* (this communal fund was important in the redistribution of the goods to the community), and the land belonging to the Inca and to the sun. In exchange he received his part of the distribution from the state warehouses. The Inca male also had to fulfill his obligations as a warrior between the ages of 25 and 52. For this system, Pachacutec had divided the empire into four parts (north, south, east and west), each of which contained 10,000 families, and these families into subdivisions of 1,000, 100 and 10.

The Maya plebeians lived in similar circumstances to the Aztec. They had a plot of land, living on what it yielded. Landa speaks at length of their cooperation in working the land and building houses, from which we may deduce the

In this sculpture from the Museo Popol Vuh in Guatemala, we seen an old Maya sorceress in a wide-brimmed hat, with some sort of animal, leaning back in meditation. The social status of such people was equal to that of their low-level neighbors who employed their services.

As in the European courts, there were dwarves for the entertainment of the lords. In late Classic Maya pottery, figures of dwarves sometimes appear, dressed differently from the rest of the people and apparently in the same way as their lords. This dwarf with the large turban may be seen in the American Museum of Natural History in New York.

The macehualtin *(the plural form of* macehualli*) were plebeian freemen who made up the main body of the Aztec workforce. They belonged to a* calpulli*, which was an ancient organization of kinship from which they received a house and a plot of land to provide for the needs of their families. Above we see a pottery figure of a* macehualli *from the Museo de Antropología in Mexico.*

presence of a certain degree of collectivism, otherwise relatively unknown among the Indian peoples.

The two lowest Aztec classes were the proletariat and the slaves. The first group was made up of outsiders whose land and possessions had been expropriated by the state, or Aztec who, for some reason or another, had lost their privileges as members of the *calpulli*. They earned their living as porters, carrying heavy loads, or working for the lords.

Slaves could be foreign boys or girls who had been received as payment of tribute, or Aztec who had fallen into such an unfortunate situation through debt. They could also be thieves who had not been able to pay back what they had stolen or children sold by their parents. Reminiscent of a classless society were teachings proclaiming that the children of slaves were always free, that the ill treatment of slaves was forbidden and that it was illegal to give slaves to new masters without first asking for the slave's consent.

In Inca society the lowest classes were the *mitmac* and the *yanas*. The first came from peoples who had been transferred to another region because they were considered to be a threat to the state. Tupac Yupanqui carried out several such deportations, but the Inca most famous for putting this policy into practice was Huayna Capac, who sent the equatorial Cañari to the south of Peru, and moved the Chachapuya from their homes in the north of Peru. The *mitmac* were always considered rebels against the state and made to live in isolation in unknown territories, surrounded by hostile peoples.

The *yanas*, or serfs, came from different backgrounds, most commonly being prisoners of war, though at times they were young men who had been recruited to serve the emperor. They were not entitled to the privileges of the *ayllu* and had no ethnic ties or affiliations. They were often given as gifts to the *orejones*, to great warriors, and to the *curacas*, to work their lands. Most of the *yanas* were servants at the imperial palace or in the temples, though they were also used to fill low-level positions such as army porter or watchman in the royal warehouses. In spite of everything, it cannot be said that they were slaves, since they were allowed to possess land, livestock and goods, which they could leave to one of their sons.

145

Maya militarism at the end of the Classic period led to an increase in the number of slaves. This Jaina ceramic figurine from the Princeton University Art Museum portrays a prisoner with his hands tied behind his back and his hair cropped, smiling enigmatically in the face of his new status as a slave.

Education
and
knowledge

The Mochica doctor (facing page) inherited the formula for preparing the poporo *potion through family tradition, while young Aztec (above) were obliged to undergo severe practices to strengthen the spirit—two examples of the great variety of methods used throughout the centuries to gain education and knowledge in pre-Columbian times.*

Learning from childhood

Education was the foundation of social order, which in turn reflected the perfect order existing in the world of the gods. Children and adolescents were the main recipients of education, though the pre-Columbian Indian either taught or was taught throughout the whole of his life. Parents taught their children, teachers taught adolescents, the elderly taught parents and grandchildren, priests taught the citizen and the leaders, and the Inca emperor taught everyone. Every time a new Inca was appointed in Cuzco or a *tlatoani* in Tenochtitlan, he would give a moralistic speech to his people, similar to those that politicians give today on achieving office. The speech given by Emperor Roca serves well here as an example: "Let the thief, the homicide, the adulterer and the larcenist be hanged without remission. Children shall serve their parents until they are 25 years of age and thereafter serve the Republic…"

Naturally, those who were most qualified to teach were members of the priesthood; they were in the privileged position of knowing the gods' wishes. Next came the great lords, some of whom claimed to be descendants of certain gods or to be directly in touch with them. But, as we have said before, every member of society felt it to be his right to teach his neighbor, believing that in this way he would be helping to keep things in their place, which when all was said and done was the sociopolitical order of each people.

For Mesoamericans, education explained the why and wherefore of the different social classes and the convenience of maintaining the status quo. They were also taught to fear the gods and offer them continual sacrifices so that they would be satisfied and not send great catastrophes, as they had done in the past. The Aztec considered education so important that Motecuhzoma and Ilhuicamina decreed that it be compulsory and established schools in all the *calpulli*. To the Inca, it was education that justified both their very existence and also their conquests. It was the sun god who had sent his own children to all the peoples in the world to preach their civilized doctrine: respect for all men, for women and girls in particular, monogamous marriage, contracted after the age of 20, obedience to the *caciques*, sun worship and the dedication of houses to the

148

This reproduction of sheet 63 of the Mendoza Codex *depicts the education of young Aztec. In the upper strip we see a priest walking in front of a pupil as they go up the mountain to make a sacrifice to the gods. In the second we see a young lad marching off to war, carrying his arms and equipment; this is followed by two teachers from the* telpochcalli *using burning sticks to punish a youth who has been caught living in concubinage. The third strip shows an apprentice priest being punished with pine needles for breaking the rules of chastity. In the fourth and final strip, we see functionaries punishing a vagabond by cropping his hair and burning his scalp.*

virgins of the sun. Since certain peoples offered resistance to such a noble enterprise, they were justified in conquering them in order to set them on the right path. It was a holy war, which the Europeans would later explain better with the appropriate theoretical foundation.

Parents were educators *par excellence*. In all of the cultures it was they who were entrusted with the instruction of the children. They taught the boys to work the land, hunt, make pottery and weave, and the girls to cook and clean, and in addition they taught them correct social behavior. This instruction was sound and consisted of both good advice and discipline. Punishment was administered when the rules of behavior were ignored. This could at times be violent, with offenders being whipped, scratched with maguey thorns and, among the Aztec, forced to breathe chili pepper smoke. According to Landa, the Maya girls in Yucatán were educated by their mothers, who "reproach them, instruct them and make them work, and if the girls do wrong they are punished with pinches to the ears and arms. If they are seen to raise their eyes, they are much reproached and their eyes are rubbed with pepper, causing grave pain." For the Inca, the father was the only educator and represented Manco Capac, the great teacher.

There are some extraordinary examples of paternal Aztec education, such as the well-known speech of father to son recorded by Mendieta, of which we shall quote only a few of the more important points: "Love all people and you will live in peace and joy. Follow not the fool, who neither obeys his father nor respects his mother, but, as an animal, leaves the true path...Look, my son, mock not the aged or sick or those lacking limbs, nor he who is in sin or has erred...Do no harm to others, nor give them poison or inedible food...Wound not others, nor set a bad example, nor talk too much, nor interrupt another's conversation, so as not to disturb him...Talk not idly, nor stop in the market nor in the baths...Be not vain nor look much in the mirror...Make not gestures as you walk, nor clasp hands with others. Look well where you walk, and thus you shall not find yourself with another, nor in front of him. If you are told to hold office, should they wish to prove you, excuse yourself as best you can and

you will be held to be sensible...Neither enter nor leave before your elders; rather, whether you are sitting or standing, wherever they may be, allow them to go first and respect them. Speak not before them, nor cross in front...Neither eat nor drink first, rather serve the others before...If you should wish to marry, tell us first the news, and do not dare to do it without us. Look, my son, neither a thief nor a gambler be...Work with your hands and eat from the fruit of your labor." As we can see, these are moral rules of courtesy and good manners. Some of the final pieces of advice are of note, such as, "When you are spoken to, my son, shuffle not your feet, move not your hands, for that is done by people of low intelligence; bite not your blanket nor the clothes you wear, nor spit, nor look about you, nor stand up frequently if you are sitting."

No less interesting is the advice given by a father to his son on sex: "For the world to continue, the joining of man and woman is necessary. This was ordained by the master of the universe. And you will discover this. But throw yourself not at it, as does the dog, who then swallows his food in all haste. Let yourself not be dragged down by carnal pleasure. You have manly enterprises to undertake. You have to build up your

manly strength and reach full and complete development. You are like a maguey; you must have offspring when you mature. And this will give you manly and marital strength. And your children will be strong, vigorous, tall, well-formed and oh so handsome...Listen to another thing; though in time you reach the fullness of your manly power, make not haste to put an end to it. True it is that you must make use of the body of your wife, as it is something of yours and part of you yourself, but act not greedily, as though you were starving to death, have not your fill too soon. That is, do it not with excessive eagerness, nor exhaust yourself with that worthlessness. Moderation, measure, calm; that is what is required." The advice given by a mother to her daughter was similar.

Not even marriage freed a man from having to listen to fatherly advice, as we can see from the advice given by an Aztec peasant to his son: "Work always and reap, and eat the fruit of your labor. Look, be not faint, nor idle, for if you are idle and negligent how will you live with another? What will become of your wife and children?...My son, make your wife take care of the things she uses to do her work and of what she must do in the house, and tell your children what

149

This reproduction of plate 64 from the Mendoza Codex *illustrates the education of young Aztec. In the section at lower left, a priest brings an apprentice to a mountain in order to sacrifice him.*
To the right a young man marches off to war carrying his equipment and arms; in the image above it two masters of "tepochcalli" punish a young man with burning sticks for cohabitating illicitly with a woman.

The upper left depicts the punishment of a priest's apprentice with pine thorns for breaking the vow of celibacy.
In the fourth and last border, various officials punish a vagrant for cutting down and scorching The Head with Fire.

is for their good. Give them good advice as parents, both of you, so that they will live as decent people...Fear not, my children, the work from which you live, for from it you will have what they will have to eat and you will clothe them with it. Again I say, my son, care for your wife and home, and work so as to have something to offer and console your parents and any who come to your house, and you will be able to receive them in spite of your poverty...Love and be pious and be not arrogant, nor do others harm but be polite and affable towards others...Wound not, nor do evil to others, and doing what you ought, extol it not as a virtue for that is a sin against the gods...Be not a roamer, nor a bad farmer; settle down and take root, sow and reap and make a home for your wife and children to be settled when you die."

The elderly constituted the second pedagogic group after the parents. Among some Mesoamerican peoples the educational influence of the elderly was enormous, since they were considered to be the trustees of two values, experience and time. For the Maya the old man in each family was considered a greater teacher than the father. According to Landa, the young boys had enormous respect for the old: "And they took their advice, and thus they could boast of being old, and told the boys what they had seen." The old woman in the family performed the same function for the young girl.

Aztec elders also felt that it was their duty to educate the young. This is a famous piece of their advice: "Eat not in haste, take not great bites out of the bread, nor put much food in your mouth lest you choke, nor swallow what you eat like a dog...Break not the bread into pieces, nor snatch at the food on the plate; let your way of eating be quiet, and not give those present cause for laughter. At the beginning of the meal wash your hands and rinse out your mouth, and having eaten, do the same again. Dress not in a curious manner, nor with too much imagination...nor wear torn garments in the street, nor walk slowly in the street, nor with haste, nor taking strides. Those who do so are called *ixtotomac cuecuet*, which means 'he who walks looking everywhere like a madman'...Neither walk with your head down...nor looking in all directions so that it may

not be said of you that you are silly or stupid or badly raised...It is wise to speak calmly, not in haste, nor uneasily, nor raising the voice...The things you hear said and see done, especially if they are wrong, ignore them and keep silent."

As the performance of important duties prevented the nobles from educating their own children, servants or teachers were entrusted with the task, something common to all societies. Sahagún states that the Aztec mother or wet nurse

This lithograph from Five Years' Expedition, *published in London in 1806, shows a Karib family from Surinam. The man is wearing a feather headdress and carries his bow and arrows in one hand and his parrot in the other. The woman is holding a young child in her arms and has thongs tied to the upper part of her calf to show that she is married.*

educated the child until it was seven or eight years of age, when it was entrusted to pages or companions: "The one who lived with the child taught it to speak in a well-mannered way, using good language, to obey and respect all those officials of the republic whom he should chance to meet." It would seem that the Purepecha, Maya and Mixtec had the same custom, and that these pages were often the older sons of the servants, who usually acted as their playmates. Muñoz Camargo states that the lords of Tlaxcala had tutors exclusively for teaching and that their classes reflected the demeanor characteristic of good breeding, as in the course of the class the pupils "squatted, and did not sit on the floor, nor look at the teacher, nor raise their eyes, nor spit, nor fidget, nor look each other in the face; on leaving the class (the teacher) withdrew without turning his back on them, his head bowed and with great modesty."

The advice given by the lords to their children had an elitist bias, like this piece of advice given by an Aztec father to his daughter: "Be careful, for you are of high birth, descended from those of high birth, and thanks to illustrious persons you were born. You are the thorn and bud of our lords…Listen, many times I have given you to understand that you are of noble birth. You are a beautiful thing, even though you are no more than a little woman. You are precious stone, you are turquoise…you are of a noble line…Look, do not bring dishonor on yourself, nor on our lords, nor on the nobles, nor on the rulers who preceded us. Do not become as the common people, do not become plebeian…This is your duty, what you will have to do: during the night and during the day devote yourself to the things of god…Awake, arise in the middle of the night, prostrate yourself on your elbows and knees, raise your neck and your shoulders. Invoke, call the lord, he who is like the night and the wind. He will be merciful, he will hear you at night, he will look on you then with mercy, he will grant you what you deserve, what has been assigned to you…And during the night be vigilant, rise swiftly, hold out your hands, extend your arms, wash your face, wash your hands, wash out your mouth, take up the broom quickly, and sweep…Pay attention, take interest, work hard to know how things are done, thus you will spend your life, thus you will be at peace. Thus you will be valiant. And prepared if our lord should decide to send you misfortune; let it not be in vain. Or if poverty should grow up among the nobles. Look well on, embrace, what is the duty of a woman; the spindle, the shuttle…Search for he who is to be your companion, but not as if in a market, do not call him, not as if it were spring, do not go with an appetite for him. But if ever you should disdain the one who is to be your companion, he who is chosen by our lord, if you reject him, you will be mocked, in truth you will be mocked and will become a prostitute."

This print from Exploration of the Valley of the Amazon, *published in Washington in 1853, shows a great Caripuna hunter named Matua, holding an unusual bow with its arrows. He is accompanied by his brother, Manu, whom he is teaching to hunt. The artist has accurately illustrated the symptoms of the intestinal parasitosis, very common in the Madeira River area, from which the adolescent brother is suffering.*

Schools for the rich and schools for the poor

Under normal circumstances, the ordinary people or plebeians did not have any sort of schooling. Inca Roca, who had been so concerned about founding schools for nobles in Cuzco, described his idea of education quite clearly with these words, recorded by Garcilaso: "It is advisable that the children of the common people not learn the sciences, for they belong only to the nobles, and thus they will not become proud and diminish the Republic. Let them learn the occupations of their fathers, which is enough for them."

As we have seen, education in Aztec society was compulsory and given in a public school called *telpochcalli*, or "the house of the young," which was dependent on the *calpulli*, and where boys were taught to be good citizens and brave warriors. The teachers at these institutions were the *telpochtlatoque*, or "teachers of the young," and were divided into two groups: the *telpochtlado*, or "he who speaks to the young," who taught general education, and the *tiachcauch*, or "captains," in charge of military instruction. There were also the *ichpochtlatoque*, or [female] teachers of young women."

Father Diego Durán states that Aztec children were taught in the *telpochcalli* "to be well-mannered, to respect their elders, to serve, to obey, given papers on how they were to serve their lords, to move among them and be polite to them. There they were taught to sing, to dance and one thousand other subtleties. Also, they taught them

exercises of war, to shoot arrows, to throw a *fisga* or rods burned with fibers, to handle well the sword and shield, making them sleep little and eat less, so that from childhood they would know their work and not be raised in comfort." The priest did not miss the point concerning the aim of being a servant, which was inculcated into the young *macehualli* and was also the reason why their education was compulsory: "To serve, to obey, giving them papers on how they were to serve their lords." Apart from this was the civic and military education, which had always been compulsory.

In addition to all this they were made to do a whole series of exercises aimed at breaking the spirit of the individual and at making him aware of his value as a member of the community. Thus, he was obliged to sweep the school, cut firewood, repair ditches and canals, work communal land, etc. Moreover, his strength was measured (with trunks loaded onto his back), as well as his abilities. Naturally, the pupil was submitted to severe moral scrutiny, but from the secular, rather than religious, point of view. It is true that he was not allowed to drink *pulche* (he would do it in secret), that he had to undergo mortification of the flesh and purification, but these were the prohibitions and obligations of any man.

After school was over for the day, a great dance was held lasting until after midnight, after which the pupils went back to the school to sleep, though the boys went one way and the young men

another, where, as Sahagún states, "there they sleep with their lovers." He added, "These young men had their lovers in twos and in threes. Perhaps one woman in a house, and the others are perhaps elsewhere." Which goes to prove that they were not educated according to the monolithic sexual abstinence preached by the priests. When the pupils of the *tepochcalli* reached marrying age, the parents asked the teachers for permission for their sons to leave the school and become full-fledged citizens.

The alliance between the nobles and the priesthood was particularly evident in the temple schools, where the priests taught the children of the nobles. The priests even shared some of their exclusive knowledge concerning the calendar and writing system, in exchange for filling the ranks of the priesthood with members of the nobility, who could then continue with their studies and finally become priests themselves. Schools for the children of nobles also existed in the Otomie society, of which Sahagún wrote, "There, in the temple lived the *tlamacazque*, and there were the little children educated. There they did penance, kept vigil, brought water, pierced their flesh with thorns, bled themselves, cut their flesh and fasted. All the night the *teponaztli* played, above in the temple."

Young Aztec and Maya nobles were also educated in temple schools, together with the future priests. The Aztec schools were called *calmecac*, the boys usually starting at the age of

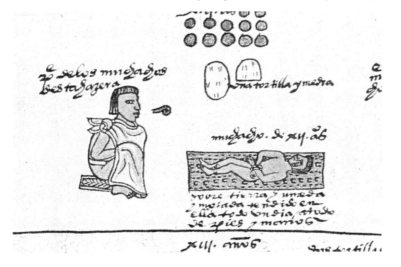

152

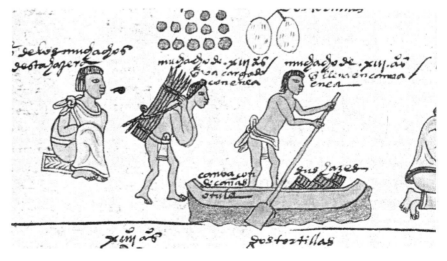

The Mendoza Codex *illustrates the education of young Aztec, and here we see the different types of education given to adolescents of 12 (right) and 13 years of age (left). The 12-year-olds are painted as blue circles, with the text below stating that the suitable diet for that age was one tortilla and a half. At right, under the eye of a teacher who remains seated, we see a boy lying on the ground and the legend, "On damp, wet earth, lying there all the day,*

with his hands and feet bound." On the left, the education of an adolescent of 13 years of age is depicted, also with the use of blue circles. At this age the ration was two tortillas, and the child carries anea *(red stalks) on his back or in his canoe. To his left, the figure of the teacher also appears, giving the boy advice (the spiral coming out of the mouth).*

The different Aztec social classes are clearly depicted in the Mendoza Codex. *Below on the left, the* tlacuilo *or artist has painted five seated* tetecuhtin *or lords. The legend states, "Telzpuchtli [that is, tecuhtli] means bossy fellow." Facing them is another* tecuhtli, *though this one is married. His wife appears behind him, spinning cotton. In the center is tribute, consisting of two blankets, perfumes, a copper axe, a basket of tamales, a stewed turkeyhen and*

a cup of chocolate. A blanket had the equivalent value of 100 cocoa beans, capable of feeding a man for almost a month. Tenochtitlan received two million blankets per year as tribute. Below on the right, different types of civil servants are depicted, dressed in blankets whose colors related to the type of work they did.

Education

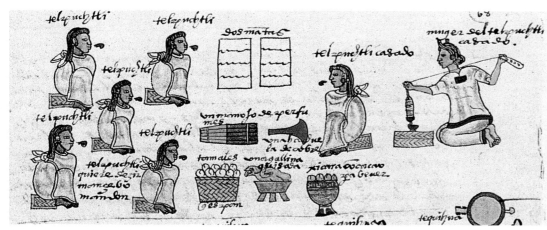

15, though some nobles preferred to take their sons to them earlier. Cortés explains that the children started "from the age of seven or eight until they were brought out to marry…They have no access to women, nor does any woman enter in the houses of religion. They abstain from eating certain types of food, more at some times of the year than at others." Together in these schools with the sons of the *pilli* or lords were also any *macehualli* children considered to have demonstrated exceptional talents or a great religious avocation.

The *calmecac* were very numerous (in Tenochtitlan alone there were seven) and the teaching was supervised by a kind of vicar general. The teaching was in three main areas: religious, cognitive and courtesy or behavior in society. The first was perhaps the most important, for it was no coincidence that it was a temple school, one that trained future priests. Sexual abstinence, fasting and religious practices disciplined the body and the spirit of the student. Thus, he was never able to sleep all through the night but obliged to get up several times at the sound of the shell horns to burn incense to the gods, prick his ears and legs with maguey thorns until they bled and bathe in the rivers and lakes. Adapting to this kind of life must have been extremely difficult, especially at the beginning, as a noble warned his son: "Every day you will cut maguey thorns to do penance…and you will also have to make your body bleed with maguey thorns, and bathe at night, in spite of the cold you may feel." Study involved reading and interpreting the picto-

graphic signs, the calendars (mainly the sacred calendar), astronomy, chronology and systems of divination. Finally, the aim of the teachings on courtesy or behavior was to teach the boy proper etiquette, the cultured language (different from that used by the plebeians) and self-control in order to always be a balanced man of great moderation and tact.

The Inca also had schools for the children of the nobles. Apparently, they were conceived by the Inca Roca himself, who, having reached the conclusion that the plebeians needed no special education so that they would not "become proud," considered the education of the sons of the aristocracy appropriate, "so that the *amautas* may teach the sciences taught to the chief Inca and those of the royal blood and the nobles of the empire"—that is to say, to the chosen class. Of course, the teaching was limited to information that could be memorized. This included a wide syllabus of religion, government, courtesy, the art of war, history, and a certain amount of poetry, music, philosophy and astrology. The teachers were called *amautas*, which was synonymous with sage or philosopher, and they were held in very high esteem. These schools were conducted in a structure called *yacha huaci*, meaning "the house of teaching," in which the *amautas* and the *haravec*, or poets, lived. Their only text was the remarkable *quipu*, a number of knotted strings on which were recorded Inca history, legislation, demography and state revenue and expenditure. Garcilaso states that "their laws were written and committed to knots in thread of different colors

which they used for their records and whose use they taught to their children and descendants."

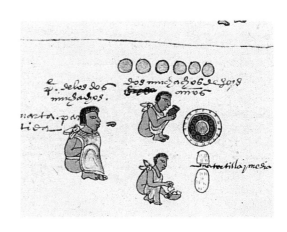

Also from the Mendoza Codex, *two boys of six years of age (represented with six circles), eat under the supervision of their father. According to the text, their ration was one tortilla and a half per day.*

153

Female education

In Mesoamerica in general, education for the daughters of nobles ran along similar lines to that of boys and was also given in temple schools. Bernal Díaz wrote, "And there nearby were other great chambers, in the manner of monasteries, where were gathered many daughters of Mexican neighbors, like nuns, until they married." As in the case of the boys, the girls were educated in these schools, living a life full of self-sacrifice and hard work until they were of marrying age, when they were allowed to leave the school (having obtained permission from the teachers) or stay on to devote their lives to their gods. Many of these girls were condemned to be priestesses from the very start, either because of their birth signs or because their parents wished it so.

Fernando Alba wrote that the young girls of the nobility entered school at the age of eight, "which was the age for them to enter the cloister; and the day having been determined for this, the relatives gathered, and she was taken to the temple, crowned with flowers and dressed elegantly in their usual attire, where she was received by the high priest; and after having reverently worshiped the false gods, burning incense to them and in their presence cutting off the heads of a certain number of quail, they took her down to the halls and place of reception, where in the presence of the mother superior and the other maids the *tequacuilli* or superintendent or vicar of these convents stood and gave with an admirable effect this elegant sermon." The sermon was, in fact, elegant, but rather soporific and alluded to the self-sacrifice the novice would have to endure and the purity she would have to attain. Then, according to Alba Ixtlixochitl, "Following this, she was divested of the rich garments she had been wearing and her hair cut off, a ceremony having to be carried out by one of the *cihuatlamacazque* or priestesses." The priestess also addressed a speech to the girl, exhorting her to self-sacrifice, obedience and the care of the temple.

Friar Agustín de Betancourt described the discipline in the schools in detail: "The routine was to arise by turns at half past ten at night and at dawn to put incense on the brazier; they went with one of the priestesses who taught them. In silence they swept the lower part of the temple, for the higher parts were swept by the children of the nobles. They ate twice each day; on holy days they were allowed to eat meat and sing and dance to celebrate the day. On the other working days, though they fasted, they wove blankets for their gods and each day, early in the morning, cooked food and took it to the altar to offer it, for they said that the gods accepted the steam from the food, and the priests later ate the food. If they were careless in their work they were punished by the old women, doing penance, for they believed that otherwise their flesh would rot. If the crime were public and discovered they received the sentence of death by stoning, as with the vestal virgins."

When a young woman reached marrying age, a meeting was arranged with the high priest of the temple on the day the girl was to leave. "The parents took cooked food, and incense, and the maid came out finely dressed and before the idol to which she had been devoted she held out a large blanket, and with great reverence placed an offering on the blanket, on painted plates made of wood: on one of the plates were *tamales* which are cakes of cooked corn, and on five bowls with three legs, which they call *molcajetes*, cooked

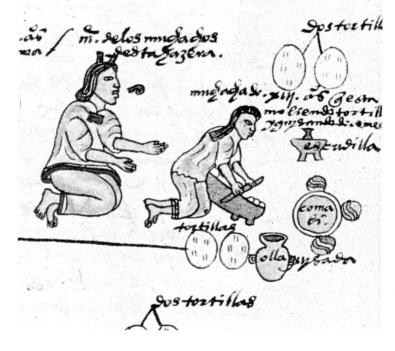

154

Aztec girls' education is also depicted in the Men-doza Codex, and here the tlacuilo has painted the stage between 12 and 13, or childhood and adolescence. The 12-year-old (above right), who ate only one tortilla and a half, is being directed by her mother (seated behind her) to get up and sweep the house during the night (the pictogram above them contains the legend "this picture means the night"). The 13-year-old (above left) ate two tortillas and did heavier duties about the house, such as grinding the corn in the metate *and cooking, all of which took place under the mother's watchful eye. Around the group we see a bowl, a* comal *or flat plate and a cooking pot.*

meat of duck and other fowl. And the satrap of that idol having made his address, she bade farewell to all and they took her, accompanied by her relatives, and thanked the *tequacuilli* or vicar of the parish, and he was appeased by the offering."

The girl's eagerness to leave the school was attributed to her forthcoming marriage, but in reality the reason must have been that she was finally leaving such a place of mortification and penance.

The life of Aztec noblewomen contrasted sharply with that of the lowest classes, who had to see to the drudgery of housework, help to grow milpa *and sometimes even sell small things in the market. In this illustration from the* Florentine Codex, *we see a weaving woman using a belt loom.*

The virgins of the sun and the wives of the Inca

There were two types of Inca women, the chosen and the discarded. The chosen women were divided up into two groups: those destined to be virgins of the sun and those chosen to be wives of the Inca emperor. The first of these two groups lived in the convent in Cuzco, near the sun temple (it is not true that this institution formed part of the temple, since women, and sun virgins in particular, were never allowed inside). The second lived in numerous convents in the larger cities, from which some were sent to Cuzco to become secondary wives of the Inca. The Spaniards became so confused with so many virgins and convents that they were finally unable to distinguish between them, but they were, in fact, very different.

The sun virgins were the true *acllahuaci* or chosen ones, selected both for their lineage and their beauty. Garcilaso wrote, "It was necessary that they be virgins and to ensure that this was so, they were taken at the age of eight downwards." They lived in a convent in Cuzco, spending the time weaving fine clothes with vicuña wool for their husband, the sun. There was, however, one snag, as Garcilaso tells us: "He [the sun] could not wear those vestments, and they were sent to the Inca as the legitimate son and heir of the sun for him to wear." When the Inca's wardrobe was complete, he ordered any remaining clothes to be offered to the sun god. It is not true that the Inca, as some have claimed, gave clothing to his nobles; this would have been sacrilege. What does seem to be true, however, is that the nuns also supplied the colla (empress) with clothes for sacred purposes. Perhaps it was for this reason that the empress frequently went to the convent.

The other *acllahuaci* or chosen women were the Inca's wives and those who lived in the convents of the largest cities. They were recruited in the provinces of the empire, the girls selected coming from different backgrounds. Many of them were of royal blood or daughters of nobles and *curacas*, but most came from the common people and were of outstanding beauty. The convents operated in the same way as did the temple of the sun virgins, with *mamacunas* and servants, but were paid for by the Inca's fortune. For this reason, a governor, a steward and a pantryman were also appointed. The *acllahuaci* also made clothing for the Inca and lived in convents full of fountains and gardens and used dishes made of gold.

The Inca's secondary wives lived in the great palace in Cuzco until they reached old age, when they were allowed to return to their places of origin with a large sum of money. Sometimes, on the death of an Inca, the successor inherited all the wives, which brought about a need for reorganization. The wives of the dead Inca automatically became *mamacunas* or teachers of the young wives of the new Inca. As for the *acllahuaci* who were not chosen to go to Cuzco because they were not beautiful enough, these stayed in the convents in the provinces, where they remained virgins all their lives. When they reached old age, they were allowed to choose between living out the rest of their lives in the convent or returning to the towns where they had been born. The "discarded" wives were married to common men.

For the Inca, virginity was held to be particularly important. Garcilaso says that many girls from the great families remained virgins voluntarily: "In their houses they lived withdrawn, honorable lives, having taken vows of virginity though not of the cloister." These were called *ocllo*, and one of them, who was a relative of his mother's, he had known when he was a child.

Institutions in Mesoamerica similar to those of the Inca are unknown, though López Cogolludo stated when describing the buildings in Yucatán and especially in Uxmal, "In some places, near to the temple building, there is another, where the virgins lived, like nuns, in the way of the Vestal Virgins of the Romans."

Punishment

The epilogue to education was the punishment of those who would not accept the established social behavior, the order of things. Methods of punishment, which made up a sort of pre-Columbian law, were recorded by the Spanish priests in their zeal to demonstrate the existence of a natural law in accordance with Christian religious principles. It is true that respect for life and the property of others existed all over Mesoamerica but within a very different frame of reference from that of Western culture. To the hunters, for example, the very idea of entitlement to ownership of the land in which the animals lived was inconceivable, and to the gatherers the term "private property" could not be applied to anything that could not be carried. Even in more sophisticated societies such as the Inca, communal goods were more important than private ones, and theft of communal goods was more severely punished.

The concept of punishment was more complex in the more complex societies. An Aztec who killed a slave was forced to become the slave of the owner, and Landa tells us that with the Maya, "He who committed murder had to pay with his life." In the case of the Chibcha this led to extreme cases, such as that in which a husband had to compensate his wife's family with his life if she died during childbirth.

It was also natural for justice to be handed out by the victim. Only the high cultures resorted to third parties or institutions to settle their differences, since they had a legal arm within the administration. With the Inca, for example, the *curacas*, the political chiefs, inspectors and a panel of 12 judges were part of the legal system. The highest authority was the Inca emperor's and that of the four viceroys of the *Tahuantinsuyu*. The legal procedure consisted of the testimony, then interrogation, then, in some cases, torture and finally the decision of the court, against which there was no appeal. It is significant, however, that even these high cultures left the punishment of the offender to the people, so that the community would act as defender of the established order.

In pre-Columbian law, punishment was applied against those who acted against the state and its institutions (especially in the high cultures) and also those who acted against the individual and the social order. Among this last group were those crimes against personal integrity, life, and the freedom and honor of the individual.

The gravest crime was naturally murder, punishable in virtually all of the societies by death. But there also existed degrees of punishment for the offense. Thus, for example, whoever in Inca society killed a *curaca* was quartered, whereas the punishment for killing a common man was only a whipping. In the same way, the crime of murder as a result of an argument or jealousy was less severely punished than if premeditated. The circumstances were also taken into consideration. For the Inca, if a person wounded another to such an extent that the victim could not look after himself, he was obliged to maintain the victim, and if he had no means to do so, he was punished with extraordinary severity, and the maintenance of the victim was paid for by the emperor. Personal integrity included one's honor, and the Aztec punished slander by cutting off a piece of the lips and ears of the offender.

There were also special sentences for crimes of a sexual nature. In the Aztec and Inca societies the rape of a virgin was punished by stoning. Stoning was also the punishment for adultery throughout Mesoamerica. "The fornicator's nose and genitals were cut off by the offended husband and the adulterer stoned." In Chibcha society punishment for rape depended on whether the offender was married or single. The single man was condemned to death whereas, the married man was obliged to give up his wife to two single men.

Crimes violating property were less severe, and punishment could consist of a warning, cutting of the hair, tearing of the cloak, whipping, or cut-ting off the nose, ears or hands. If the offender was a noble, the punishment was more severe and increased with each new offense. As far as theft was concerned, the gravity of the offense depended on what had been stolen and where. The Aztec, for example, did not consider it a crime to steal an ear of corn, provided it was taken from the first few rows of a maize field and if the offender had stolen it through poverty, but it was considered a crime if the ear had been taken from farther inside the field (because it spoiled the field). Theft on the highway was punishable by death (since it threatened trade) and also in the market, but if the theft had taken place inside a house the punishment was only slavery (only in Texcoco was it punishable by death). For the Maya, the gravity of the crime of theft depended on the social status of the thief. If he was an important person, it was considered extremely serious. Bishop Diego de Landa wrote, "The

156

Maintaining social order depended on certain codes of behavior whose infringement was severely punished in the high cultures, where the privileged groups had most to lose. Only these groups resorted to third parties or to institutions in order to have the offender punished, for normally it was considered that whoever was affected by the crime committed should be the one to deal out the punishment. Third parties and institutions, also dealt with crimes against the state and its institutions, and punishment was extremely severe. In the other cultures, crimes were usually committed against other individuals and usually involved attacks on personal integrity, life, freedom and honor. In this scene from the Matritense Codex, *we see Aztec criminals being hanged and beaten with clubs.*

Cowardice in the face of the enemy was considered a capital offense in many Amerindian tribes. This print by Jacques le Moyne shows the execution of two deserters from a tribe of Indians of the Florida Peninsula.

people assembled and the prisoner's face was cut from chin to forehead along the sides, in punishment for great infamy." In Inca society, crimes concerning property were only punished when the property belonged to the community. Thus it was a crime to draw water from a communal well without permission, hunt on communal land, burn bridges, etc.

But not all sentences called for the life or property of the offender; jails also existed. Mendieta recorded that the Aztec "had their jails in a dark building and these they made their cage or cages, and the door of the house was small like the door of a pigeon house, closed from the outside with boards and with large stones placed against it." Some Spanish chroniclers wrote that the Inca had cells full of wild animals in which they placed suspects. If the suspect was still alive after two days, he was considered innocent. Huaman Poma described one of these underground prisons, in which a common criminal was surrounded by wild animals in one cell, in contrast to a noble sitting patiently in another, awaiting torture or death, a depiction of justice that was not equal for all.

Punishment of crimes that we would nowadays call common offenses fell into a rigid penal system in which the accused was submitted to various degrees of torture dictated by custom and usage. Among the Aztec, the degree of punishment dealt out to the culprit was extremely severe, as we may see in the picture at the top of this page from the Tudela Codex, *which shows how thieves were bound and then stoned to death. In the picture above, from the Men-doza Codex, we see that the punishment for adultery was to have stakes driven into the skin.*

157

The mysterious codices

There is an air of mystery surrounding the pre-Columbian scribes. They were so secretive about their profession that we still know little about their work. We do not know if there were official scribes or if the authors of the works also wrote them down. Those who illustrated the Aztec codices, called *tlacauilo* or painters, were venerated as the men who used red and black ink,

as if it were something almost magical. We do not know whether they were priests or laymen, whether they did their work in the temples or in their homes or even how they learned their profession, but only that their work was so respected that those who painted were always great Aztec lords. The writers worked wonders with words. Less mysterious were the codices' readers. Read-

ing was the province of the priesthood, who were always consulted to fathom the destinies of men in the great books of wisdom. No one knew who had written them.

The Amerindian codices are the best source of information on the inhabitants of pre-Columbian America. Unfortunately, there are only a few in existence, first because only a certain number

Pre-Columbian libraries

The Aztec kept their books, or codices, in liraries called *amoxcalli*, built close to the temple schools. The librarians were called *amoxauque* or "keepers of the books" and were often sages or *tlamatinime*. The largest library in the Aztec world was in Texcoco, destroyed during the Spanish conquest. There were many *tonalamatl* (from *tonlli*, day, and *amatl*, paper) or "books of destinies" in the temples, used to read the future. (The name comes There were, five books, as Motolinia tells us: "The first tells of the years and the times. The second of the days and holy days that they had during the year. The third of the dreams, delusions, vanities and auguries in which they believed. The fourth of baptism and the names they gave to their children. The fifth of the rites and ceremonies and auguries that they had for weddings." The few codices that have survived are both pre- and post-Hispanic, of a historical and religious nature. There are three Maya codices, thirteen Mixtec, nine Aztec and a few others of miscellaneous origin. The Maya codices, all pre-Columbian, are: the *Dresden Codex* (the oldest, from the beginning of the 13th century), a treatise on divination and astronomy; the *Trocortesian Codex* in Madrid (the most modern), containing horoscopes and almanacs; and the *Peresian Codex* in Paris, on ritual, and prophecy as well as the 52-year cycles. In 1971, a fourth codex, made of balsa wood and dating from 1230, was exhibited in New York, but many doubts exist as to its authenticity. The only pre-Columbian Aztec codex is the *Bourbon Codex* (now in the Bourbon Palace in Paris) dealing with ritual and chronology. Worthy of note also are the *Tira de la Peregrinación* in the Museo de Antropología in Mexico, on history, the *Tlaxcala-Puebla-Mixtec* and *Borgia Codices* in the Vatican library, the *Fejérváry-Mayer Codex* in the University of Liverpool and the *Laud* at Oxford University. The best codices on the Mexican culture of the southeast are the *Becker* and the *Vindobonensis*, both now in Vienna.

158

The Aztec invented a writing system in which pictography was combined with ideograms and phonetic constructions. Thus, for example, the night was represented by a black sky and a closed eye, while defeat was represented by a temple in flames. Chronological signs, however, were ideograms. The phonetic constructions were numerous: a (atl, water), coyo (coyoctic, a circular hole), icpa (icpatl, a ball of thread), mi (mitl, an arrow), tlan (tlantil,

teeth), etc. Ideograms were often combined with phonemes. Thus, the name of the city of Otlatitlan was written with the ideogram for cane, which was otwatl *and a phoneme,* tlan, *which was represented by teeth. Some parts of the codices—above we see a page from the Maya Trocortesian Codex—could not be exactly transcribed, and these were repeated and explained in the schools.*

The Aztec codices were made by the tlacauilo, *who used red and black inks. It is not known whether or not they were priests, but their craft appeared to have magical properties. Neither is it known where they were taught, but in any case they were held in such high esteem that some great lords took pleasure in writing codices. The book was made by sticking leaves together to make a type of screen. On the facing page is a page from the* Trocortesian Codex.

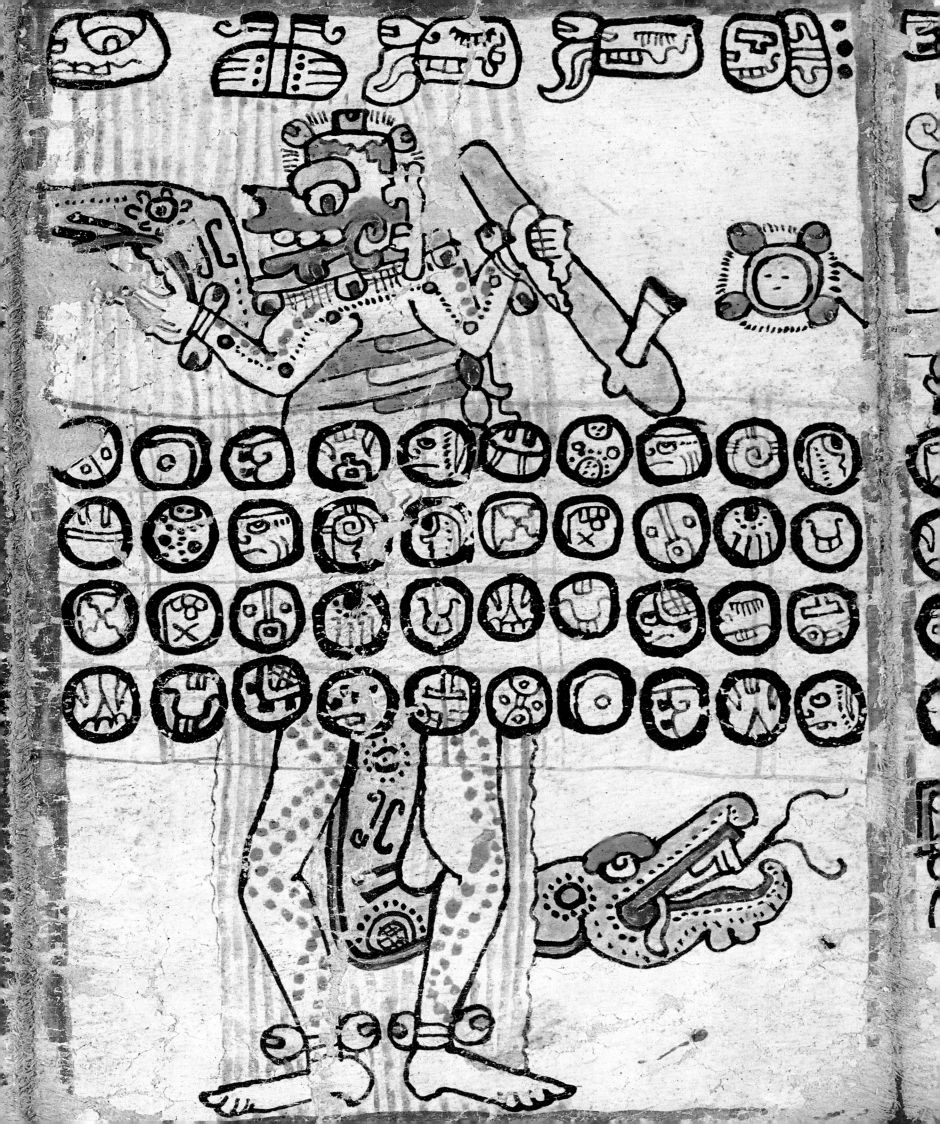

of the cultures had a writing system, and second because many codices were destroyed, either by the Indians themselves or by the *conquistadores* (when Tenochtitlan and Texcoco were taken, for instance, the main libraries were destroyed), or by the Spanish priests, who considered them to be works of the devil. Curiously, the most zealous codex destroyers such as Friar Juán de Zumárraga and Bishop Landa later became champions of the Indian cultures. Zumárraga, the archbishop of Mexico, destroyed many Aztec codices and yet introduced the printing press into Mexico and was one of those to promote the University of Mexico. Landa, meanwhile, carried out an *auto-da-fé* in Mani (south of Mérida) in 1562 on the Maya codices, and then wrote his *Report on the Things of Yucátan*, which is the best and most accurate account of the Maya culture. He left us two great contributions in particular: his description of the Maya system of measuring time and the Mayan alphabet.

All of the known codices are from Mesoamerica (those written by the Nicarao on animal skins are lost). The peoples from southeast North America (Muskogee and Iroquois) created pictographs; the only remaining examples are painted on bison skin capes or on the tents of the Dakota, Mandan and Hidatsa Indians and tell of warfare or tribal events. Attempts to decipher the language of the Inca based on the reading of marks on kidney beans have unfortunately been fruitless, and the *quipus*, which Sarmiento de Gamboa claimed to be a register of historical facts and traditions, are no more than mnemonic systems, as we shall see later.

Maya writing is the most complex of all the systems and most of it is still undeciphered. Landa recorded that the Maya alphabet consisted of 27 symbols, but understanding the language is not so simple. The Maya used pictography, ideograms, logograms, syllables and signs representing forms, the system varying, moreover, from one region to another. The most common symbols would seem to be glyphs but used with affixes, prefixes and suffixes, sometimes in chains. Some 80 glyphs are known but, in spite of the aid of computers, all attempts to discover the mechanics of the system to date have failed. It must be taken into consideration that one sym-

160

The only codices to have come down to us belonged to the peoples who lived in Mexico. Unfortunately, those made by the Nicarao on animal skins have been lost. The peoples of southeast North America (the Muskogee and the Iroquois, for example) used pictographs, but all that remain of these are to be found on bison-skin cloaks and on Dakota, Mandan and Hidatsa tent coverings. These tell of wars and events of importance to the tribe. Above we see an

Apache skin cloak with certain attributes for carrying out magical cures. The illustration is from The 9th Annual Report of the Bureau of American Ethnology.

This Maya cup, from the late Classic period (600–800 A.D.) and now kept in the New Orleans Museum of Art, shows a figure of a monkey scribe. According to tradition, Hun Bat and Hun Chuen, whose names are sometimes transcribed as One Monkey and One Artisan, were changed into monkeys by the Twin Heroes, their stepbrothers. Maya scribes are no less famous than those of the Aztec.

bol frequently represents several ideas. Thus, *Po* is the name of the moon goddess, of the patroness of weavers, of one of the months and also means "frog."

Aztec writing is better understood, since fewer ideograms and more phonetic symbols were used: It is made up of pictures, symbols and hieroglyphs. Thus the spoken word is represented by means of a spiral coming out of the mouth and a path with footprints. (The word "star" is represented by the ideogram of an eye.) The development of the language, however, meant an increased use of phonetic writing, and it is probable that if the European invasion had not taken place, the Aztec would have developed a completely phonetic system of writing.

A wide range of materials was used for writing: stone was often employed, but soft materials such as leather and paper were more common. It is possible that the Maya used books made of deer skin and maguey fiber but their oldest codex is the *Dresden*, made of the bark of *Ficus cotinifolia*, which is very common in Yucatán. Of the 700 species of Ficus that exist in the world, 50 grow in Mexico. They also used a type of paper made with the bark of the fig tree called *huun*, which was also used for making tunics. The bark was first pounded, then covered with a coat of calcium carbonate and water, thus carefully sealing the pores. Finally a coat of paint was applied

A cylindrical Maya cup found at the Peten site in Piedras Negras (Guatemala), featuring a figure in a large feather crest and adorned with an enormous necklace who is sitting in such a position that he seems to be declaiming or orating. The use of ceramics as a form of graphic expression was common; the complicated Maya form of writing grew with the independent development of polychrome cylindrical cups.

to the sheet, which was now ready for writing on. The Aztec made paper from *amatl* (*Ficus petiolaris*) by polishing the bark with a stone, the *xicaltetl*, and then covering it with stucco. They held paper in very high esteem, and they used it to adorn their gods.

Books themselves were made by sticking leaves together in the shape of a screen. Landa wrote, "They [the Maya] wrote their books on a long folded leaf and all was closed within two boards which they made very well; and this paper they made from the roots of a tree and they gave it a white luster which was very good for writing on, and some of the important lords through curiosity had learned this science and for this

were held in high esteem, though they did not use it in public."

The Inca's infallible accountants

Many Amerindian peoples used elementary mathematics, but the Maya and the Aztec excelled in this field. The Maya created the accounting system that was used all over Mesoamerica for centuries. The Aztec developed the most advanced accounting system known in any society without a writing system.

The Maya mathematicians invented an arithmetical system based on 20 with a conventional notation for the smallest units. The unit was written as a dot, every five units as a line. A dot over a line was six and two dots over three lines would be 17. The base unit or score was four lines. They also discovered the zero, represented by an inverted shell. To represent higher units they moved vertically. Each higher level was derived from the previous one, multiplied by 20. Thus, the units were placed in the first position, in the second the 20s, in the third the multiples of 400, and in the fourth the multiples of 8,000. The Maya's enormous preoccupation with chronology and historical dates obliged them, however, to modify the third level, which they brought down to multiples of 360, from which point they continued with multiplication by 20. The fourth level was thus changed to multiples of 7,200 (369x20), etc. The Maya applied mathematics greatly to daily life.

The Inca used the decimal system, which was much simpler, enabling them to collect and distribute goods with great precision. It has been said that the Inca knew perfectly how many llamas and how many men he had at his disposal at any given moment. This, of course, is an exaggeration, but it gives a rough idea of the usefulness of the accounting system used by the Inca. It has always been thought that the system went back to the times of Pachacutec. The Spanish chroniclers were amazed when they saw that Inca society was divided into groups of 10, 50, 100, 500, 1,000 and 10,000 units, but in practice the system could not have been so simple, since births and deaths must have affected the production and distribution units each month, with the bureaucratic machine being unable to keep completely up to date. Wedin believes that the decimal system was used for military purposes and that its use in relation to the civilian population came later if at all.

The great problem for Inca accounting came at the moment of recording the information, since there was no written system. This was solved by using the very simple *quipu*, the knotted strings employed by the extraordinary men called

To keep an account of the numbers of men, cattle and goods, the Inca employed quipucamayoc, *experts who used a decimal system to collect data of interest to the state. The* Poma de Ayala (top) *illustrates such a civil servant. Each expert passed on his information to his superior, who in turn did the same, until finally all the information came together in Cuzco. Above, in this lithograph by Balbuena from the Museo Postal in Madrid, we see an ideal-ized interpretation of a* quipucamayoc *in a canoe, in which he is transporting tribute.*

quipucamayoc or accountants. The *quipucamayoc*, who had a keen memory, registered with knots the loads of corn or wool coming into the royal storehouses, and even the number of births in a certain area. There were *quipus* to record production, distribution, and population. Color and order was essential. Thus, yellow meant gold on the *quipus* recording wealth, and corn on those recording production. On the demographic *quipus*, statistics on men were recorded first, then women and finally children. Cieza de León distinguished two types of *quipu*, those used for accounting and those to represent words.

The *quipucamayoc* recorded and reproduced data swiftly. They never made mistakes, since a mistake could cost them their lives. Certainly the technique was difficult, though each one was a specialist in his own field (military, economic, or demographic). He passed his records on to his superiors, who in turn sent them on to Cuzco, where all the accounts of the empire were kept. It has been said that a *quipu* could be read only by the person who had made it, but the *quipucamayoc* taught his system to one of his sons, who could take over when necessary. In this way, the continued operation of the accounting system was assured.

The Inca also established a system of weights and measures, including the fathom, half-fathom, the cubit (from the elbow to the fingertips), the span (8 in.; 20.3 cm.) and the *jeme* or *yuku*, which represented the space from the index finger to the thumb in an outstretched hand. For volume, they used the *pokcha* (almost 28 liters; 29.7 qts.) and the *runcu* or basket, which was further divided into one-half, one-quarter and one-eighth. To measure surface areas, they used the *papacancha* or *quincha* for *papas* of approximately 20x20 *varas*, one vara equaling 2.8 ft. or 85 cm.

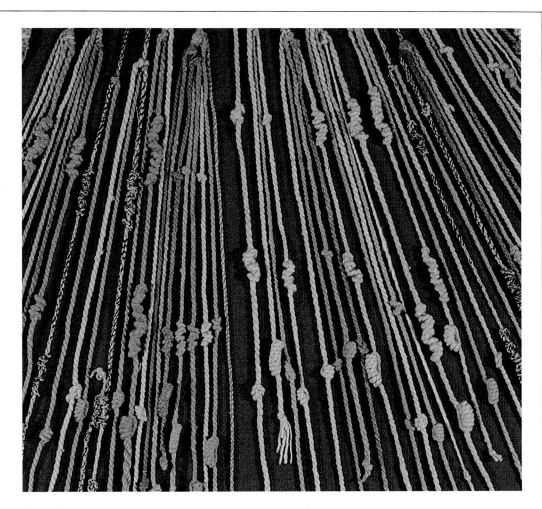

The quipu

The distributive fairness that existed in the Inca empire would not have been possible without the *quipu*, which facilitated the exact calculation of production and expenditure. The *quipu* was in fact a mnemotechnic system of accounting, whereby a horizontal cord with other braided cords of different lengths branching off from it was used. Knots were made in these braided cords at certain intervals and had some relation with other knots made in other cords when the *quipu* was spread out. The knots nearest to the main cord indicated 1,000s or 100s, depending on the type of accounting being done; those next along the cord were 100s or 10s, and those lower down were the 10s or units; finally, nearest to the ends were the units or nothing at all if no knot were made. Short sticks and a small amount of colored wool were tied to the main cord to indicate the type of item being computed on the *quipu*. It is believed that amounts registered never went above 1,000 and that zero did not exist. In spite of the system, it is likely that only the *quipucamayoc* could read his own *quipu*. According to tradition, it was thanks to the *quipu* that the Inca emperor could know at any time how many llamas he had and how many men he could send to war, and this was all due to the incredible skill of the accountants whose talents were passed down from father to son. Thus the knowledge for using these primitive but effective instruments of mathematical control, similar to those pictured here, lived on.

Calendars and
sun clocks

Two schools of thought, the civil and the religious, determined the two types of calendar that were used to register the passing of time, demonstrating the active participation of the religious sector within the field of science.

All the Amerindian peoples were aware of the passing of yearly cycles, though measuring this was somewhat difficult. The Haida, for example, measured by marking the position on the west wall of a building the first ray of sunlight coming through a hole made in the east wall. At solstice the beam of light fell in the same place for several consecutive days, indicating the beginning of a new cycle. All the marks on the wall made up the calendar, which they divided into 12 lunar months.

Through their sun cult, the Inca achieved accurate measurements and were able to calculate the summer solstice (June 21) and the winter solstice (December 21). The span of their territory across two hemispheres enabled their discovery of the equatorial zone and the equinox, where the midday sun did not cast the shadow of columns or pillars on certain days. This discovery was made in Quito, which they thought was much

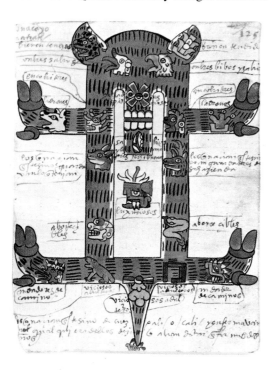

nearer the sun than anywhere else, possibly influencing Huayna Capac in his decision to transfer his court to Tomebamba (Cuenca, Ecuador).

The Inca astronomers established a calendar of 365 days, each of which had a *huaca* or sacred place dedicated to it. Every 10 of these *huacas* represented a week, and three of these weeks made up the month or *quilla*, 12 of which constituted a year. This calendar dictated farming schedules and holy days, and is confirmed by Huaman Poma. Some scientists believe that the system of measuring the solstices using stone columns was taken from the equatorial Cara Indians, a people known to be great astronomers.

The greatest astronomers, however, were the Maya, who established a solar year of 365 days and another religious year of 260 days. The latter was based on a combination of two factors, a series from 1 to 13 and another from 1 to 20, and

had a name for each unit: *Imix, Ik, Akbal, Kan, Chicchan, Cimi, Manik, Lamat, Muluc, Oc, Chuen, Eb, Ben, Ix, Men, Cib, Caban, Etz'nab, Cauac* and *Ahau.* The combinations were made like the following: 1 *Imix,* 2 *Ik,* etc. up to 13 *Ben,* the first series starting once more in combination with the remaining parts of the second, i.e., 1 *Ix,* 2 *Men* up to 7 *Ahau,* when the first series continued and the second started, i.e. 8 *Imix* at the end of 260 days, thus making the yearly religious or *tzolkin* cycle. The combinations lent themselves to divination and prophecies, as can be observed in the *Chilam Balam.* The combination of these two civil and religious calendars would be the result of multiplying the 365 days of the first by the 260 of the second, giving 18,980 days or their equivalent, 73 *tzolkin* or 52 *haab.* This kind of cycle of 52 solar years was commonly found among the Classic and Post-Classic cultures.

Aztec calendar of the deer in a drawing from the Tudela Codex. *The symbols drawn in this picture are associated with the auspices reserved for the newborn under the various signs of the calendar. To be born under signs considered favorable was fundamental for the fortune one could expect in life.*

The famous Intihuatana stone or sun clock in Machu Picchu is capable of calculating the summer solstice (June 21) for the grand celebration of the sun god. The best solar observations were carried out by the Inca in Quito, on the northern frontier of the empire, where it was discovered that on certain days of the year the midday sun did not cast a shadow, leading the astronomers to believe that that part of the empire was nearer than any other to the sun king. Thus

they had a pragmatic idea of the equator and of the days of the equinox. However, this took on scientific, rather than religious, significance.

The snail, pictured here, was built in Chichén Itzá and is without doubt the most representative aspect of Maya astronomy. It was the Maya who achieved the highest precision in the measuring of time, determining that the solar year was made up of 365.2420 days, which was extremely near to the real number of 365.2422 days as used in the Western World. They also discovered that the lunar month lasted 29.53059 days. In order to make up for certain inconsistencies they made corrections, as in 687 A.D. when all the Maya cities agreed to count the next new moon as the starting point of lunar cycles. Another correction was made in 756 A.D. to accommodate the leap year.

The Aztec used similar calendars. The solar, or *xiuhmolpilli*, cycle was made by combining a series from 1 to 20 with the name of the month. These took on the meanings of "growth," "the waters cease," "flaying of men," "little vigil," "great vigil," and "drought," among others. The sacred calendar was called the *tonalpohualli* (book of destinies), in the charge of the *tonalpouhqui*, and worked in the same way with the series of numbers from 1 to 13 and the names of the 20 days. The series of 20 was as follows: crocodile, wind, house, lizard, serpent, death, deer, rabbit, water, dog, monkey, grass, cane, jaguar, eagle, turkey buzzard, movement, knife, rain and flower. When the 52-year solar cycle came to an end it was feared that the sun would not come out again, and the last five days were considered to be ill-fated. On the last day of the last year of the cycle all hearth fires were extinguished and the people kept vigil all through the night, while the astronomers and priests examined the sky in search of favorable or unfavorable signs. When the *mamahuaztli*, or mizzenmast, constellation appeared, close to the Pleiades, it was considered a sign that the world would go on. At dawn a fire was lit on the chest of a human sacrifice on the Estrella hilltop and sent out to all the hearths, where heat and light were reborn.

It seems that the Aztec had a leap year every four years and were aware of the synodic cycles of Mars and Venus and the comets, which they believed brought bad luck. Shortly before the arrival of the Spaniards, a priest of the god Huitzilopochtli warned Moctezuma that a comet had appeared in the east.

A major factor in the integration of the pre-Columbian peoples was engineering, which they applied in the construction of bridges and roads in some of the most inaccessible parts of the world. Less than a century ago, in 1911, a completely unknown city was discovered in the Andes at 88,590 ft. (2,700 m.) above sea level—the now world-famous Machu Picchu—and in 1975 the "Lost City" of the Tairona was discovered in the north Andean region of Santa Marta (Colombia), circled by several truly monumental roads. The commercial development of the Maya and Aztec would be incomprehensible without the existence of a system of roads.

The best pre-Columbian engineers were undoubtedly the Inca, who created the mightiest road system on the continent. It was called the *Inkario* and connected southern Colombia with Chile. As in many other aspects of their society, the Inca gained from previous cultures, in this case from the Huari, who had already begun work along the southern fringe of Peru.

The *Inkario* was an immense road network extending over a known distance of at least 14,490 miles (23,319 km.) and possibly as much as 24,855 miles (40,000 km.). It was an essential lifeline for Cuzco, since it was by this route that news was received from the distant provinces, production surpluses were redistributed and the army marched on its way to win conquests and suppress rebellion. It stretched from Quito, extending northward as far as Quillacinga de Pasto in Colombia to the Maule River in Chile. In Peru there were two main highways, one from the coast and one from the mountains, connected at various points by branch roads. As they did not support heavy traffic, the foundation work was rudimentary and the *Inkario* was actually a surface road that followed the terrain. In the steepest sections it took the shape of a stairway cut out of the rock and in the flat areas it became a wide avenue of up to 23 ft. (7 m.) in width. Where it crossed the Atacama desert there were just a few markers called *moles*.

165

America still retains secrets of its urban past. In 1911, the archaeologist Hiram Bingham found a complete undiscovered city situated 8,856 ft. (2,700 m.) above sea level on a steep hillside in the Andes. This now world-famous city was Machu Picchu—the last refuge of the Inca. Not long ago, in 1970, Colombian archaeologists found the remains of another city built in the Santa María territory of the Chibcha-speaking Tairona Indians. It has been re-

The *Inkario* had to span great ranges of elevation in the Andes caused by rivers and torrents, which in turn led to the development of advanced techniques in bridge-building. There were various types of bridge, such as the rope bridge, the hanging wood, the hanging basket, the hanging bridge and the floating bridge. The first was no more than a rope made of hemp cord stretching from one side to the other, tied at each end to trees or rocks. To cross this bridge, a person had to pull himself along the rope using his hands and feet, while hanging on for dear life. The second type had a piece of *curca* wood, which slid along the rope; a person tied himself to the piece of wood and was pulled across like a sack of potatoes. The third type had a fiber basket in which the person crouched and was pulled across from the other side (sometimes the person himself could pull the basket along, using his hands). The hanging bridge was made of three or four fiber ropes held on both sides by pillars or stones. One rope was used for sliding the feet along on, the other two acting as handrails. The four-rope bridge had a reed floor between two of the ropes, and two other ropes served as handrails. The floating bridge was made of mats placed on reed rafts like

those used at the mouth of the Desaguadero River.

Tambos or warehouses containing arms, food and clothing were built all along the Inkario, making it possible for the army to advance swiftly, with no need to waste time collecting provisions. They were also a means of ensuring that news traveled quickly in the Inca empire.

166

Sorcerers and surgeons

It was believed that illness was the result of sinfulness, of spells, of evil spirits entering the body and also of the breaking of taboos. The curing of illness was therefore the job of those with special powers in this area, such as priests, shamans and sorcerers. We shall discuss priests at length in the next chapter. Their therapy consisted of prayer, fasting and mortification—none of which were very effective. The shamans and the sorcerers were more successful.

The shamans or medicine men (and women) were found all over the continent. They were individuals whose mien clearly indicated they had been specially chosen; they might be extremely hot-tempered, epileptic or crippled. The Shoshoni or Yuma acquired their magic powers during dreams in which the supreme being or another god appeared to them. The power of the Yurok and Hupa medicine men came from certain substances left by spirits in their bodies. They learned their profession from a master over many years and very often with the help of narcotics, hallucinatory drugs and long periods of fasting. They were taught how to diagnose an illness, the use of sacred objects for seizing and expelling evil spirits, prayers and incantations, and the use of natural medicines. Many of them were talented conjurers (in order to be able to show the illness to the patient) and others, like the *machi* or Araucanian shamans, were good ventriloquists. Although they apparently lived like the common folk, their behavior always differentiated them from the rest of the community. The Haida shamans of North America, for example, did not eat

seaweed or whale blubber, bathe, or cut or comb their hair, though they adorned themselves with curved bones pushed through the nose and wore bone necklaces carved with animal figures. Many wore women's clothing.

In many areas the sorcerer also functioned as shaman, and in others he was a failed shaman who had not completed his apprenticeship. The healer was also a sorcerer. It often happened that each family had its own "family sorcerer" who cured common complaints or expelled "household" evil spirits when a member of the family reached one of the important moments in his life. Among the Alacaluf Indians, for example, all old men of standing in the community became sorcerers. The sorcerer did not make a living from his profession, as did the shaman, though he was

paid for certain services. Women also followed this profession, as was common among the Aztec.

There were also sorcerers or shamans who worked evil spells. The Shoshoni called the sorcerer *pohagant*, which means "he who has power," and his evil counterpart *tidjipohagant*, meaning "he who uses the power maliciously." The *tidjipohagant*'s services were very expensive, due to the danger involved in unleashing evil.

The greatest healers were the shamans, followed by the sorcerers who practiced medicine on a smaller scale. The family sorcerer was important since at times it was necessary to be repeatedly purified, as when one was in contact with a pubescent girl, with a new-born baby or

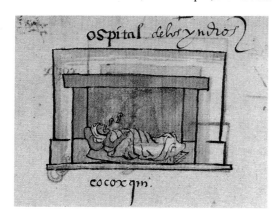

It was not easy to know whether illness was the result of some evil spell or of sins committed. In order to discover the cause, the Aztec patient went to his doctor, whose first task was to diagnose which of the two was the reason for the illness. In this picture from the Magliabecchi Codex *(top) two patients explain their troubles to a doctor. After speaking to the patient, the Aztec doctor discovered the cause of the illness by throwing grains of corn onto a piece of*

cloth or into a vessel containing water. According to how the grains scattered or floated on the water, the doctor was able to discern the cause of the illness. Above right, a scene from the Magliabecchi Codex, *in which a healer is using this process to discover the cause of the patient's ailment. On the left, from the* Osuna Codex, *the "Indian Hospital," with one of the patients.*

This extraordinary Mochica vessel depicts in detail the everyday work of a doctor examining a patient, who is possibly pregnant. His headdress bears the figure of the animal from which he draws his supernatural powers, and he is also wearing earrings and a necklace. The Inca received many of their curing traditions from the coastal cultures. This piece is in the Museo Nacional de Arqueología y Antropología in Lima.

This scene, taken from The History of the Orinoco, quite faithfully reproduces a cure performed by a shaman or sorcerer from either the Amazon or Orinoco region. Below, left, he inhales a hallucinatory drug (yopo or caapi) through the nose using an instrument made from long bird bones. Thanks to the drug, he sees the cause of the illness in the second stage of the process (top left), and then goes on to cure the patient by blowing tobacco smoke over him (center). This drives the evil spirit away. Finally, the doctor performs a song and dance to the accompaniment of a rattle or maraca (right) and orders the evil spirit to leave the patient's body and never to return.

the cooking utensils of a deceased member of the family, and it was not practical to be continually calling in the shaman for such matters. To do their job the sorcerers had to use very complicated procedures, usually linked with sympathetic magic or homeopathy.

The rituals for healing, purification, and expelling evil spirits were mixed with such useful remedies as purging, bleeding, piercing of the flesh, poultices, massage, medicinal tea, steam baths and cold water baths—all with surprising results. The Haida shamans applied heat to inflamed areas or cut them open and dressed them with soft plant material and silver tree pitch.

The Aztec had extensive knowledge of the human anatomy, as a result of their human sacrifices. Their continuous wars enabled them to make advances in trauma treatment (they used splints on broken bones, for instance). They applied coagulants and cicatrizants to wounds and bled patients with obsidian knives. They also knew how best to treat snake bites, as Sahagún recorded: "Medicine against snake bites is then

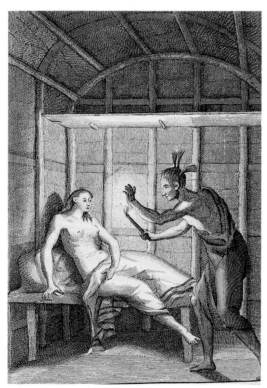

The ways in which the Huron shamans cured their patients were similar, as may be seen in this photograph from the work Manners and Customs of the Peoples, published in Paris in 1814. The only difference is that instead of expelling the evil spirit with tobacco smoke, a firebrand was used.

170

[immediately] to suck the area where the snake has bitten and dry it and put around it a very thin and transparent poultice of maguey leaves, and when the bite is heated by sitting near the fire, it is rubbed with ground picietl [tobacco]."

The use of medicinal herbs and plants was of great importance, and many of the treatments are now used the world over. The Inca used coca against vomiting, hemorrhaging and diarrhea. Balsam of Peru and at times sarsaparilla were used to cure ulcers. For purging they took the root of the huachanca plant, brews made from molle (a pink fruit from the false pepper) or green corn husk dissolved in an alcoholic drink. The sap of the molle was also a good cicatrizant for wounds. Quinine bark (chinchona) reduced fever, as did the sap of some types of cactus and certain types of yellow flower boiled in water. They also used the leaves of some edible plants. Quinoa leaves were used for sore throats, yucca leaves for rheumatism, and apichu leaves (mixed with grease) were used against ticks. Oca juice was used for inflammation of the kidneys, smoke from the

quinaquina cured migraine, chilca grass was used for pains in the joints, and matecclu grass for eye problems. A small amount of tobacco dissolved in water and drunk on an empty stomach was an effective diuretic, and the water obtained by boiling datura was taken to induce sleep.

Even more surprising than the number of remedies used by the Inca was their knowledge of surgery. Inca doctors practiced advanced trauma treatment for broken bones and even surgery for amputation, but undoubtedly the most amazing practice was that of cranial trepanation, which called for great skill. The patient was put to sleep with cocaine, which was made by mixing coca with llipta, a powerful alkali of quinoa ash and lime. The cranial walls were then perforated with a T-shaped metal knife of gold or copper called a tumis, whose upper part was sharp and curved. Then a rectangular hole was made in the cranium and the affected area cut out. The bone growth of the cranial walls seen through X rays shows that patients who underwent this operation could live for several years. Some crania have been found showing that trepanation was carried out several times (as many as five times on one example) on the same patient.

The Aztec also used a great number of natural remedies for purging and as emetics, diuretics, sedatives and narcotics. Tobacco was used to relieve headache and *quanenepilli* (passiflora) bark for pains in the chest. Sahagún devoted most of one volume to the medicinal herbs and plants used by the Aztec; through him we know that balsam of Peru, root of Jalapa, sarsaparilla and *iztacpatli* were used to fight fever, *chichiquahuitl (Garrya laurifolia Hart)* to fight dysentery, *iztacoannapilli* as a diuretic, *nixtamalxochitl*

The snake dance of the Hopi Indians

Used to bring on the rains, the snake dance is probably the most famous of the North American Indian dances and was still performed until just under a century ago. As a preliminary to the dance, the priests of the clan collected all the snakes they could find in the area. Without taking any precautions, they would put their hands into the nests of the snakes and, when they found one, sprinkle it with holy flour, strike it lightly with a whip made of feathers, seize it by the neck and put it into a bag. All the snakes caught in this way were taken to a *kiva* (house) while different preparatory rites were carried out (songs, prayer and ceremonial dances).

On the morning of the ninth day, two snake priests went all over the village with bison horns and the snake brotherhood then held a race. After the priests had purified the snakes by washing them, a man dressed as a warrior put his hand in the bag, took out a handful of snakes, placed them in a bowl of medicinal water and let them fall onto the sand to dry. The Hopi boys then played with the snakes as if they were

harmless, though there would be many rattlesnakes among them.

Finally came the great ceremonial dance in which the priests, sounding their rattles, their bodies painted black, white and brown, danced around the square and made their way in threes to a grove where each was given a snake. He held the snake in his mouth or rolled around his neck while he danced. One of his colleagues struck the snake with a whip made of feathers. After dancing around the square three or four times, the first dancer gave the snake to the third of the group, who danced with

it. The snakes were then placed within a magic circle, where the women sprinkled them with flour. At a prearranged signal everyone sprang into the circle, picked up handfuls of snakes and ran with the snakes to the plain, where they placed them on sacred altars made for the purpose.

No one knows why, but it usually rained a short time after the dance. Neither is it known why the snakes did not bite the children, the women or the dancers, though the Indians explained this away easily by saying that the snakes were their relatives, their totem.

as a revulsive, valerian against spasms, and *matlalitztic (Crommelina pallida)* against hemorrhaging. Francisco Hernández, a Spanish doctor sent by the king of Spain to Mexico in the 16th century, recorded the use of more than 1,200 plants in Aztec medicine. Unfortunately most of his work was lost in the fire in the Escorial in 1671.

As important as the cure were antisinning purifications, pilgrimages to holy places, rituals for the expulsion of evil spirits and things as useful as purges, bleeding, puncturing of the skin, poultices, massage, medicinal tea, cold baths, steam baths, unguents and medicinal herbs—with which quite astonishing results were often obtained. To inflammations the Haida shamans applied heat or else cut them open and treated them with soft vegetable matter or fir

pitch. In this 1839 English lithographic print, a Mandan native begs for the protection of certain idols.

Music and culture

Tambor de guerra de dos varas y media de largo.

The shell horn, the drum, the whistle, the ocarina, the flute, the rattle, the cascabel and the trumpet were only some of the instruments played by Amerindian peoples in pre-Columbian times. On the facing page we see a Maya shell horn from the beginning of the Classic period (250–400 A.D.), now on display in the Kimbell Art Museum in Fort Worth. Above is a war drum from the Natural History of the Orinoco.

Musicians, singers and dancers

For the Amerindians, music was an integral part of life, and one only has to see the musicians in the Bonampak fresco (*below*) to understand the degree of professionalism that was reached in music. In the *Becker Codex* we may also see Mixtec musicians, whose names are Five Movement, Eight Deer, Nine Flower and Twelve Movement, performing a dance in commemoration of a great battle won in 1048 A.D. Music was so important that it was studied by many of the Mesoamerican lords. One famous musician was Tlacahuepan, the brother of Moctezuma. Moreover, the *huey tlatoani* liked to dine with musical entertainment. The dance of the Tezcatlipoca flautist shows that music was accompanied by dance, though not by song, but this was unusual

since the Aztec considered that music, dance, song and poetry were essential and inseparable in true poetic expression. The word for poetry was *cuicatl*, which also means song and music. The poet and singer was the *cuicani*.

Pre-Columbian music was of a religious rather than an aesthetic nature. It formed part of ritual and prayer. In fact it was considered to be of divine origin, as can be seen in the *Popol Vuh*. Secular music did exist, however, at least in Aztec society. Castellanos claims that popular and religious music have coexisted, the latter being played on wind instruments by very select groups of musicians.

There were many kinds of instruments: snail shells (the Aztec used a bone or clay mouth-

piece), both single and double drums, whistles, ocarinas, Pan pipes, single, double, triple and quadruple flutes as well as those made with animal shells (the Maya used turtle and the Guarani, armadillo). Metal instruments were also common in South America, reaching Mesoamerica in the Post-Classic period. Among these were timbrels, bells and trumpets. Of special interest among the metal instruments was that used in the temple of Netzahualcoyotl in Texcoco, which Ixtlilochitl described as "a metal instrument that they called *tetzilacatl* and served as a bell and had almost the same sound." Some instruments had onomatopoeic names such as the *chilchil*, a copper disk beaten with two sticks and used in Peru, Nicaragua and Mexico. The *teponaztli* or sacred Aztec

This parade of the musicians in the Bonampak frescoes is one of the most famous scenes in pre-Columbian art. It shows a grand celebration from around 800 A.D. in the Maya city, in which musicians march past playing enormous trumpets, maracas and other instruments. The frescoes were discovered in 1946 and display all the splendor of court life, in which music naturally had a prominent place. Secular music, apart from the great religious music that the Maya undoubtedly had, was a gift from the gods, as is stated in the Popol Vuh.

drum also seems to have come from South America. In Ecuador it was called *tunkuli*, in El Salvador and in Guatemala *tun*, and in Yucatán *tunkul*. It was possibly the Toltec who spread its use throughout Mesoamerica.

All over America there were whistles as well as whistling vessels, which made a hissing sound when the liquid they contained was moved. Mesoamerican whistles were double, triple and quadruple barreled, made of pottery and usually decorated with pictures of animals, though some depicting human figures have been found. Bird-shaped ocarinas, sometimes bitonal, were common in Ecuador and Colombia. Flutes, some with a double diaphragm, were of various shapes. The Hopewell culture and others from the Mississippi basin used human bones. The Guarani played reed-grass flutes as well as other larger flutes made of bone. Especially well known are the high-pitched ones played by the Aztec in their Tezcatlipoca festivities, made of very thin clay and able to produce five different tones. These had a mouthpiece and a flower-shaped end.

Mesoamerican drums greatly impressed the Spaniards. Father Landa said that the Maya had "small kettledrums that they beat with their hands (*huehuetl*) and another drum of hollow wood, of a heavy and sad sound, that they beat with a longish stick with the milk of a tree at the end (*teponaztli*)." The Aztec had the *huehuetl* or single-skin drum, which they beat with their fingers. One of these, made of wood and deerskin, was kept in the great temple of Tenochtitlan, and, according to the *conquistadores*, the sound was "lugubrious." They also had *teponaztli*, which were grooved, sometimes H-shaped wooden drums, played with the hands or with sticks whose ends were covered with India rubber. When Tenochtitlan fell, one of the most significant signs was the silence; the drums and shell horns were still.

Inca music was characterized by the use of flutes or *quenas*. These were sometimes vertical, made of cane or bone, with holes that produced between two and five notes, or were similar to Pan pipes, made of several cane, wood or clay tubes of different lengths. The multiple flute is always associated with Lake Titicaca, its sound

evoking the sound of the wind in the Andean peaks, the solitude of the llama shepherd or the heat of the sun on the *altiplano*, but it was also found elsewhere in Mesoamerica. It was played, for example, by the Maya. Besides the famous *topoto* or shell horn, the Inca played llama-skin drums and timbrels, ocarinas, bells made of large broad beans or metal (which they placed around their ankles), and trumpets made of baked clay (like those of the Mochica), of wood, pumpkin, metal (copper and gold) and seashell. The Inca used the pentatonic scale.

Virtually all of the American people practiced some form of dance. This was usually combined with singing and was almost always related to magical or religious ceremonies. The Iroquois celebrated all their holy days, and particularly their new year festival, with dances, accompanied by music played on timbrels and drums. The Cueva Indians performed their famous sun dance when a person lost a close relative at the hands of an enemy tribe. After a series of very complex

rituals, the mourner began a frenetic dance, to the sound of a whistle and drum, until he fell exhausted to the ground. He was then led to his bed, where he remained until he had a vision of a defeated enemy—a sign to the warriors to seek revenge. But the most famous of the North American Indian dances was the snake dance of the Hopi Indians, which was performed to bring rain.

The Maya were masters of both song and dance, and their performances were regularly used for religious purposes. Besides giving praise to their god, the content was also moralistic, as may be seen with the "Singers of Dzibilchaltun." In 1942, a manuscript was discovered (possibly from the 18th century) titled *The book of the dances of the ancient men which it was the custom to perform here in Yucatán in the villages when the white men had not yet arrived.* It is a compilation of 15 songs, possibly written by Ah Ban, grandson of the great Ah Kulel, at the beginning of the Spanish conquest. Alfredo Barrera Vásquez comments, "Although we call all the texts in the Codex songs, some are more like narratives." But the Maya also had secular songs, as Sánchez de Aguilar stated: "They sing of fables and ancient customs." The chronicler was undoubtedly alluding to the existence of songs on imaginary themes and historical traditions.

True professionals were responsible for Maya dance, song and music. These professionals were called *hol pop* and it was their duty to teach the three arts. Aguilar says, "They had and have their principal singer who intones and teaches what is to be sung, and they venerate and revere him and call him *Holpoop*, and in his charge are the kettledrums and musical instruments." These masters were highly respected and given special places in the temple during the festivals.

Maya dance was performed individually and in groups, the dancers richly adorned, wearing masks and using a combination of simple and complicated dance steps. A surprising fact is that they actually danced on tiptoe; in the *Dictionary of Motul* it is stated, "*Ba del cuxtel*: walk (dance) on tiptoe, as in depictions of some Maya dancers." It is also curious that they used triple dance movement (the legs facing one direction, the body another and the head a third), a custom dating back to Pre-Classic times.

Dances were performed at religious ceremonies, family celebrations and public festivals. Among the first group was the dance performed on the day dedicated to the god Itzamna Kauil. According to Father Landa, "In this festival danced the old women of the village who had been chosen to do so, dressed in certain garments." Another dance was that performed in the ceremonies of the year Muluc, when the people went with their god, "accompanying him all with devotion and dancing war dances." Another dance was that performed at the Chacuuaya festival, when old women danced with dogs.

Among the popular dances were the cane dance or the *colomché*, the flag dance, and the fire dance. The cane dance was performed in a ring with the young performers painted in black and adorned with feathers and garlands of flowers. They danced to a poetic composition sung in chorus accompanied by high-pitched flutes. Two dancers came out of the ring to the center, where one threw sticks to the other. They then returned

176

The two ceramic sculptures seen here show the interest of the Andean noble classes in music, an interest that was shared in Mesoamerica. The pieces come, however, from two very different and distant places. The one on the left is from the Jama Coaque culture in Ecuador, on the edge of the Inca world, and depicts an orejón *dignitary, with beautiful earrings and intricate headdress, playing a* quena. *The piece may be seen in the Museo de Arte Precolombino in*

Santiago de Chile. The other piece is of a Mochica orejón, *wearing a headdress with disks, seated and playing a flute. It is in the Museo de Arqueología y Antropología in Lima.*

to the ring and another pair took the stage. The chroniclers report that the dance could last all day. In the flag dance, up to 800 men took part, waving flags and dancing to a war-dance rhythm. The fire dance took place over a day and a night, fires being lit when darkness fell. Other common dances were the battle dance, the dance of the fishermen, of the shooting of arrows, of the healers, of the fliers, of the hot ashes, and of the Flowers. In the *Popol Vuh* the dance-songs of the stilts, of the weasel, of the armadillo, of the centipede and of the owl, among others, are mentioned.

In the territory of the Aztec triple alliance, poetry, song and dance were arts taught in small conservatories called *cuicalli* or "houses of song." Children from the age of 12 onward were taught in the *cuicalli* by famous poets, musicians and dancers paid by the *tlatoani* himself. Besides the *cuicani*—a singer or poet—who wrote the works, the *cuicapicqui*, supplied the theme and the first version of the composition, and the *cuicaito* directed the whole performance, aided by the directors of the choir and choreography. Acording to the chroniclers, the compositions made use of sharp and grave tones, the *crescendo* and certain rhythmic combinations. Sahagún wrote down 150 or more of the rhythms that accompanied the songs. In Clavijero's opinion, most of the composers were religious men: "The composers were normally priests who taught the poems to the children, so that they would be able to sing them when they were older."

The Aztec had various types of dance, including the dance of embrace and possibly a precursor to the belly dance. Sahagún describes the dance of embrace: "Those who went at the front [dancing], being those most experienced in war, held the woman around the waist; the others, who were not experienced, had no license to do so." Dr. Francisco Hernández drew up a very complete list of Aztec dances and songs in the 16th century and published it in his *Antigüedades de Nueva España* (Antiquities of New Spain). The dancers often wore masks, a custom in Mesoamerica dating from the times of Teotihuacan.

The usual way of dancing was in a group, the dance depending on the number of people taking part. Sahagún relates: " The dancers held flowers

177

The origins of the Andean quena *are extremely ancient and difficult to place geographically. This figurine shows a flautist wearing a beautiful breastplate, with disk-shaped earrings and a large hat. It comes from the Chancay culture and is on display in the Museo de Arqueología y Antropología in Lima. The Chancay culture developed along the coasts of Peru, 30 miles (50 km.) north of the Valley of Rimac, a thousand years before the ceramics of the Mochica and Nazca cultures appeared. It was characterized by a proliferation of ceramics for funeral offerings. In some tombs as many as 50 ceramic objects have been found, the most typical among them being figurines with slanting eyes who are known popularly as* chinos *(Chinese).*

in their hands and were adorned with feathers. They all shook their bodies and hands and feet at the same time, an impressive sight and extremely ingenious. All movement was made to the sound of the drums and *teponaztli*. With all this, they all sang in great concert and with very sonorous voices the praises of that god they were feasting…as they use very diverse shakes in their dances and tones in their songs." Acosta speaks of another group dance: "In these dances they made two rings of people; in the middle, where were the instruments, went the elderly and lords and most solemn persons, and there, quietly they danced and sang. Around these, at a distance from the center, came out the rest, two by two, dancing more freely in a group and doing diverse movements and making certain stops and then came to make a large wide ring."

For the Aztec, the religious dancing and singing were also the most important. Their masters of song were priests called *tlapixcaltzin* who performed virtually the same duties as the *hol pop* of the Maya. This person was described by Sahagún "as a choirmaster who taught and directed the song to be sung in honor of the gods of all the festivals." He added that among all the

priests who served each of the gods there was always one called "the *ometochtzin* who was like a master of all the singers, who sang in the *cues*; it was he who made sure that all came to do their duties in the cues." Some of the religious dances had secular variations, like the dance of the roses, of which Durán wrote, "The dance that they most liked was that in which they danced with roses, with which they made crowns and bedecked themselves…and they made houses of roses, and made trees full of sweet-smelling flowers, where they sat their goddess Xochiquetzal."

There is no doubt, however, that the Aztec also had secular songs and dances. Durán reports: "There were differences in their songs and dances, for some songs were strong and solemn, sung with great moderation and tranquility by the lords on solemn occasions and on occasions of great authority. There were others of less gravity and more lively that were songs with dances of pleasure." Logically, the secular songs and dances were performed by laymen.

There were, moreover, different musical styles. On recounting a party given by the Tenochca in honor of the ambassadors of Cholula and Tlaxcala, Tezozomoc wrote, "They danced and

sang in four ways: first, the Malahuacuicatl, the true song; second, the song of Huexotzinco; third, the song of Chalco; and fourth, the song of Otomi." Evidently, the "true song" was the Mexican one.

As we have said, dances were performed by a great many other Mesoamerican peoples. As one example we may cite the Mixtec with their *volador*, gladiator and arrow-shooting dances. In South America, mainly in the Amazon region, virtually all of the peoples had their own dances. The great mastersingers of the Inca were the *amautas* and the *arawicuj*, who will be discussed later with poetry. In any case, it seems that song and dance together were not as common with the Inca as with the Aztec.

The Inca's greatest dance was the *way-yaya*. This was performed in the main *plaza* in Cuzco, presided over by the Inca emperor, his family and the mummies of previous emperors. Men and women made two lines, holding hands, the dancers advancing toward the emperor slowly and rhythmically to the sound of a drum, taking two steps forward and one back. One variation on this dance was the dance of the snake, in which the men stood on one side and the women on the

178

Inca culture is full of traditions. In South America each people had their own dance, especially in Amazonia, where the European illustrators often distorted the truth. In the lithograph, above, from the work The Indian Tribes of Guyana, *published in London in 1868, is a rendering of a Koria Arawak Indian dance that called for great skill and in which women offer a drink to those taking part. Top, a ritual Amazon Indian dance, according to the roman-*

tic view of Picturesque America, *a famous collection of prints from the last century contributed to by various authors who had traveled in South America. The dancers, dressed in loincloths and feather headdresses, play flutes and shake vegetable rattles tied to their calves.*

The print at bottom corresponds to the many images that form the graphic album entitled Galerie aguable du monde, *a fantastic choice of prints cataloged in the 17th century; one of these scarce examples is preserved in the Biblioteca Nacional de Madrid. This image responds to a Baroque idealization of the dance of the* zancos, *an exercise in equilibrium culminated in the presence of the Aztec emperor, who observed the evolution of the dancers, while the*

drummers increased the rhythm of the music, inciting many of the participants to collapse.

other, holding a long rope or cable whose end was shaped like the head of a snake.

There were also popular dances, such as the dance of the llama herders, performed around a number of the animals, for which the dancers were adorned with hoops covered with llama wool. In the *pulis-pulis*, performed to draw out the birds of that name, which the Indians hunted, those taking part bedecked themselves with feathers. Another dance was the dance of the *parianes* (a stork-like bird), performed when the leader of the *ayllu* took charge of irrigation channels. In the dance of the *chaco*, the hunting of wild animals was mimed, the men dancing with their slings in their hands, the women holding sticks. The most famous of the peasant dances was the *huaillia*, performed in pairs. The dancers traced small steps, which gradually became faster and faster. A completely secular Inca dance was that performed by the *orejones* in their palaces. The man danced with two women, whom he took by the hand and twirled around.

179

One of the aspects of Indian culture that most benefited from cultural exchange was music, as may be seen here in this simple print from The Natural History of the Orinoco *(1791, Museo Naval in Madrid), in which Mapue Indians dance to an indigenous wind instrument, accompanied by a flute and drums of the colonial period.*

Wind and percussion instruments were the most common in pre-Columbian America. Among the first were Maya trumpets and Andean flutes, culminating in the *quena* (1). There were also Pan pipes capable of producing extremely delicate notes, like the one pictured here (2), ending in a conch shape, as well as double, triple and even quadruple flutes, as in (3), and this extremely complex one (4) with four openings out of a circle. In their celebrations in honor of the god Tezcatlipoca, the Aztec used flutes ending in a flower shape (5) that were capable of producing exquisitely mournful tones, perhaps befitting the tragic fate awaiting the Indian cultures. The most widespread percussion instrument was the drum, found

3

4

6

1

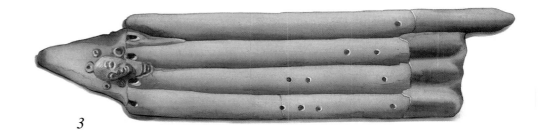
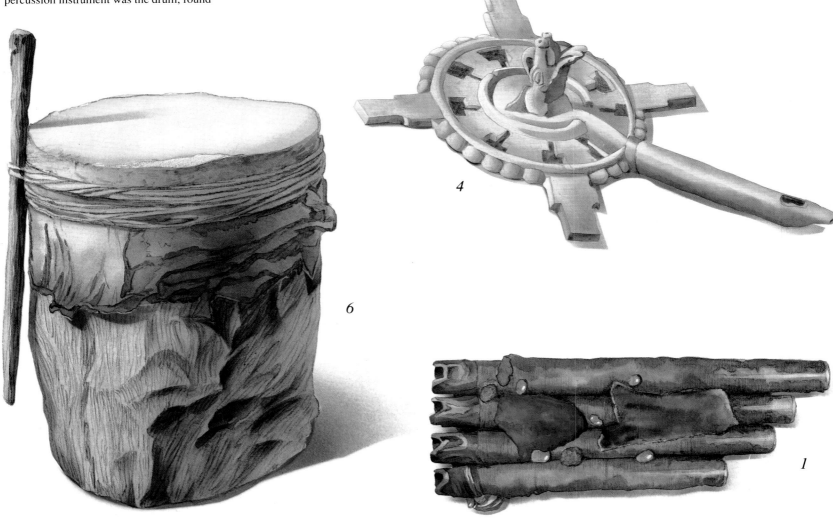

2

5

7

8

throughout America, with origins going to ancient times. The simplest were skin drums (usually deerskin), as shown in (6), which were played with the fingers. More complex were those with an H- or M-shaped slot, as shown in (7). These may have come from South America or the Amazon region but spread all over Mesoamerica and were also used by the Aztec. The most famous type of drum is the *teponaztli* or great Aztec kettledrum, which was played in the great *cu* in Tenochtitlan and may be seen in the Museo National de Antropología in Mexico. It is faithfully reproduced in (8). It is of stone and carved with attributes of Macuilxochitl, the god of dance. Its double skin produced a very special sound, forever ingrained in the memories of the *conquistadores*. Sahagún refers to it on several occasions. String instruments were less common, but those that existed were extremely ingenious, one example being the vibrating bow, with certain types played by using the mouth as a soundbox.

Playwrights and comedians

Although it may be said in general terms that theater did exist in many pre-Columbian cultures, it may only truly be classified as such in the case of the high cultures, where, apart from the religious ceremonies—themselves veritable shows—there existed popular theater.

The Maya had theater directors who worked in collaboration with the music and choreography directors, discussed earlier. According to the *Dictionary of Motul*, it was their task to "look after the dancers and players." In fact all the elements of theater were employed since, as Landa suggests, they performed to the sound of the *tunkules* or the kettledrums, of the flutes and turtle shells played with deer horns, and they sang allegorical, historical and mythological poems.

The Maya performed their plays and comedies in theaters, of which Landa wrote, "They had before the north stairway [of the castle], at some distance, two small theaters made of stone, at the top of four steps and tiled above, in which it is said that they perform their plays and farces for the amusement of the people." Its proximity to the temple may indicate some religious purpose, but in any case, there is no doubt as to the existence of nonreligious performances. Sánchez Aguilar wrote, "They had and do have plays that represent fables and ancient tales...I saw that there were songs and mimicking that they do of the singing and talking birds and most especially of one which sings a thousand songs." Landa says that they had "most gay entertainments, and principally players that perform with much comedy." These, then, were farces or imaginative plays situated within the context of the theater.

Some, however, were more of a historical nature, as was *Rabinal Achi*, which tells of the capture of an enemy warrior, the conversation between himself and his captors, and of his trial and subsequent sacrifice to the gods. The play

was transcribed in 1850 by Bartol Zis, after a Quiche tradition. Fortunately, the abbé Breasseur de Bourbourg, appointed parish priest of the village of San Pablo de Rabinal, Guatemala, allowed the play to be performed in 1856, later translating it into French and thus preventing its loss to posterity. Other plays were more like comedies, as Landa observed, and the *Dictionary of Motul* confirms nine titles in this genre: *The Small Seat in the Sky, The Turkey Vendor, The Pot Vendor, The Chili Pepper Vendor, He Who Sells Entanglements, He Who Governs the High Sierra, The White-mouthed Macaw, The White-headed Boy* and *The Cacao Grower*.

Another type of theater was mythological drama. The *Popol Vuh* alludes to the work *The War of the Gods and the Heroic Deeds of Hunahpu and Ixbalanque*, which recounts how two young brothers take revenge on their elder brothers for their humiliating treatment. Their suffering is reflected in this brief passage: " They were loved neither by the grandmother, nor by Hunbayt, nor by Hunchouen. They were given food to eat only when the meal was over and their brothers had eaten...But they were not vexed, nor did they become angry but suffered in silence for they knew their station and took account clearly

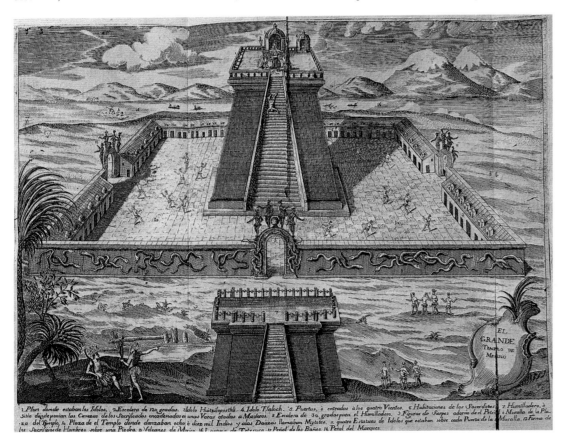

Aztec ceremonies to the gods Tlazolteotl, Cinteotl and Xipe Totec were invariably theatrical, and this was obviously noticed by the artist who made this imaginative print (above) of the Great Temple in Tenochtitlan in 1768, which is now kept in the Museo de America in Madrid. In it we see a sacrificial victim rolling down the steps while a great ritual dance is being performed in a large patio. Ceremonies similar to these were performed in all of the Aztec temples, though mainly in that of Quetzalcoatl in Cholula. According to the Ramírez Codex, *this temple "had a medium-sized patio where on the day of the celebration great dances were performed with rejoicing and humorous interludes . . . where they feigned to be deaf, to have rheums, to be lame, blind and done-armed . . . others came out as vermin, others dressed as beetles and others as toads."*

Apart from their ceremonial dances, the Aztec also had lay dances, and these were performed to entertain the lords as well as the common people. In a print (top) from one edition of The True Story of the Conquest of Mexico, *written in the 17th century and now in the Biblioteca Nacional in Madrid, we see this acrobatic dance performed, while in the background several natives do pirouettes on a tightrope tied between two posts.*

of all that happened. They brought birds when they came each day and Hunbayt and Hunchouen devoured them, giving nothing to either." Their revenge, incidentally, was to trick the elder brothers and change them into monkeys.

There was a similar range of theater in Aztec society. Some of their religious ceremonies relating to the cults of Tlazolteotl, Cinteotl and Xipe Totec were dramatically theatrical. Imagine what it would mean to the audience to see a victim of human sacrifice flayed on the top of the pyramid, a priest putting on the skin and then performing a ceremonial dance. But as in the case of the Maya, the Aztec also had nonreligious theater. Several chroniclers, José de Acosta among them, wrote of the theater in the temple of Quetzalcoatl in the holy city of Cholula. The best description comes from the *Ramírez Codex*: "[The temple] had a medium-sized *patio* where on the day of the celebration were held great balls, rejoicing and amusing farces, for which there was in the middle of the *patio* a small theater of thirty feet square, curiously painted white, bedecked and adorned for that day with all possible neatness, surrounded all by arches made with all manner of roses and plumage, and hanging at intervals were many birds and rabbits and other placid things…where they performed farces, feigning to be deaf, to have rheums, to be lame, to be blind, to lack one arm…others came out as insects and reptiles, some dressed as beetles, others as toads, others as lizards and other things which greatly pleased the audience, for they were most ingenious.

"They then feigned to be butterflies and birds of diverse colors, bringing out boys from the temple dressed as such, who climbed trees in a grove that they did plant there, the priests shooting darts at them, at which droll remarks were made in defense of some and in offense of others, which greatly amused those present; and when this was done, all these persons performed a great *mitote* or dance to conclude the celebration; and this were they accustomed to do at the principal celebrations."

The development of the theater gave rise to small groups of comedians who earned their living by entertaining the lords. Torquemada wrote, "[These balls] amused those at the palace and

183

Among the large number of Mesoamerican games was the volador *(the flier), which was practiced by the Mixtec. It became very popular during the colonial period and has survived even to modern times. Curiously, it was one of the few games not adopted by the Aztec, in spite of the fact that they knew of its existence. A long pole was stuck into the ground, and from the top four men hung upside-down, covered in feathers. Slowly they came down, turning in circles around the pole. The game is undoubtedly related to the Maypole and other fertility rites, but there was also a certain element of enjoyment involved in taking part. In the picture we see the* volador *on a screen from colonial Mexico of the 17th century. It is in the Museo de América in Madrid.*

The Jama Coaque culture of the north of Manabí in Ecuador is representative of Mesoamerican influence in the country, in spite of its early development (500 B.C.–500 A.D.). It is possible that the musical art of this people, which is depicted in many of their ceramic figurines, also came from Mesoamerica. Below we see a group of musicians and dancers (now in the Banco Central de Ecuador). (It should be realized, of course, that each figurine was made in isolation, and they were never intended to form a set.)

also those in the city; the audiences were large and receptive and the lord went to the entertainers and ordered them to dance or they came from the village to dance in the palace that service and recreation…that they call *Netotiliztli*." These *netotiliztli* were dances for pleasure and amusement performed to music by acrobats, contortionists, dwarves and hunchbacks. One of them consisted of a man dancing while supporting two of his companions on his shoulders, each of whom held flowers and feathers in their hands. Another was the classic test of lying on one's back on the ground and rolling a log with the feet. Bernal Diáz wrote that Moctezuma "had also a large number of dancers and clowns; some danced on stilts, others flew when dancing, and all of this was for the entertainment of the monarch. One entire district was inhabited by these buffoons, who knew no other occupation."

These clowns and comedic characters appeared in many cultures—not only for the amusement of the great monarchs but also to amuse the people. They usually performed while holding some sort of stuffed animal as if it were a scepter and acting the role of guardians of morality. They were found among the Pueblo, Hopi and Zuñi Indians, in the *baldzam* or buffoon houses of the Maya, in the Yaqui *chapayecas* and in the Quechua *chunchus*.

The Inca *amautas* combined dance with music recitals and created a theater whose main genres, apart from the religious, were comedies and tragedies based on events in Inca life, or "the intimate life," as Garcilaso called it, including two types that historical researchers call the *wanka* and the *aranway*. The first of these evoked historical events, while the second was a type of humorous play set to music and song. The show took place in the *wallki* or sacred center of the theater.

So that the common people would be able to hear of and even relive events within the empire, reenactments were performed in the streets of Cuzco, particularly those commemorating an Inca victory or the death of some famous sovereign. Sarmiento de Gamboa wrote that Pachacutec ordered important events in the lives of his ancestors to be acted out in the presence of a macabre audience of the mummies of these same ancestors. Martínez de Arzanz states that in 1555, eight plays dedicated to the history of the Inca were performed in the Imperial Villa del Potosi.

In spite of the literature compiled by the chroniclers and the oral traditions of the Inca empire, only one Inca tragedy has survived. This is titled *Ollantay*, written in the 18th century by Espinosa Medrano, the choirmaster and archpriest of Cuzco Cathedral, on what is undoubtedly a traditional pre-Hispanic native theme. Ollantay was one of Pachacutec's generals who fell in love with Star of Joy, one of the king's daughters. When he found that he was not able to marry his beloved, he rebelled against his monarch. He then had many adventures until Pachacutec was succeeded by Tupac Yupanqui, who managed to capture his rebel general and have him brought to Cuzco, where he pardoned him. The ending is a happy one; the daughter of Ollantay and Star of Joy appears and frees her mother from the cave in which she is held prisoner, so that Star of Joy and Ollantay can finally marry.

184

A Mayan ship displayed at the Museo Nacional de Antropología de México D. F., depicts the capture of a prisoner, guarded by a Maya warrior; this sequence carved in stone uses the theme of the dramatic work, Rabinal Achi, *a historic and militaristic play dealing with the capture and sacrifice of prisoners of war. (Nacional de Ecuador)*

The ancient occupation of comedian is represented by this Olmec statue of an acrobat in the Museo de Antropología de Mexico. Contortionists, acrobats, dwarfs and hunchbacks, accompanied by musicians, danced for the enjoyment of villagers and aristocracy alike. These dances were called netotiliztli *by the Aztecs.*

Poets and writers

Except for a few Aztec and Inca poems, no examples of Amerindian poetry remain. We know the Aztec excelled in poetry, written in a form of high language called *tecpillatolli* (spoken in the *cuicalli*), quite different from *macehualtolli*, spoken by the common people. Thus the general public would not appreciate the more subtle verse and poetry reserved for the well-educated upper classes. Tecayahuatzin, the lord of Huexotzinco, gathered wise men and poets around him at his palace. Another great poet was Netzahuacoyotl, lord of Texcoco.

In the central part of Mexico alone there were four major areas in which great poetry was written: Texcoco, whose school was of spiritualist inspiration. Of particular importance were Netzahuacoyotl, Netzahualpilli, Cacamatzin, Cucuahtzin and Tlaltecatzin; Tenochtitlan, whose poets were more concerned with epic themes. Among its authors were Tochihuitzin, the son of the emperor Axayacatl, who wrote poems on the theme of military defeat, and the poetess Macuilxochitzin, princess and daughter of Tlacaelel; Tlaxcala and the surrounding areas (Huexotzinco and Tecamachalco), whose school was concerned with the literary process; and Chalco, which produced a great deal of anonymous poetry. The only poet whose name we know was Chichicuepon, who lamented the military misfortunes of his homeland.

186

There are, naturally, many examples of court poetry and literature from the times of the great Aztec tlatoani *Axayacatl, but most surprising is that the king himself should have become one of the main characters in one of the satirical* cuecuechcuicatl *or impudent songs—popular songs that show that the literary genre had come down to the people itself. The particular song in question is about the defeat of the king in Chalco, which gave rise to the women of that province singing lines that cast aspersions on the monarch's virility. The illustration seen above is from the* Dúran Codex *and shows the king receiving some of his* tecuhtli *or counselors.*

Georges Baudot classified Nahuatl poetry into six different categories: divine, frank, martial (of the eagle), erotic, of flowers and of anguish. Many of these are well-known through the examples that have come down to us. One of the most difficult to find is the *cuecuechcuicatl* or the shameless, impudent poem, which must have been banned by the Spanish priests. Let us take a look at an extract from the poem that the women of Chalco mockingly dedicated to the Aztec king Axayacatl, who was defeated by fellow Aztec warriors:

Another woman: I only need to lift my worm and I make it stand up straight:
With it I shall give pleasure to my little baby Axayacatl.

The three pictures inserted into the text on this page belong to the Florentine Codex *and show the special devotion of the Aztec people for the music and dance associated with the poetical chants, of which the popular and the aristocratic classes were equally fond. In the scene at the top left, a group of women are dancing at a feast. In the scene at the right center, a group of musicians perform their dances around a drum, while in the scene above, the percussion and*

Oh, my pretty little king Axayacatl,
If in truth you are a man, here you have something to keep you busy.
Are you impotent then?
Take my poor ash, come now, and do your work on me.
Come take it, come take it, my joy:
Oh, my little boy, give it to me, my little boy.
With merry pleasure shall we laugh,
We shall be happy and I shall learn.

The first woman: Not yet, not yet…do not rush, please,
Oh, my little one, king Axayacatl…
Now you move, now you move your little hands,

I see, I see you wish to clutch my tits:
Nearly, nearly, my dear little heart!
Perhaps you will spoil
my beauty, my integrity:
with beautiful flowers
I surrender my womb…there it is,
to your driller, I offer it to you as a gift…

The *icnocuicatl*, or songs of anguish, are the most beautiful of Nahuatl poetry. It is well worthwhile to look at an anonymous poem from Huexotzinco, lamenting death:

Weep; I am a singer.
I see the flowers in my hands
which delight my heart: I am a singer.
Wherever roams my heart, roams my mind.
As a handful of turquoise, as a gleaming emerald
I held my song and beautiful flowers in esteem.

wind instruments are brought into the exhibition of the performers.

The Aztec schools of song and dance

Aztec were taught to sing and dance in schools built next to the temples. Friar Diego Durá described them in these words: "In all the cities there were next to the temples great buildings where resided masters who taught singing and dancing, which houses they called *cuicalli*, meaning 'House of Song,' where was no other exercise but the teaching of boys and girls of singing and dancing and the playing of instruments…The singing and dancing commenced, and he who could not do the back step to the sound and rhythm of the music was taught with great care, and they danced until late into the night…The boys took pride in knowing how to sing and dance well and in being able to lead the rest; in the dances they took pride in keeping time with the feet and coming in on time with their bodies to the movements that they made, and with the voice also, for the dance is not only governed by the sound but also by the high and low notes which are sung in their songs, for they sing and dance at the same time, and for these songs there were among them poets that composed them, giving to each song and dance a different melody."

187

Song and dance were usually performed together at the great Inca celebrations. These were very frequent, there being one associated with the food production cycle at least once a month. They were group occasions in which there was nevertheless a degree of discrimination—the women would dance on one side and the men on the other. The most important of all was the way-yaya, a great dance performed in Cuzco before the Inca emperor, in which the women danced holding hands. The scenes of celebration below appear in Trujillo of Peru, an 18th-century work by the famous Bishop Martínez Compañón, the original of which is kept in the Biblioteca del Palacio Real in Madrid.

Be merry, my friends: no one shall remain on the earth.
I shall not take with me my beautiful songs, nor my beautiful flowers.
Be merry, my friends: no one shall remain on the earth.
And so I weep and scatter my flowers.
Will you, perchance, go with me to the land of mystery?
I shall not take my flowers although I am a singer.
Be merry, we are still alive: you are hearing my song...

The Inca poets were the *amautas* and the *arawicuj*, also known as the *haravicus*. The first group were sages, great writers of verse, authors of religious songs and possibly even composers of music. It has been said that they were the more cultured poets, in contrast to the *haravicus*, who were the popular ones. Without doubt the *haravicus* wrote *arawi* and *taki*, a lyrical, intimate type of poetry that the *amautas* did not use. However, their differences were not so clearly defined for it seems that the *haravicus* collaborated with the *amautas* as well. Their great mastery of language and music enabled the *haravicus* to write beautiful poetry on both important and delicate themes which was appreciated by large groups of people. The *haravicus*, however, must not be considered second-rate *amautas*, for they were also held in great esteem by the aristocracy.

The great Inca poets wrote *jailli* or liturgical texts. They also wrote lyrical poems on nonreligious, often historical, themes, often for recitation in public, during work in the fields and when constructing. Other highly appreciated poetic forms were the *arawi* and the *urpi*, poems of a more personal nature, the main theme being unhappy love affairs. Inca verse was based on variations in tone rather than meter and rhyme. A beautiful extract from an *arawi* poem (from *Ollantay*) illustrates Inca sensitivity. It tells of two enamored doves, separated by the snow and death.

Two enamored doves
sigh, weep and grieve,
for the snow separates them.
On a dry, woodwormed treetrunk

188

one sees that
in the desolation of the moors
her sweet and tender love,
from whom she has never been parted, is lost.
The other dove also suffers,
remembering his love,
thinking she has perished,
and sings to her so:
…Where, my dove, are those eyes,
that delicate breast,
that heart that enveloped me in its tenderness,
that tender voice that called my name?…
And she who remained alone
wanders, lost, among the rocks
and sobbing disconsolately
moves among the brambles.
And asking all things in existence,
cries…Where are you, my heart?"
stumbles in her weariness,
and, exhausted, finally dies.

As regards Nahuatl prose, we have already
seen examples of the advice given by parents and
the elderly. Quechua prose is also well worth
examining. In the oral tradition of Peru we find

*The streets of Cuzco, which we see at top, right, in
this colonial print of the 17th century belonging to
a collection in the Biblioteca Nacional in Madrid,
served as the stage for Inca plays performed to celebrate great conquests or funerals of emperors, as
may be seen above in a print belonging to the same
collection. The main genres in Inca theater were the*
wanka, *which was historical in nature, and the*
aranway, *which were humorous. Both were accompanied by song and dance.*

many pre-Columbian literary pieces. Two such
examples are the stories "The Covetous Brother"
and "The Butterfly." The first deals with the
traditional theme of the poor brother despised by
the rich brother. In it, an old man gives the poor
brother a spell by means of which the rock, the
puna (bleak, arid tableland) and the *pampa* yield
to him gold, silver and copper. When the rich
brother discovers what has happened, he tries to
extract the same riches, but the rock gives him
horns, the *puna* fur, and the *pampa* tail, so that he
is turned into a deer who thereafter wanders the
puna and *pampa*. The story of the butterfly con-
cerns unfounded jealousy. The husband of a
happy family goes away on a journey. His wife
stays at home with the child, and one night a
butterfly comes into the house. The little boy asks
his mother what it is and she replies that it is her
lover, who comes every night to keep her company. The father returns from his journey when
his wife happens to be out of the house. He asks
his son what his mother has been doing at night
while he has been away, and the boy replies that
she spoke to her lover, who came to her every
night. Mad with jealousy, the husband finds his
wife and kills her. One night long after, when the
husband is with his son, he hears him cry, "There
is mother's lover, the one who kept her company
at night." He sees him point to a butterfly flutter-
ing around in the light. The husband then realizes
that he has made a mistake and dies of dismay
and grief.

189

Historians and philosophers

History was kept alive in the oral accounts of events told at the great religious festivals. It was usually the elderly members of the community who passed on the stories to the younger generations. The high cultures, however, had professional historians, though these men did not treat historical fact with particular respect, since the governments they worked for obliged them to modify events to suit their purposes—which, from the point of view of objectivity, makes them extremely unreliable. This may have been what led Mesoamerican historians to use concrete, factual language, in contrast to the reiterative, flowery style used in speeches on morality, poetry, etc. The most extreme cases of subjective historical interpretation are provided by the *amautas*, authors of epic poems on imperial conquest. Upon the death of an Inca emperor, the *amauta* was called in to relate the memorable deeds of the monarch, but first a supreme council decided which deeds would be related and which would not. The *amauta* was given the list, and composed his work accordingly. No pre-Columbian work of this kind exists today, though they are alluded to by the chroniclers. The only known work is *The Death of Atahualpa*, which was written during the colonial period.

The Maya also had professional historians, one of whose duties was to pass on their knowledge to two other persons so that it would never be lost. According to Las Casas, "This man al-ways instructed two of his brothers or relatives in things relating to history, and made them practice it while they lived and come to him when they had queries." The priests, kings and lords went to the historians whenever they were uncertain as to proper behavior. Las Casas adds, "And not only [did] new historians [go], but kings and priests, with questions on ceremony, rules of conduct in religion and in festivals, on the gods, and on any matter concerning ancient governments and lay matters of importance, consulting them on these things." Maya historians would seem to have had very extensive knowledge and served as a sort of living library on the cultural experience of the nation.

The case of the Aztec must have been similar, though one great codex, the *Boturini*, also known as *The Roll of the Pilgrimage*, has survived, detailing the migration of the Aztec from Aztlan to the lakes in the Valley of Mexico. The task of writing the *xiuhamatl* or annals was given to historians in Mexico, Texcoco and Tlaxcala, with instructions to pay special attention to genealogy. We do have numerous Aztec historical stories, such as the *Mexicayotl Chronicle* from Tezozomoc, the *Toltec-Chichimeca History*, the *Annals of Tlatelolco*, the *Chichimeca History* by Ixtlixochitl and the *Annals of Cuauhtitlan*, but all of these belong to the post-Columbian period. Finally, part of the *Ubin Codex* and the chronicles of Sahagún should be mentioned.

The question of whether or not there were intellectual philosophers in Amerindian society has always been hotly debated. There is no doubt, however, that Maya, Aztec and Inca thinkers all held their own metaphysical concepts of life. The *amautas* or Inca sages were true philosophers whose wisdom was deeply rooted in their culture.

In the previous chapter we examined Aztec views on morality, which followed the philosophical premise of man's basic goodness. Man was the "owner of a face, owner of a heart," the Aztec believed. A concept of the relationship between body and soul existed, to the point that the good man expressed "the action that gives wisdom to the face" and "the action that enriches the heart." Unfortunately, philosophical texts are extremely rare, and we have only what Sahagún compiled when he traveled among the natives of Tepepulco and Tlatelolco.

Much of what the Amerindian sages wrote on the mystery of life and death, on the suffering endured in the world of the living and the promise of the afterlife, remain lost to us forever.

The Aztec codices contained many historical passages. The Dúran Codex speaks of sacrifices of birds and other offerings made at the Acuecuexatl fountain, a spring between Huitzilopochco and Coyoacan, which King Ahuitzotl made use of to have an aqueduct built to take drinking water to Tenochtitlan, the Chapultepec aqueduct no longer being able to supply enough for the needs of the people. The aqueduct burst and the city was flooded, resulting in the deaths of a great many people and the destruction of the fields. To cope with the tragedy, Ahuitzotl had birds sacrificed and the hearts of numerous civil servants offered (above). On seeing that this was not enough, he ordered divers to seal the leaks in the aqueduct and had the Acuecuexatl fountain covered over with mortar.

The great Aztec historical codex is the Boturini, also known as the Issue of the Wanderings (facing page), which tells of the great migration of the Aztec from Aztlan to the lakes of Mexico, where the sign appeared that their god had told of: an eagle perched on a nopal cactus. It was there that they settled and founded the great city of Tenochtitlan, which became the capital of the empire.

tenochtitlan

colhuacan. pueblo.   tenayucan. pueblo

Warriors
and priests

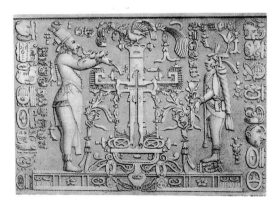

War, as symbolized in the Maya warrior on the facing page, and life, as expressed in this print reproducing the famous Palenque Cross—the symbol of the tree of life made by the corn—are the introduction to a world of warriors and priests in pre-Columbian America. The warrior is in the Denver Art Museum and the lithograph comes from the Atlas of Mexican Antiquities.

The barbarian invasions

Pre-Columbian American peoples, unfortunately, were well versed in warfare, this being one of the aspects that the New and Old Worlds had in common. Even the objectives were similar, including the expropriation of the land and labor of others, usually justified as a divine cause. Thus, warriors in society were men of great prestige and were held to have carried out the will of the gods. They were the sword of the gods. Although the last period in pre-Columbian American history is usually called the military period, it must be taken into account that such a name in fact refers only to events that took place within the territory of three of the peoples—the Maya, the Aztec and the Inca—though the other peoples also took part in armed combat, as we shall see later. The struggles of the Maya all but ended along with their urban culture at the beginning of the 15th century, and by the time the Europeans discovered the continent such struggles had ceased. Their military structure was very similar to that of the Aztec, having been introduced with the invasion of the Toltec.

War, defined as an action carried out by a whole nation with a collective motive, an action organized by chiefs, using military tactics and skills to carry out a series of attacks to the bitter end, was practiced extensively by the Aztec and Inca. For others, warfare was temporary and sporadic. There were even quite "civilized" ways of settling one's differences, such as regulated and expiatory combat. One such example was to be found in the Maidu people of California, who engaged in a virtually bloodless method of fighting. The two groups shot arrows at each other until one man was wounded, which was the signal to cease combat and declare winners and losers. The two groups then sat down to a banquet, at the end of which the winners paid the losers compensation for the injury of their man. The Botocudo of eastern Brazil settled their differences of opinion over territorial limits or hunting grounds. Opponents fought in twos, thrashing each other with sticks. The same method was employed by the Kaingang, from the same region, using sticks and stones. Unfortunately, these methods were all too rare.

Far from what certain military governments like to believe, war is not the consequence of any

This Eagle Knight head is kept in the Museo Nacional de Antropología in Mexico. The Eagle Knight was the ideal of what the Aztec warrior should be: noble, brave and respectful toward the gods. Every Aztec man was trained for war in the telpochcalli *before he was allowed to march off to war as a kind of shieldbearer to a great warrior. The Aztec had different orders, such as the Eagle Knight, the Tiger Knight and Arrow Knight. The army was centered around veterans or professional soldiers called the* quachic, *who swore never to retreat and also took up the most dangerous positions in combat.*

Pre-Inca cultures also engaged in warfare, as is demonstrated by their fortifications and representations of warriors. Below, we see a Moche warrior armed with a great club and wearing a headpiece bearing the image of an animal, the emblem of his people. The figure is from the Museo de Arqueología y Antropología in Lima.

natural human instinct but an artificial cultural complex, striving to achieve specific aims. For the Amerindians, such aims were simple. The Tupinamba of Brazil and the numerous Carib-speaking peoples of Colombia, Venezuela and the West Indies fought in order to take prisoners, who would then serve as food in their ceremonial banquets. So too did the Chorotega of Nicaragua, who performed wholesale human slaughter for the same purpose. Main reasons for war between the peoples of El Chaco were violation of territorial limits, to kidnap women and to satisfy family vendettas. The Aztec made war in order to obtain prisoners to sacrifice to their gods.

Similar reasons must have led to the great campaigns embarked on before the arrival of the Europeans though little is known about them. The Spaniards believed that the peoples they encountered had lived in the same place since ancient times, but that was not the case. We have mentioned the invasion of Mesoamerica by the Nahuatl-speaking peoples, the last of which were the Aztec, and we have mentioned the arrival of

195

War was an everyday event in the agricultural and theocratic culture of the Mochica, which developed over the first seven centuries of this millennium on the northern coasts of Peru. Along with their fortifications, we have their pictographs and ceramic sculptures, among which are warriors leading their bound captives. Above, we see a captive with a rope around his neck being pulled up by the hair as the warrior, wearing large earrings and a handsome headpiece, demonstrates his power over his prisoner. The piece is from the Museo de Arte Precolombino in Santiago de Chile.

Apart from those made of metal, which were relatively uncommon, the Indians used a variety of weapons, particularly projectiles, which had been used since the times of the mammoth hunters (11,000 B.C.).

Some projectiles, such as the poisoned arrow and the *boleadoras*, were typically American. The former was smeared with *curare* and used for hunting and only very rarely in warfare, while the latter was usually made up of two balls tied to each end of a string. The Inca, however, used a special kind called the *sillo*, a string with three cords, each of which had a metal ball tied to the end. When thrown, it wound itself around the enemy's legs. The bows used for shooting arrows were cylindrical, flat or plano-convex in shape, made from a wide variety of woods (Brazil wood, palm, etc.) of different lengths. Those used by the Ge Indians of Brazil were more than six feet (two meters) long, and those of the Patasho (who lived in what is today the state of Bahía) were as much as nine feet (three meters) long. Bowstrings were made of agave in the tropical Amazonian region, whereas they were of leather in North America and El Chaco. Arrows, too, were extremely varied, with tips made of wood (double-edged or cross-shaped), stone or bone, with or without feathers.

Other projectiles, such as the sling and the lance, were similar to those of the Old World. The lances were made with special types of American hardwood (Brazil wood, palm, etc.). Heads were made of bone or stone fixed to the ends (as used by the Maya, Mixtec, Chinantec and Mixes). The dart-thrower, used by Europeans in prehistory, was also very popular, especially with the Aztec (who called it an *atlatl*) and the Chibcha, among others. It was a rod with two stone or bone hooks attached to it, one for the finger and the other for resting the dart on.

Assault weapons were the most unusual of all Amerindian weapons. First came the club, a tremendously heavy weapon, both hands being needed to wield it. Some, like those of the Araucanians, were jointed, with sharp stone chips encrusted in the ends. Others had star-shaped heads or rings made of stone at the ends, like those of the Nicoya Indians of Costa Rica, the Cañari of Ecuador and the Inca. The lance was also common. Made of hard wood with pointed ends, it was usually of great length and could also be used as a projectile. Later the wooden sword was introduced, usually made of palm wood and sometimes shaped like an oar. The Aztec fixed obsidian blades to the end, making it a terrible weapon. Stone axes were also used, although the axes used by the Maya were made of copper, which they imported (probably from the Zapotec). Finally knives, made of flint, obsidian or simply of stone, came into use.

The first weapon used for defense was naturally the shield, usually made of wood, wicker or leather. The leather ones

were round and convex with two straps inside for gripping and were found west of the Inirida River. Jibaro shields were round and made of wood, while those of the Mojo and Omaua were oblong and were either of wood or wicker. Aztec shields were round, and those of the Inca either round or rectangular, covered with leather with painted figures. Other defensive weapons were used for protection against arrows, including clothing padded with cotton, as worn by the Aztec and Inca, protective cotton pads, as worn by the Nicarao, and bandages wound around the extremities, as used by the Maya of Yucatán. The head was protected by a helmet made of wood, wicker or even of metal.

Toltec groups in Yucatán. The best-known case, however, is that of the Carib-speaking tribes, who set off from Amazonia northward, displacing the Arawak peoples who had settled in Venezuela. The Caribs went on from Venezuela to the West Indies, and by the time the Spaniards arrived were displacing the Taino. The Arawak went on to Colombia, where they in turn displaced the Chibcha peoples, who went to the interior of Magdalena. Another great migration, though little is known about it, was that of the Tupi, who traveled down from north of the Amazon to upper Tapajoz and crossed Paraguay, finally reaching the coast of Brazil in recent, though still pre-Columbian, times. Thus there was a veritable invasion by barbarian peoples similar to that which took place in Europe after the fall of the Roman Empire.

In North America the Apache and Navajo Indians migrated southward, circling the Rocky Mountains, reaching the southwest, and settling in the region where the Pueblo and Pima Indians lived. The Muskogee emigrated as far west as the Mississippi and settled on the plains that extend

east of the river. The Iroquois came from the southeast, passing through Ohio to their final destination. The Algonquians advanced south, crossing Ohio and Chesapeake Bay, the vanguard reaching the Savannah River. The Sioux nation spread out eastward with the migrations of the Algonquians and Iroquois, reaching the upper Mississippi, Virginia and North Carolina.

The famous prairies of North America, therefore, were only a point of transit for numerous migrations. As was seen in chapter one, contrary to 19th-century American literature, at the end of the 15th century there were no nomadic hunters on the plains, only a few sparsely populated farming settlements. The arrival of the Sioux tribes in this area was a direct consequence of two effects that the Indians obtained from the Spaniards and the French—the horse and the firearm. The farmers who lived in the area then became nomadic hunters and abandoned their ancient settlements.

The Algonquians were excellent warriors who lived in the southern part of Canada and northern part of the United States of America. Their nation was made up of many peoples, such as the Ojibwa, the Sac and Fox, who lived in the southwestern region of the Great Lakes and who are seen here fighting a naval battle on Lake Superior. Intertribal warfare in North America served as a false justification for the white men to invade the Algonquians' territory. The illustration is from Information in Respect of the History, Condition and Prospects of the Indian Tribes of the United States, *published in Philadelphia in 1813.*

The influence of Romanticism in the 19th century brought forth all kinds of fables regarding the fighting capacity of the Amerindian. In this 19th-century print from History of the United States, *a tribe marches off to fight in the way of the European armies of the time.*

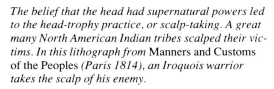

The belief that the head had supernatural powers led to the head-trophy practice, or scalp-taking. A great many North American Indian tribes scalped their victims. In this lithograph from Manners and Customs of the Peoples *(Paris 1814), an Iroquois warrior takes the scalp of his enemy.*

Declaring war was always a deadly, definitive decision, which immediately put the enemy on a war footing. There were many ways of declaring war: In El Chaco and in some parts of North America, the method was to shoot arrows into the ground. The print seen here comes from History of the United States, *an album of art from the 16th to the 19th centuries.*

The fate of the prisoner

The barbarity of the warriors reached its climax when victory was obtained over the enemy. Pillage, rape and murder were the inevitable consequences of triumph and it was common to take the head of the enemy as a trophy. The popular belief that all the supernatural strength of a man was contained in his brain made the head a most coveted object. Head-taking was common practice all over the Amazon region, especially in Tupi territory. The Munduruku Indians cut off their enemies' heads, mummified them and then decorated them with feathers and artificial eyes. In east Xingu and in the Andean region, the "skin trophy" was customary, the skin of the face and the scalp being removed in one piece. A variation on this theme was the famous Jibaro art of *tsantsa*, which continued up until only a short time ago: the head of an enemy defeated in combat was transformed into a type of talisman by reducing it to the size of a fist.

As the soul of the enemy was in the head, it was logical that he would wish to take revenge. A feast was therefore held to neutralize the enemy's power. During the celebration, the head was immersed in a magic liquid, which could reconcile the spirit of the dead enemy with his killer, changing him thereafter into the killer's protector. The head was then tied by the hair to a belt worn around the waist. For most North American peoples as well, the finishing touch to any great victory was to cut off the head of the enemy and take the scalp as a talisman. This custom became more and more popular during the Spanish colonial period.

The Araucanians celebrated their victories in an extremely cruel way, torturing their prisoners by quartering them over a period of time—while doing their best to keep them alive—and eating the limbs. The skulls would later be used as drinking cups and the long bones made into flutes. The Diaguita Indians were less vicious, only cutting off the enemy's head. Some of the peoples of Ecuador had the macabre custom of flaying the enemy and using the skins to cover the great drums used during their celebrations. With each drumbeat the head and arms would move grotesquely.

For the Aztec, war was something sacred, as it provided prisoners whose blood would feed the gods. The object of war, therefore, was not to kill the enemy but to capture him alive and take him to the sacrificial altars. Warriors were trained to wound or knock out an adversary, but not to kill him. Boys or novices came behind the warriors in battle to tie the hands of the wounded and unconscious so that they could later be brought back alive. The bravest prisoners, such as the Tlaxcallan or the Huexotzinco, were of greater value and thought to be a more pleasing offering to the gods; capturing one of these warriors meant a military promotion. Another objective of war was to spread the ancient Toltec culture through its heirs, the Aztec, to the areas previously controlled by Tula that had fallen into the hands of evil intruders.

Though wars were fought with the noblest of aims, justifying any sacrifice, there were other practical pretexts for declaring war. The most common was to defend the *pochteca* or merchants. The Aztec were zealous advocates of free trade and believed that their *pochteca* were entitled to do business anywhere. When any difficulties arose, they went to war in order to reestablish free trade. They used this argument, as

Suplicio de los prisioneros en el Perú

The fate of prisoners of war depended exclusively on their captors, who usually used extremely cruel torture techniques. On this page we see two romantic views of the torture given to captives. At top right, from the Biblioteca Arcaya in Caracas, an Iroquois prisoner is being burnt with torches. Above, a prisoner from a jungle tribe in Peru is punished in this print from the History of America, *in the Museo Naval in Madrid.*

The Aztec held warfare in such high esteem that they considered death in combat to be one of the greatest sacrifices made to the gods. In this way there arose the gladiatorial sacrifice, depicted here in this sheet from the Tudela Codex. In this type of sacrifice a prisoner (the legend reads "slave") was tied to a large round stone and given mock weapons (a sword and shield) to defend himself and die fighting against a warrior, who appears on the right.

Ixtlilxochtl tells us, for their attack on the central cities and to invade the Tehuantepec isthmus (where all the members of a caravan of merchants had been killed) and even to fight Coyohuacan when the city guards seized fish, ducks and frogs belonging to Aztec women who had gone there to sell their wares. Other pretexts were that Aztec messengers had been murdered, or that it was suspected that an attack was being prepared against the Aztec, as was the case when Tlatelolco attacked Tenochtitlan.

Eventually, there was no practical cause for war, when the empire already stretched from coast to coast. Still, the Aztec feared that the supply of blood to the gods would dry up—which would mean the end of the world—so they established what is known as the "flowery war." This was a pact whereby a permanent state of war would exist between Tlaxcala, Cholula and Huexotzinco, thus ensuring supplies of prisoners for sacrifice. The pact was made in 1450, in the wake of a terrible famine, attributed to the lack of sacrifices. Dates were fixed and battles held, enabling the bloody machinery of war to continue functioning. Despite the pact, other conflicts arose, resulting in great animosity between the peoples participating in the flowery war.

Somewhat contradictory to the act of war was the protocol surrounding it. Ambassadors were sent to persuade the leaders of the enemy city to submit peacefully. The first ambassadors came from Tenochtitlan. If they had no success, then after one month (20 days), ambassadors were sent from Texcoco. If these were also unsuccessful, then one month later, ambassadors came from Tlacopan to deliver an ultimatum. After one more

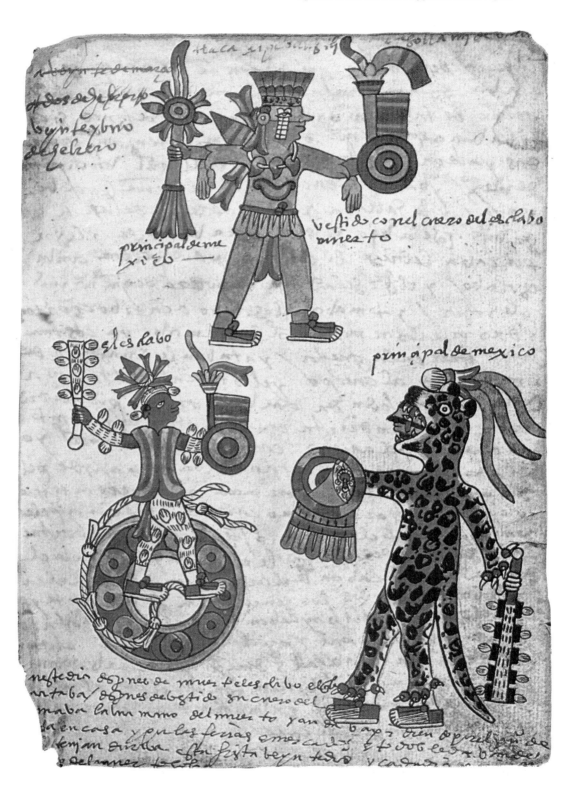

For the Aztec, the war against Azcapotzalco in 1428 meant both independence and the beginning of a social hierarchy with its pipiltin or lords and macehualtin or plebeians, which came into being as a result of the pact made between the two. At that time the tlatoani of the Aztec in Tenochtitlan was Itzcoatl. The print above belongs to the John Carter Library collection in New York.

Maya Warriors

Militarism was one of the distinctive traits of the Post-Classic Maya civilization, something much different from the peaceful classical Maya. In the Temple of the Warriors of Chichen Itza, bas-reliefs and paintings of combatants occupy the places once dedicated to parades of gods and priests. The activities of war entered Yucatan with the invasions that occurred during the 9th and 10th centuries. These involved Mexicanized populations, such as the Putum, or genuine Mexicans with Toltec traditions. They carried slings (atlatl) and arrows, with which they easily defeated the Maya who lived in the region, whose sole weapon seems to have been a lance with a flint point. The pointed helmets and badges are reminiscent of those of the knights of the orders of the eagle and tiger of Mexico. All of this is narrated on the doorways and pillars of the temple, which show the conquest of the Yucatan by the Itzae. The victors and the defeated thus constituted the new Maya society, even if the fusion

was slow and difficult. The true Maya continued for many years to define the invaders as "strangers" or "coarse ones," as "people without father and without mother" and so on. In the society that finally emerged, war continued to form an important part, but it had become professionalized. It was conducted by holcanes, professional soldiers. Mercenaries were sometimes imported from other areas, as happened around the beginning of the 13th century, when certain Mexican troops took the field and introduced the use of the bow and arrow. War was directed by the batab, or governor of the city-state, and the nacom, or the true head of the military operations, elected for three years, during which time he could have no relations with women and could not eat meat. Strategy was based on the ambush, prepared with great secrecy and carried out with all the cunning needed to terrorize the enemy. They hurled turtle shells, yelled, blew trumpets. The black and red pictures served the same function. After a victory, the holcanes were suitably honored, most of all if they had captured high-ranking prisoners.

month, war was declared. In this way, it seemed that the Aztec had had no desire to go to war, when in fact the opposite was true. But there was a reason for using this method: The set periods of time gave the gods the chance to approve or disapprove of military action.

It was the duty of every Aztec male to serve as a warrior. Thus he was initiated in the art of war at the age of 15, when he first went to the *telpochcalli*. When he reached 20 years of age, it was his right and duty to go to war. The *macehualli* or common man could leave the army to marry, but the nobles were warriors for life. Sagahún wrote that when the son of a lord reached the age for going to war, "His father and relatives feasted the captains and old soldiers; they gave a feast and gave blankets and embroidered *maxtles*, praying them to take great care of the lad in battle by teaching him to fight and protecting him from the enemy, and when some war was to be fought, the soldiers took him away. They took great care of him, teaching him all those things necessary for defense and also for offense against the enemy, and when the battle was fought, did not lose sight of him, and taught him, pointing out those who captured enemies, in order that he also could do thus so."

The army was centered around those veterans or professional soldiers called the *quachic*, who had vowed never to retreat in battle and always took up the most dangerous positions in combat. They were considered mad and likely to live short lives, though they enjoyed certain privileges, such as being allowed to dance with the courtesans at night in the *cuicalli* or house of song. Sahagún wrote: "They were called *quaquachictin*, which is the name for deranged albeit valiant men in war…also *otomi otlaotzonxintin* which means '*otomis* shorn and reckless.'…They were great slaughterers but held to be incapable of taking command."

All military affairs were referred to a military council, which was also represented in the supreme council. Final decisions were taken by the *tlatoani* himself. Battles began at the time indicated by the priests as being the most favorable for victory. Tactics in warfare were not very sophisticated, being limited to false retreats to lead the enemy into ambush, taking positions at

strategic points, and hiding in ditches covered over with branches and jumping out on the enemy. Sometimes scaling ladders were used, as in the taking of Icpatepec, or attacks were made in canoes on the lake cities (one may be seen in the *Nuttall Codex*).

Combat began with the sounding of shell horns, blowing of whistles and the throwing of projectiles. Then came hand-to-hand combat, during which the Aztec were able to demonstrate their skill in leaving the enemy *hors de combat* without killing him. Victory was determined when one group managed to enter the enemy's city and set fire to its temple. This is why the Aztec sign for conquest was a temple in flames pierced by an arrow.

Once the war was over, terms of peace were negotiated. The vanquished admitted to the power of Huitzilopochtli over their own gods, bowed down before the victors, begged their forgiveness and offered tribute, which had been calculated previously by the pochteca. Conditions were stated and agreements made. The city and surrounding territory, kept largely intact, would now become part of the Aztec confederation.

The entire Aztec military system (the ambassadors and peacemakers, the taking of live prisoners for sacrifice, and peace talks in which tribute was negotiated) was condemned to failure when faced with Hernán Cortés and his men, for they made war in a different way.

In Amerindian societies, being a warrior meant social prestige. The warrior depicted above is on a ceramic piece of the Classic Maya period. We can see certain characteristics that set the warrior apart from other citizens: the thick eyebrows and the imposing mustache, to heighten the impression of aggressiveness. He is also wearing an enormous turban and padding to protect his neck, and he carries a rectangular shield. The piece is in the Art Museum at Princeton University.

Inca warfare

The Inca did not make war to obtain prisoners for human sacrifice to their gods but rather to civilize the world, in accordance with the instructions they had received from the children of the sun. Like the Aztec, they had no wish to kill their enemies but simply to submit them so that they would understand the advantages of forming part of the civilized world—the *Tahuantinsuyu*. Thus, before they marched off to war, they took great pains to try and persuade the enemy to surrender without resistance. If this was unsuccessful, they then resorted to intimidation, and if this did not work, they tried to bribe the enemy leaders. Only if none of these tactics was effective did they go to war, first sending out spies to find out the number of soldiers and strong points of the enemy and consulting the gods as to when was the best time to attack.

Much has been said to support the view that the Inca were an extremely militaristic nation, but in fact all they did was perfect a tradition of the Peru region, particularly the coastal region, where a permanent state of war had existed since the Classic period. All Inca men between 25 and 50 years of age were required to serve in the army, although they did not have to be permanently on active service, for even in wars, troops fighting at the front were relieved. Units were made up according to the place of origin of the men, possibly because certain regions specialized in the use of certain weapons. The high-ranking officers were always Inca, and the supreme leader was the Inca emperor himself, though at times he would pass control to one of his generals or relatives, usually his son or brother.

Combat was preceded with a parade aimed at intimidating the enemy. The soldiers marched along displaying their special insignia, many of them, the Cañari and Chanca in particular, with their faces painted red (with dye from the arnotto tree) or black (from the inaja palm). The general was borne in his litter, carrying in his hand a *suntur paucar*, the symbol of command. It was, in fact, a long staff, embellished with gold and decorated with feathers. By his side walked men from the most "Incanized" provinces. If the emperor himself was commanding the troops, his litter was surrounded by his personal guard of

204

Inca militarism perfected a tradition for warfare mainly in the coastal region, with the Mochica able to create a powerful empire. On their vessels they painted or carved a great many scenes of war, which was for them a fact of everyday life. The warriors carried different types of weapons, the most common being the conical-tipped mace, round or rectangular shield and thick armor made of quilted cotton. They also wore masks and headdresses with animal forms. In this figure from the Museo Nacional de Arqueología y Antropología in Lima, the warrior has wings and his face is covered with a bird mask.

Cañari warriors, followed by a standard-bearer displaying the royal emblem—a small, square flag, made of cotton and wool on which was a rainbow (the symbol of the Inca) and the personal coat of arms of that particular emperor—a jaguar or a condor, for example. Bringing up the rear would be an idol, escorted by honor guards, followed by the concubines of the leaders, porters and, finally, more troops.

The alarm was sounded as soon as the enemy was sighted. The general or the emperor reviewed the troops from his litter. Next the enemy was harangued, resulting in a lot of shouting. Finally the attack was launched. Archers and

slingmen shot their arrows and stones. Other warriers used their spear-throwers. After this came hand-to-hand combat, in which the terrible "rings" and *macanas* or double-edged wooden swords were used. Lances, skull-crushing star-shaped maces and axes also came into play. The captains fought in front of their men, distinguished by feather crests and other insignia. The general or the emperor, if he went to the battle, watched from his litter, following the fighting with interest and sending reinforcements wher-

The discipline and organization employed in military supplies was perhaps the key to the Inca army. It marched in formations of archers, slingers and pikemen, each of whom had their own special distinguishing features and was usually grouped according to their place of birth. The scene painted on this kero *depicts a typical warrior. The piece is in the Museo de la Universidad de Cuzco.*

This Chimú huaco *shows a typical warrior with his club and shield and wearing a headdress with a feline head on it. During the Inca period the dress of the warrior did not change. It consisted of a kind of tunic down to the knees, decorated with drawings. The piece is in a collection belonging to the Museo de Arqueología y Antropología in Lima.*

205

ever they were needed. The battle ended when one side managed to capture the idol of the other (as with the Chanca) or when the leader was captured (as with the Colla) or simply when the superiority of one side over the other became so evident that there was no point in going on with the slaughter.

Victory was celebrated with a triumphal entry into Cuzco. The parade would be led by the victorious troops, the captains in their finest military dress, marching to the sound of the drums and shell horns. Behind these came the prisoners, their hands tied behind their backs and their wives and children begging for mercy. The enemy leader was carried naked, on a litter, and surrounded by drums made of the skins of his dead relatives. Next, the spoils of war were displayed, guarded by soldiers bearing the severed heads of the enemy captains on pikes. Next came *orejones* dressed in ceremonial attire and behind them young chosen women of the emperor, singing and dancing and shaking timbrels. Next came the high functionaries, walking by the side of the Inca's litter. Bringing up the rear were the Inca's relatives, the princesses, borne on litters, and finally more troops. Thus they reached the great *plaza* in Cuzco, where the emperor performed the rite of crossing the square by walking over the backs of defeated warriors lying on the ground. The occasion ended with singing and dancing and offerings to the gods.

The power of the Inca army lay in two main strengths: good leadership and strict discipline. The *tambos* or state warehouses, which held both arms and food supplies, were placed strategically at regular intervals along the roads, enabling the troops to advance continuously without having to lose time in searching for provisions or disturbing the civilian population when doing so. Whenever the troops went beyond the limits of the *Tahuantinsuyu*, they took herds of llamas along to carry food and arms. Discipline was strict in the extreme. It was forbidden for a soldier to break file, even when the troops were approaching Cuzco in complete safety. One famous general, Capac Yupanqui, brother of Pachacutec, was sentenced to death for allowing the Chanca soldiers in his army to desert and for continuing beyond the limits of the *Tahuantinsuyu* on his military campaigns when he had not been told to do so. This was in spite of the fact that his campaigns had been highly successful.

The Inca were not often cruel to the civilian peoples they defeated, especially at the beginning of their territorial expansion. Prisoners were returned to their homelands, and the *curacas* and leaders who had not shown themselves exceptionally hostile to the Inca were restored to office. Later, public buildings were constructed and Inca arts, crops and cattle introduced into the conquered area. It would seem, however, that in the latter years of the empire the degree of cruelty to the enemy increased. In one of his paintings, Poma de Ayala shows a prisoner kneeling on the ground with his hands tied behind his back while his eyes are being put out. It is also known that during the civil war between Huascar and Atahualpa, women and children, Cañari and Chachapoya in particular, were slaughtered.

The Inca were so convinced of their military superiority that they paid not the slightest attention to a group of adventurers led by a bearded chief who ventured into the empire. The emperor, Atahualpa, did no more than arrange to meet with them in a city where he planned to bathe in the thermal waters, convinced that he would be able to have them easily killed there. The name of the city was Cajamarca.

Sacsahuaman and Machu Picchu

Most fortifications were built in the Peru region. Tribes in Amazonia built palisades, while the Pueblo Indians built their villages on inaccessible *mesetas* and lived in houses without doors or windows. During an attack, the Zuñi Pueblos took their women and children to an easily defended *meseta* called "the hill of thunder." The Diaguita (in northern Argentina) built their villages "in the form of castles," according to the chroniclers, from which they could hurl down stones on to the enemy.

The Inca system of fortifications was the most magnificent in the whole of the New World. The greatest of these was Sacsahuaman, which overlooked Cuzco. Built on a nearby hilltop, it was triangular in shape with walls forming a zig-zag with heights of 21 ft., 16 ft. and 10 ft. (6.5 m., 5 m. and 3 m.), with battlements and ingeniously positioned entrances. Its water supply came from a secret aqueduct, which brought water from a hidden spring. More fortifications were built in case of attack by barbarians from the jungle areas on the main access routes to the *Tahuantinsuyu*, such as in the Paucartambo and Vicañota valleys. These were permanently garrisoned by soldiers who also worked the land. There they maintained houses, their families and even temples.

The most typical example of a fortress-city is Machu Picchu, the last refuge of the Inca Manco after the Spanish conquest—undiscovered until 1912. It is situated 8,200 ft. (2,500 m.) above sea

level in the *sierra* with the Urubamba River below forming the shape of a horseshoe. Built on terraced land, it had a double wall on the side facing the river, with two fortlets built on each of the points that overlooked the *sierra*. A moat ran around the inside wall and its entrance could be blocked with wooden boards. Stone steps ran from terrace to terrace, and an aqueduct running below the wall brought springwater to 16 stone fountains.

Scenes of warfare are common on Mochica ceramics, which are found in museums all over America and Europe. Depicted are warriors with their captives, who are usually naked or have the top part of their bodies uncovered. Their enemies are also seen wearing wearing macabre headdresses, such as head-trophies or arms, and they are armed differently from the Chimú. Professor Kutscher believes that they were a people from a country inland of the coastal region, possibly belonging to the Recuay culture. His hypothesis is that, after unifying the coastal territories, the Mochica launched a campaign for imperial conquest toward the mountains. The piece on the facing page is from the Museo Amano in Lima.

The priests

The priesthood was able to gain power in Amerindian society by proclaiming itself the intermediary between the human and the divine. In moments of difficulty or in times of catastrophe they attributed the disastrous situation to the anger of the gods and warned that circumstances could become even worse if men did not appease the gods and lead better lives, as they had always preached. In this way they were able to control the peasants and ally themselves to the leaders, whom they declared divine, as well as to the warriors, whose warlike mission in life they declared sacred. They thus gained prominence within society, striving to maintain a conservative social order from which they themselves benefited greatly. The result was that everyone, rich and poor alike, ended up at the service of the religious hierarchy.

The holy men normally belonged either to the noble or priestly class, though occasionally boys with exceptional qualities from the lower classes were accepted into their ranks. The priests were trained in the temples together with the nobles, later completing their studies under other teachers and in the service of the gods.

Training consisted of the study of metaphysical knowledge (both cosmogonical and cosmological), ritual, sciences that were the priests' sole patrimony (the calendar system, chronology, divination), healing and above all self-knowledge. It was this last point that distinguished the priests as saintly, and this was achieved by punishing the body by means of prolonged periods of fasting and penance, such as the taking of cold water baths at night and self-mutilation. A life of chastity was also common among the priests. Aztec and Inca priests were celibate and the punishment for fornication was death. In order to demonstrate their austere view of life, they rejected all frivolity, usually wore their hair long and disheveled and put on somberly-colored clothes. Extraordinarily respectful of order, they had an internal organization in which it was necessary to rise step by step. The novices often performed the duties of servants, and there was even a type of lay priest charged with the heavier work.

A distinct priesthood existed among many of the peoples. The Chibcha priests, called *moxas*, were the epitome of saintliness, which is surprising if we consider that they did not choose the post but inherited it through the mother's line. In the case of the Chinantec and Mixtec cultures, they were obliged to abstain from sex for the seven years they served in the temples. The Kougi or Ijca priests (*mames*) were allowed to marry but spent their lives continually fasting, in prayer and on pilgrimages to the highest peaks of the Andes.

At the top of the priestly Aztec hierarchy were the pontiffs Quetzalcoatl Tlaloc Tlamacazqui and Quetzalcoatl Totec Tlamacazqui. Those below were divided into two categories: the *tlamacazque* ("those who give things" or "offerers") and the *tlenamacaque* ("those who give fire"), as well as the novices. Educated in the *calmecac*, they devoted their lives to the cult of the deities and to the care of the temples. They dressed in black and wore their hair long as a symbol of austerity and holiness. The priests took part in the quotidian celebrations in the citizens' lives as well as the religious ceremonies. A well-structured calendar enabled them to impress the people from time to time with their esoteric knowledge.

It would seem that the Inca priests had greater influence at the beginning of the empire, when positions in the priesthood were hereditary and they aspired to positions in public administration. Defeated by the nobles, they were forced to give up their prerogatives, including that of refusing commoners entry into the priesthood. The Inca pontiff, *Villca Humu*, was always the brother or nephew of the emperor, and was revered by all. He was supposed to remain celibate, but Cieza states that he in fact had concubines. The pontiff ate only herbs, drank only water and fasted completely for up to eight days at a time. He lived in the country, not far from the capital, and wore an ankle-length woolen tunic and a gray, brown or black blanket. On ceremonial occasions, he wore a white blanket and a golden breastplate in the shape of a half moon, gold armlets and anklets and a gold mitre bearing the symbol of the sun. He was the supreme judge in all matters relating to religion and presided over the supreme coun-

The deep religiousness of the Andean peoples dates back thousands of years into ancient times, as is testified to by the magnificent Kotosch temple in its Chavín de Huantar pre-Classic splendor. On the coasts of Peru, religion spread extensively during the times of the high cultures of the region. The Sun and Moon pyramids and Mochica religious ceramics are fine examples, and religion was perhaps behind the warlikeness of the Mochica. The fresco above from Penamarca (Peru) shows one aspect of an enigmatic Mochica ritual. We see a high priest dressed in a large cloak, carrying a glass with the religious offering. He is followed by several acolytes, one of whom bears the ceremonial fire. The fresco is in the Museo de Arqueología y Antropología in Lima.

cil, which was made up of either eight or ten high priests. It seems that it was he who appointed the higher clergy, who in turn appointed the lower. The common priests were called the *hatun villca* and looked after the affairs of the cult and of the sacrifices. Their most important tasks were divination and listening to the confessions of their parishioners. Below these were the *humu* or *nacac*, who did not serve as priests all their lives. Finally came the servants, called *legos* (lay friars) by the Spaniards.

Famous for their saintliness and wisdom were the Maya priests. It seems that those who lived in Yucatán or "the New Empire" were no longer required to remain celibate, like the ancient Maya, at least below the level of senior priest, for as Bishop Landa wrote, "He was succeeded by his son or a near relative." He also says that the Maya priesthood hierarchy was made up of priests, *chilanes*, sorcerers, doctors, *chaces* and *nacones*. It was the task of the first to "try to teach their sciences and declare emergencies and their remedies, to preach and officiate on their holy days, make sacrifices and administer their sacraments. The task of the *chilanes* was to give the people the replies of the demons. They were so highly respected that they were carried on the shoulders of others." The Maya priests had the monopoly on the knowledge of the sciences, and their training included "the count of the years, months and days, the holy days and ceremonies, the administering of their sacraments, ill-fated days and times, the manners of divination, the remedies for ills, reading and writing with their letters and characters." They spent their lives in a truly saintly manner, making sacrifices (of copal, India rubber, chicle and humans) and practicing self-mutilation using obsidian knives, flint razors, shark's teeth and maguey thorns. They drew blood from the tongue, ears, arms, legs and even from the penis, as a shocked Landa recounts: "At other times they made filthy and unpleasant sacrifice, gathering in the temple those that did it, and, one after the other, made two holes in the male member, askance, from the side, and passed all the amount of thread through that they could, remaining thus strung together."

The main activity of the priests after attending to the cult of their gods was to make sure that sins

The holiest of all holy men were the Maya priests. These devoted their lives to prayer and sacrifice, frequently offering their own blood to the gods through self-inflicted wounds made with flint knives, shark's teeth and maguey thorns. They extracted blood from the tongue, ears, arms, legs and even from the penis. This was described by an astonished Father Landa: "They did make two holes in the male member." This impressive ceramic figure from the end of the Classic period shows a Maya noble carrying out the sacrificial rite on his penis. The figure is in the American Museum of Natural History in New York.

were not committed by others to offend the deities. As this was extremely difficult, they could be appeased through confession and penance. The Inca went frequently to confession, the Aztec only once in their lives. The transference of guilt to the confessor gave rise to an accumulation of sins, which every so often the priest needed to expiate through special purification ceremonies like those that took place in Cuzco. The Ijca and Kougi *mames* or priests purified themselves by bathing in the waters of a certain Andean lake.

Other duties of the holy men were divination and curing illness (practiced by the Pimas, Pueblos and others). They carried out their cures by diagnosing the cause of the illness from which the patient was suffering—always determined to be sin. Diagnosis was made by hearing confession or divining (the reading of unfavorable omens, often in the entrails of a llama or through the ingestion of hallucinatory drugs). Therapy,

usually consisting of purificatory fasting, bloodletting, offerings to the gods and even pilgrimages, was then prescribed. If the patient's condition did not improve, it was because the gods were still offended, and if he died, then it was because his sins had been so great that he had not been worthy of forgiveness. The holy men were also responsible for making rain.

The subject of religion in Amerindian societies is quite complex. The people did not worship a single god, and it was believed that the inclusion of the gods of other peoples could only strengthen a native religion. Some gods displayed conflicting traits, while others duplicated similar functions. This was especially true of the Aztec, who through their conquests incorporated into their religion Ixcuinin, the Huaxtec goddess of carnal love, sin and confession, calling her Tlazolteotl. They likewise adopted the god Xipe Totec (the flayed one) of the Yopi people of the southwest.

Even rites practiced by other peoples were adopted, such as the flaying of human sacrifices, a practice of the Tlapanec. Their phallic dances came from the Huaxtec and the snake dance from the Maztec.

In addition, a single god could appear to be both one and many beings, representing contradictory or opposing concepts: good-evil, young-old, man-woman. In this way the Maya god of creation, Itzamna, was during the daytime both the sun god, Kinich Ahau, and Bolon Dzcab, the patron of royalty. The Aztec had four *Tezcatlipocas* (black, red, blue and white), each of which was one, single god: the red god was Xipe Totec, the blue was Huitzilopochtli (god of war and at the same time the midday sun), and white was Quetzalcoatl, god of the Cholula merchants; the black god, of darkness and sorcery, retained the name Tezcatlipoca. It has been said that the 166 Aztec gods were all manifestations of the

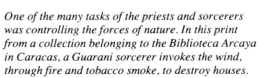

Along with other tribes from El Chaco, the Charrua of Paraguay shared the belief that death could be caused by evil spirits. The hopeless case was left to his fate so that he would not affect the other members of the group and was expected to dig his own grave, as we see depicted in this print from Manners and Customs of the Peoples, *published in Paris in 1914 and now belonging to the Biblioteca Arcaya in Caracas.*

One of the many tasks of the priests and sorcerers was controlling the forces of nature. In this print from a collection belonging to the Biblioteca Arcaya in Caracas, a Guarani sorcerer invokes the wind, through fire and tobacco smoke, to destroy houses.

The shaman's powers of healing had to be demonstrated by an immunity to poisonous creatures capable of killing normal human beings. Not only were they able to cure bites inflicted by snakes, scorpions and other malignant creatures, but they would also play with these to demonstrate their great gifts. In this print from The Indian Tribes of Guayana *(London, 1868), we see a shaman from the Orinoco region.*

Most religious beliefs were based on animism. The Canella and Kainkang of Brazil believed that all of nature was divided into opposites. This print, from Natural History of the Orinoco, *shows a ritual dance performed by Brazilian Indians in which evil spirits were expelled through the inhalation of tobacco smoke and the sound of rattles. The ground is possibly being made ready for sowing.*

same deity. Though this is an oversimplification, it reveals the complex nature of the Amerindians' belief.

By the time of the arrival of the Spaniards, religious integration, particularly in the case of the Aztec, was still not complete, making matters even more contradictory. Thus their god of creation, Tloque Nahuaque, was worshiped only by an elite group of poets and priests, yet hardly at all by the common people. King Netzahuacoyotl, the great intellectual, erected a temple to Tloque Nahuaque, but there was no idol or representation of the god in the temple because he remained an abstraction.

It is difficult to distinguish between the religious (the world of the beliefs controlled by the priests) and the magical (that of the sorcerers and shamans). The one group petitioned the gods, while the other claimed some of their power, but in any case the two became interwoven. In fact, in Amerindian religious, magical, animistic and fetishistic phenomena all coexisted. Animism was widespread across the continent, particularly among those peoples who lived in forests and jungles. The practice of animism was derived in large part from the belief in the soul or spirit of the dead, as we shall see. The Algonquians believed that all living things, objects and natural phenomena contained latent energy, a spiritual force given by the powers of the supreme being who had created the world. This force was called *manitu* and was different from the soul of the object. The Inca believed in the *huacas*—material beings with supernatural powers. These could be rivers, strange-looking rocks, a pair of twins—in all cases, something extraordinary. Some were good, others bad, and offerings had to be made to them. The most elementary of these beings were the *apachitas*, which lived in places where it was difficult to pass. Travelers normally added a stone to a pile when they had to pass.

The Taino believed that the spirits who lived in woods and wild places shook the branches of the trees. In order to harness this power, they cut down the trees and made idols with the wood. The peoples of the Caribbean islands also thought that the woods were full of *mapoya* or malicious spirits, like trolls, against whom it was necessary to defend oneself by carrying a talisman made of

wood in the form of a small idol. The Canella and Kaingkang of Brazil believed all of nature to be animist and classified their world into opposites: day-night, sun-moon, drought-rain, red-black. The Algonquians saw the existence of good and evil spirits on the earth and in the water. The Araucanians held that there were an infinite number of evil spirits in nature—some of which materialized in the form of snakes, comets, vampires—and that each man had another self, a double spirit that left the body to walk in the world of the dead while the first slept. According to the beliefs of many Amazonian peoples, this other spirit could work evil magic and discover truths unknown to others.

There existed in the Amerindian world both sympathetic and homeopathic magic, the two often working together. One example of the former was the Zapotec custom of tilling a new field and transferring to it the fertility of an old one by means of an ear of corn fashioned into a talisman,

which was buried in the virgin soil. One example of homeopathic magic is the Inca custom of making sure that no one had access to their spittle, hair or nail parings so that these could not be used for evil purposes against them. The realm of magic was immense, while, unfortunately, what we know of it remains incomplete.

The afterlife

The existence of life after death was not a universally held belief among the Amerindians; even less so was the view that there was a direct relation between life after death and one's moral behavior during life. For them, the spirits of the dead could go to a celestial world or heaven, to an underworld, or nowhere at all. In some areas it was even believed that the afterlife existed only for the great lords and not for the common people.

Nonetheless the idea that the dead went to *some* place, from where they sometimes tried to escape and return to the world of the living, was widespread. In Amazonia, for example, it was thought that the spirits of the dead wandered in the jungle, taking on the form of dwarves, giants and animals like the *yurupary* (or jaguar for the Tupi of the eastern regions), constantly lying in wait to pounce on man. The peoples of El Chaco believed that the spirits took on the form of old people or winged children and harassed the living; old people and children for whom there was no hope of recovery from illness or an accident were killed to prevent their bodies being taken over by these spirits. The Chiriguano and Chané Indians of the Alto Pilcomayo and Santa Cruz de la Sierra regions believed that the spirits of the dead took on the form of the fox, visiting the living during the day and returning to the east, where they held their feasts, at night. The Kagaba, a group from the Colombian Andes region, believed that the dead dwelled on the highest peaks, making journeys into the mountains dangerous.

Perhaps it was because of these fears that the dead were commonly transported to a place so distant that it would be difficult for them to return. For the Algonquians this site lay in the west, on the other side of a great river that could only be crossed by a narrow bridge made of a springy and slippery tree trunk. For the Araucanians the dead went to a sort of paradise beyond the sea, where they would be happy and would not wish to return. The journey to this place was full of danger and had to be undertaken with the help of the sorcerers, who changed themselves into canoes or whales to help the traveler across. The Chimú sent the spirits of their dead beyond the sea to the Guano islands, believing that seals accompanied the traveler on his journey. Of course certain peoples—the Inca particularly—

Great cemeteries were built in the Valley of Chancay and even in Ancon from the end of Tiahuanaco until the age of the Inca, when funeral bundles painted red (a magic color of protection) were buried and surrounded by offerings to the gods. These bundles, from the Chancay culture, had false heads, which were covered with wooden or cloth masks similar to those above. Prominent noses imitating the beaks of birds, and on many occasions human hair and cloth headpieces, were added as shown on the right. The mask on the left has two eyes of shell. The masks are in the Museo de Arqueología y Antropología in Lima.

The Chimú culture, heir to the Mochica though much later in time (between 1100 and 1460, when it was dominated by the Inca), also expressed its belief in life after death in its ceramics. Bound for the world of the dead, the soul of the deceased set off on a long journey by sea, called Ni. *Carved on this Chimú pitcher is the journey taken by the soul on a* totora *boat, similar to those so common today on the coasts of Peru and on Lake Titicaca. The craft is rowed by an expert oarsman. The piece is in the Museo de Arqueología y Antropología in Lima.*

did believe that the afterlife was linked to one's moral behavior on earth. Those who had been good went to paradise, while those who were bad were condemned to hell, where it was always cold and they ate only stones.

It was more common to determine the destination of the spirit according to a person's station in life or with the way in which he had died. The Araucanian leaders and warriors went to the volcanoes and clouds, while the poor were consigned to an underworld, where they suffered eternal poverty. The Aztec believed that men who had died in combat or had been sacrificed and women who had died in childbirth went to the heaven of the sun. Once there they accompanied him on his daily journey through the sky, the men in the morning and the women in the afternoon. Those who were struck by lightning, died from drowning, or suffered a bloating illness (like dropsy or gout) went to a different world, called *tlalocan*, where the rain god, Tlaloc, lived, ruling over a paradise of trees, plants and food. The rest of the dead went to *mictlan*, an underworld in the north, where Mictlantecuhtli and Mictecacihuatl, the lord and lady of death, lived. This required a difficult four-year journey on which it was necessary to pass a series of ordeals, such as crossing rivers and snow-covered mountain peaks.

213

Creation myths

The explanation of the origin of the world and of man greatly influenced beliefs about one's conduct in life. The different cosmogonies gave rise to literature of great beauty, most of which has unfortunately been lost. Curiously, some peoples thousands of kilometers apart were found to share the same myths, suggesting hitherto unknown migrations of peoples in the remote past. Both the Algonquian Denes and the El Chaco Chamakoko and Matako, for example, believed that man was born of a woman mating with a dog. Both the North American Muskogee and the Aztec believed that their ancestors had emerged from caves in the west. The Sioux, like the Maya, believed in the legend of several defective versions of man being made before he was finally perfected. The central Californians had one of the most interesting explanations of all: The supreme being created heaven and earth from nothing and then made man and his world, being constantly hindered by the coyote, the cause of all the world's troubles and imperfection.

South America offered some extraordinary examples of cosmogonical legends as well. The Chibcha believed mankind was created by Bachue, a female deity who appeared on the Andean Lake Iguaque with her son, mated with him and gave birth to the human species. Bachue later returned to the lake and changed herself into a snake (the symbol of fertility). Men sinned against the code of Bachue and the god Chibchacum punished them by sending a deluge that flooded the savanna of Bogota, the Chibcha's homeland. There then appeared the great hero Bochica, riding in from the east on the rainbow. He dropped his golden scepter at one end of the mountain range, breaking the mountain and creating the Tequendama Falls, thus draining the savanna and enabling the Chibcha to farm their land once more. Bochica then pun-

The highest pre-Columbian cultures in Colombia were the Tairona and the Muisca, both of which belonged to the Chibcha-speaking linguistic group. Their greatest ceremonial center was San Agustín, in the department of Huila, near the village of the same name. Here a complex culture developed several centuries before Christ and flourished until the 12th century A.D., when it vanished for still unknown reasons. The Mesoamerican and Andean peoples of

Olmec and Chavín influence converged in San Agustín though with the passing of the centuries these merged. Characteristic of San Agustín are large monoliths of as much as 13 feet (4 meters) in height, carved with figures of priests, workers and gods with broad noses and feline mouths, with protruding and crossed jaguar fangs. Above we see two such figures, possibly ceremonial masks.

ished Chibchacum by making him carry the world on his shoulders; earthquakes occur when he is shifting the world from one shoulder to the other. The legend of the flood was also common in Ecuador, where it was believed to have been caused when the children of the first man killed a mythical serpent, the symbol of the phallus of the father.

The coast dwellers of Peru tell the myth of Pachacamac: The sun, Con, made the fruit and maize grow but his heat turned the coastal region into a desert and Pachacamac, the creator of men, expelled him from the region. Another legend tells of how Pachacamac killed the son of the sun, dismembered him and planted the pieces, which became the fruit of the earth. Another of Con's children then appeared, chased Pachacamac away and set fire to the air, burning the earth and changing the men fathered by Pachacamac into stones. Con then made gold, silver and copper rain down from the sky, which gave rise to the present race of men. Many of the peoples of Amazonia, such as the Makushi, the Bakairi, the Tupi and the Yurakare believed that the animals were the masters of the plants until the twin sons of the sun came along and took them away, giving them to men.

One of the most important legends was that of the four ages or four suns. It has been considered pre-Maya and pan-Mesoamerican but it is, in fact, pan-American, as it was also recorded in the Andean region. The Maya version is to be found in the *Popol Vuh*, where the failed attempts of the gods to create man are recounted. The myth begins with these words: "This is the story of how all was still, all quiet, in silence; there was no movement, no sound, and the whole of the sky was empty." The myth tells of how men were first made of clay, then of sticks and then of straw. They were unable to move, understand or speak and so were destroyed. The creator then made men of corn—the Maya—who could move, understand, speak and revere their maker.

Closely linked to the myth of creation was the understanding of its place in the universe—also propagated by the priests and magicians. It was commonly believed that the world was the center of the universe, the sun, the moon and the stars moving around it. The world was thought of as a

216

The Maya believed that flint and obsidian had been created when the rays of the sun hit the surface of the earth, and it is for this reason that they associated the two materials with the origin of the world, consequently ascribing to them sacred qualities. Above, flint gives form to the god K, through the act of smoking. The spiral of smoke crowns the head of the god as hair. The unique carving of these Classic period axes required the most careful of techniques to transform the sacred material into a religious object. The piece is in the Cleveland Art Museum.

Though according to the Popol Vuh *man was made from the thoughts and words of Tepeu and Gucumatz, the god of the heavens (which were divided into 13 layers) was Itzamna, who was represented either as a reptile made up of a snake, the crocodile and the iguana—as may be seen below on the ceremonial altar in Copán, Guatemala—or as an old, toothless man, who also appears in the codices. The Maya also believed that the surface of the earth was a reptile called Itzam Cab Ain, who was possibly another manifestation of Itzamna. Below the surface was the underworld, divided into nine compartments, each of which was ruled by one of the nine lords of night.*

flat surface, at times seen as having emerged from the waters. The Maya believed it was an island or an alligator with 13 heavens above, each one ruled by a different god, all of whom, in turn, were ruled by the iguana-reptile god Itzamna. Below the earth were nine underworlds, each with its respective god who together were the nine lords of night and were known as the *bolontiku*. This is naturally a Post-Classic interpretation, with a strong Mexican influence. For the Aztec, there were 13 heavens, where all the gods lived, each heaven presided over by a particular deity. They believed that there were nine layers of the underworld and that from the ninth down was the domain of Mictlantecuhtli, the lord of death. The sun rose in the east, climbing through the 13 heavens. When it reached the top at noon, it began its descent until it reached the west and commenced a pilgrimage through the perilous underworld, where it could be captured.

217

The useful gods

The rain god, Tlaloc, was deeply venerated by the Aztec and, together with Huitzilopochtli, occupied a special place in the great temple of Tenochtitlan. He presided over the group of fertility divinities and was adopted by the Aztec from previous cultures. He was represented in various forms; below, from Veitia Codex, *he appears as a warrior holding a snake as a weapon.*

The Amerindian found gods everywhere, and for every purpose. The supreme god was not necessarily always the creator, nor did he have to be male, nor be the most worshiped. Nonetheless, a belief in a supreme being was common. The Algonquian Ojibway tribes believed that their principal god communicated with men through an intermediary called the great hare. The Patagone, Ona and *pampa*-dwelling tribes also believed in a supreme being. The Patagone called this god Sesom, who lived in the sky and viewed the affairs of man with indifference. For the Yahgan of Tierra del Fuego he was called Watinanauewa, meaning "the very ancient one," and he was the lord—though not the creator—of the visible world, the master of all the animals and the guardian of moral law. It was he who sent a soul to each man when he was born and recovered it when he died. The Taino called their supreme being Yocahu. He lived in the sky and gave them *yucca* (a Taino word) to feed them. They could not address him directly but had to do so through the *zemi*, or small idols made of wood or stone in which he lived. The creator and supreme being of the Witoto people was Moma, who made men, the animals, the plants and the sky. He lived beneath the earth and each year renewed the vegetation.

The supreme being of the Chorotega was female and lived in the volcano Masaya. The Kagaba of Colombia also believed in a female creator and called her Gauteovan. The Cueva Indians had a supreme being as as well, and the Araucanians called theirs Ngune Mapun or "lord of the earth." The Botocudo believed that theirs was responsible for natural phenomena and sickness and that he killed men and then devoured them. To the Nicarao he was called Tamajestad. The supreme god of the Maya was Itzamna, who was represented as a reptile and iguana. For the Inca he was Viracocha— the word used by the Spanish chroniclers. It was he who made the earth, the sky and a generation of men who sinned against him, for which they were turned into stones. Viracocha created the sun and the moon and placed a lord called Alcaviza in Cuzco. He then traveled to the north and later to the west across the sea. Statues at Tiahuanaco commemorate him.

In addition to the supreme being, various other gods inhabited the heavens. Apart from the well-known cult to the sun, there were also those to the moon and, to a lesser degree, the stars. The Chimú believed Si, or the moon, to be more important than the sun, as it could shine not only at night but also sometimes in the daytime and was even able to blot the sun out during eclipses. Si's servants were the stars. The moon was also worshiped by the Chibcha (called Chia), by the Araucanians (who completely ignored the sun), and by the Inca, who called it Quilla and believed it to be the wife and sister of the sun. The Cayapo of eastern Brazil also worshiped the moon, and when there was an eclipse, they shot fire arrows up into the sky to give it back its light, while at the same time singing mournful songs. For the Aztec, the moon was Coyolxauhqui, who was decapitated by Huitzilopochtli when she was born. A figure of Coyolxauqui is positioned at the foot of the main temple in Tenochtitlan.

The god of the rain was the most widely worshipped of all deities. This god was, in fact, worshiped all over Mesoamerica from the time of Tenochtitlan onward. To the Maya he was Chac and was always depicted with a large proboscis. The Aztec called him Tlaloc and kept his image next to Huitzilopochtli's on the main altar

The rain god was worshiped all over Mesoamerica from the Formative period onward and was represented in different forms, according to the culture. In these lithographs taken from the Atlas of the Ancient Mexicans, *we see two such representations. The one above is a Zapotec funeral urn from Oaxaca, in which he is wearing a large headdress and numerous ornaments. The figure at bottom right is Pitao Cozobi, a divinity associated with the rain*

god; Pitao Cozobi was also the god of the fruits of the earth, as worshiped by the Zapotec.

The 18 months of the religious calendar included days celebrating various gods, two of which are depicted in these illustrations from the Veitia Codex. *The one on the left is Xilomalisti, whose day was in March, in honor of the water; the one on the right is Huchpanitzli, whose day was celebrated in September.*

at Tenochtitlan. Other natural phenomena, such as storms, thunder, rainbows and lightning were also worshiped. The Diaguita honored both the

thunder and the lightning. The Cueva worshipped the goddess of thunder, whom they called Dobayba. The Inca revered storms, whose god was Illapa, the thunder and the lightning. They believed that when he used his sling the thunder sounded and that the stone he threw created the lightning. The stone broke a pitcher full of water carried by his sister, and this was the reason for rain. The brilliance of his clothes when he walked flashed in the sky.

Another group of gods was identified with the earth, the sea, the mountains and the lakes. The Chimú goddess of the sea was called Ni and her sacred creature was the whale. The Cañari and Chibcha, as well as many other Andean peoples in Ecuador and Colombia, worshiped the lakes, the snow-capped mountains and the volcanoes. Among the Cañari, the Purhua worshiped two principal gods, one male and one female, who lived in Chimborazo and Tungurahua. The Inca also worshiped lakes.

The cultural heroes who had taught men how to cultivate the land, weave, build houses and other important skills were also considered gods. The deity of the Lenca (who lived in what is now El Salvador) was a woman called Comizahual or "flying jaguar," who had given men civilization and her own sons as princes. She went up to

heaven in the form of a bird, to the accompaniment of thunder and lightning. The cultural hero of the Ona was Kenos, who had been a compan-

The Inca also had religious festivals, which were held once a month, portrayed in the work of Huaman Poma. Here we see those held in August and September. August, Ocpac Quilla *(at right), was ruled by the sun and the moon, who appear in the top corners of the picture. September,* Ocoya Raymi Quilla *(above), was ruled by the moon and associated with female fertility.*

219

This imposing sculpture of Coatlicue (below) measures almost seven feet (two meters) tall, from the Museo de Antropología in Mexico. Coatlicue was the mother of all the Aztec gods, and the sculpture perfectly represents a terrifying power. A necklace of human skulls, hands and hearts rests below a double snake head with terrible fangs. Her skirt is made of entwined snakes, while at her feet is the earth monster, in the form of tiger's claws. Among her in-

numerable children was Huitzilopochtli, the god of war, who was conceived when Coatlicue was made pregnant by a feather that had fallen from heaven (the soul of a human sacrifice).

ion of the creator, Temaukely, and given their ancestors a code of morality. The Patagone had a similar hero. The Maya praised Itzamna, who had taught men how to write. The hero of the Aztec was Quetzalcoatl, the civilizer, a figure they had adopted from the Toltec. The Nicarao also identified their creator with the civilizer of the world, so that theirs was a god similar to Quetzalcoatl.

Another class of god were the patrons of the merchants, the potters, the weavers, etc., and there were as well the many house gods. One of the greatest of these was Huitzilopochtli, the Aztec god of war. The Aztec had brought him along on their long wanderings and according to tradition he was the son of Coatlicue ("she of the skirt of snakes") or the earth goddess, who had had many children before Huitzilopochtli. These included the moon, Coyolxauhqui, and the stars or Centzonhuitznahua ("the innumerable ones of the south"). Coatlicue was made pregnant by a feather that had fallen from heaven (the soul released in a sacrifice), which offended her children, who decided that the only way to put right such a disgrace was to kill her. When she was on the peak of Coatepec (the mountain of the serpent), her children made ready to carry out their plan, but it was then that Huitzilopochtli was born, coming to the world fully grown and heavily armed. He cut off the head of his sister, the moon, and his other brothers and sisters took flight. He chased, caught and killed them all. This myth is in reality an explanation of the succession of day and night, when the sun kills the moon and stars. It was depicted in the great temple of Tenochtitlan, at the top of which (as in the temple at Coatapec) stood the god Huitzilopochtli and at the foot a stone block bearing the image of the moon.

To appease the anger of the gods or simply to ask favors, it was necessary to perform certain ceremonies. These ranged in complexity, depending on the importance of the occasion. The simplest of all was prayer or dancing, one common example of this being the snake dance of the Hopi, the object of which was to bring rain. The most complex of the ceremonies was the Aztec human sacrifice. A ceremony was usually held in the temple. After prayer, songs and dances, something of great value was offered to the gods. In

the Classic period, the Maya burnt *copal*, India rubber, *chicle* and food. The early Inca offered human sacrifice, but later used coca, *chicha*, feathers, guinea pigs, fine cloth made by the virgins of the sun, and especially llamas. Every day at dawn a white llama was killed in the temple

of the sun in Cuzco. It was placed facing the *huaca* and its head cut off. Its heart and lungs were then torn out and the image of the sun sprinkled with its blood. At some of the major celebrations hundreds of llamas were sacrificed. If the ceremony was not performed with extreme

221

legend of the four suns, their cosmogonical myth, the gods in Tenochtitlan had sacrificed themselves so that mankind could live. It was due to this fact that the sun existed, but it continually needed life fluid, blood or *chalchihuatl* to remain alive. If it did not have this succor, the sun would lose its strength, cease moving, go dark and bring about the end of the fifth sun.

The sacrificial victim was placed on a slightly concave stone, four priests holding his arms and legs while a fifth opened up the chest with a flint knife, took out the still-beating heart and offered it to the gods. More human sacrifices were made when a new *tlatoani* was crowned or a new temple consecrated. Durán wrote that in the consecration ceremony of the great temple of Ahuizotl, 80,400 human sacrifices were made. This figure, however, can only be an exaggeration.

The sacrifice ended with the ritual of cannibalism, which symbolized the communion of men with the sacrificed god. By eating part of the flesh of the man who had been the living representative of the god, men could become gods themselves. This ceremonial banquet has been the subject of several scientific interpretations,

Bloody sacrifices were made, to a greater or lesser extent, to all the Aztec divinities to ensure their continued protection of the nation. In this picture from the Tudela Codex, *we see one of the many gods of* pulque, *possibly Patecatl, the husband of Mayauel and god of medicine, with blood pouring out of his mouth. Mayauel was the goddess of the maguey as well as fertility.*

care, great misfortunes such as droughts or torrential rain could ensue. The temple where these rites were performed was not where the sun god was worshiped, which took place in the great *plaza* opposite the temple.

Human sacrifice was performed by many of the peoples of pre-Columbian America. Among these were the Nicarao, the Chibcha (who sacrificed children on hilltops), the Tarasco (in honor of the sun), the Zapotec, the Totonac, the Purhua of Ecuador (who poured the blood of the sacrifice down the gullet of a clay idol), the Cañari (who sacrificed 100 children each year to ensure a good corn harvest) and the Chimú (who sacrificed children to their moon deity). The Maya offered human sacrifices in the final stage of their empire, and the Inca resorted to it in times of crisis, such as when they were at war, when there were epidemics, when the Inca emperor was seriously ill and when a new Inca came to the throne.

The idea of human sacrifice and the subsequent ceremonial banquet on the flesh is certainly something difficult for modern man to understand. Let us for a moment try to view this phenomenon within the cultural context of the Aztec, the people who practiced it most often. In the

one of which is that human flesh supplied the Aztec with the proteins that were missing in their normal diet. But the amount of flesh eaten would be minimal and, moreover, those eating the flesh belonged to the best fed group in Aztec society—the nobles—whose abundant supply of proteins came from fish and game. In any case, the Aztec diet already consisted of much protein, as they ate large amounts of kidney beans. Another theory

222

The Aztec practiced self-mutilation to offer their own blood to the gods, as we see in the picture below from the Tudela Codex. *One is piercing his ear with a knife, while another pierces his tongue. The ultimate sacrifice, a human life, is shown at the top of the picture. Human sacrifice was practiced in times of great catastrophe, the victim being placed on a stone slab and held down by several priests, while another cut out the heart with an obsidian*

knife. The heart was then offered to the god, shown here with a heart between its claws.

holds that human sacrifice was a form of population control, but this is not likely either, since the greater part of the victims were prisoners of war, and the number of Aztec children sacrificed was much lower than the number of adults.

The Aztec obsession with preserving the order of their world reached hysterical proportions every 52 years, when the ends of the religious and solar calendars coincided. On that last night, all the fires in all the hearths in the land were put out, the women shut themselves up in their houses, those in labor were afraid of giving birth to monsters and men did penance, while the priests studied the sky to see if there would be a new dawn or not. When the astronomer-priest thought he had found favorable signs, he gave the order for the sacrifice to be made. A prisoner was placed on the ceremonial stone on the Estrella hill, his chest opened and the fire stick introduced. By means of some clever manipulation, a flame would be made to burst forth from the chest of the victim, signaling a new dawn and giving rise to general rejoicing. Messengers then lit their torches from the flame and took the sacred fire to

all the hearths, where hope was reborn. Slowly the sun would begin to appear over the horizon, and all men could once more bask in its heat and light. Thanks to the Aztec's human sacrifices, the sun would continue its journey.

After the sacrifice, the victim's flesh was devoured in a great ceremonial banquet, which horrified the Spaniards. In this picture from the Tudela Codex *(above), we see a priest distributing the limbs of a victim while others eat. Some dishes are full of arms and legs, and the terrible legend "Here they eat human flesh" is included.*

223

Epilogue: the monsters thrown up by the sea

Early in the morning of October 12, 1492, the Taino of Guanahani Island saw several strange and gigantic sea monsters come up to their shores. The monsters stayed there all night long, as if lying in wait. At dawn they saw that the monsters stirred, and when the sun reached its greatest splendor canoes carrying men different from themselves came out of the monsters and landed on the beach. These men spoke an unknown language, their bodies were completely covered, and they had hair on their faces. They used sticks that cut the flesh when one ran one's hand along the edge. It seemed that they wished to trade, for they displayed objects that the Indians had never seen before, in exchange for cotton thread, parrots and gold ornaments. The Taino were unable to warn the Amerindians of this amazing visit, but the gods did, alerting especially the Aztec and Inca, for it was they who revered the gods most of all.

The first warning was given to Motecuhzoma Xocoyotzin (Moctezuma). A priest of Huitzilopochtli told him that a comet had appeared in the east. The *tlatoani* was surprised that his astrologers had not given him the news and went over to the observatory in person to see for himself. Indignant, he had the astrologers arrested and starved to death for their carelessness. It was not long before another priest from Texcoco told him that a local peasant had had a fantastic dream, which foretold evil things. He had said that he had been snatched by an eagle and had been taken up into a cave, where he had seen Moctezuma. The local *tlatoani* had given him some roses and a smoking cane and told him to breathe in the smoke. Then he had told him to go to Tenochtitlan and wound his king in the thigh with the smoking stick and tell him that his reign was about to end. Moctezuma was astonished, for he had had a similar dream and on his thigh was a burn from a smoking cane. He then consulted his augurs, who were unable to advise him.

A short time later, even worse news arrived. A man from the coast had seen moving hills on the sea. The *tlatoani* had him locked up as a madman, but he had the story verified in secret and discovered that several coast-dwellers had said that houses had appeared on the sea and that

men with hair on their faces and dressed in a type of blanket they had never before seen had come out of the houses. Fortunately, they had gone back and left in the same houses they had arrived in.

Several moons later, the *tlatoani* was told that many houses of the same kind had arrived and spat forth a great number of those strange beings on the beach at Ulua. Moctezuma ordered food to be taken to them to see if they needed to eat like human beings and asked that pictures of them be painted. His orders were carried out at once, and Aztec painters faithfully reproduced what they had seen on their *amatl paper*. When the *tlatoani* saw the paintings he was very troubled and called his sages and aged counselors to ask them if they had ever seen their like in the ancient scriptures. Some said that they had seen scriptures that spoke of men with one eye in the middle of the forehead, others that they had seen books in which there were paintings of men who were half man and half fish, but none had ever seen anything like the bearded creatures in the paintings.

Moctezuma then called in an old man from Xochimilco who was famous for the great number of prophecies he had in his possession. This man explained that in some books it was written that men similar to those in the paintings would come riding in wooden carriages. They would be white and dressed in many-colored clothes, with round objects covering their heads. The prophecy warned that these men would take possession of the land and would multiply. The *tlatoani* ordered the book brought to him, and when he saw it, he could see that the men mentioned in it seemed to be very much like those who had come out of the wooden sea-houses. And so he was convinced that his reign was coming to an end.

The gods also warned the Inca Huayna Capac. The *amautas* announced that odd things were happening in the empire and that the sky, the sea and the earth appeared strange. A comet had been observed in the sky, and in the *plaza* in Cuzco two extraordinary birds had fought to the death.

Finally, in July 1528, the Chasqui brought grave news. The sea had thrown up some strange creatures, human in shape but with heads adorned with snow and red wool below the mouths. Their feet were covered in black stars, and they had slings that made a sound like thunder when they were used. Huayna Capac was in Quito at the

The arrival of the Spaniards was preceded by strange events foreboding the coming disaster. Throughout the year a column of fire was seen in the middle of the night, and two temples were destroyed, one suddenly by fire and the other by a bolt of lightning that came without thunder. Later a comet appeared that had not been predicted by the astrologers. Moctezuma himself saw it and had the astrologers starved to death in punishment. Another strange sign was the appearance of waves on the lake at Texcoco. Finally, monsters appeared and the huey tlatoani himself had a dream in which he was told that his reign was soon to end. In this picture from the Durán Codex *we see Moctezuma gazing at the strange comet.*

Moctezuma was warned, but he refused to believe that houses would come out of the sea bearing men with hair on their faces who wore blankets such as had never been seen before. In 1519 this very thing happened in Cempoala. The sea threw up many of those strange creatures onto the beach. Moctezuma ordered his tlacuiloque *or painters to take account of everything that happened and to record it on paper. This they did, and the* huey tlatoani *was able*

to see something similar to this picture from the Durán Codex*: houses that moved on the sea and the men who came inside them. When he saw them he was puzzled and consulted the wise men, one of whom told him that these creatures, who would come to kill the Aztec, had been mentioned in a certain book of prophecies.*

time and did not pay much attention to the reports. He simply hurried on his journey back to Cuzco.

But the Chasqui again brought disquieting news. From the coast to the mountains a terrible illness was raging, killing men, women and children of all classes. It had reached the convents where the emperor's wives were dying. Even the virgins of the sun and the noblest families in Cuzco were falling victims to the terrible scourge.

The emperor himself began to feel ill and ordered the Pachacamac oracle consulted. The oracle advised the Inca to soak up the rays of the sun. But Father Sun could not stop the Inca from dying of smallpox in Quito and leaving the empire on the verge of civil war between Huascar and Atahualpa at a time when the sea would throw up onto the shores of Peru many more of the men with red wool on their faces.

The houses and hills that moved on the sea continued to bring bearded men, and the hurricane of the conquest devastated the American peoples. This is how the *Chilam Balam de Chumayel* recounts the arrival of the Europeans in Maya territory:

"In the 11th Ahau Katun, the first that is counted, is the first katun. Ichcaansiho, Face-of-the-birth-of-the-sky, was the seat of the *katun* which saw the arrival of the foreigners with the red beards, eyes of the sun, the light-colored men.

"Alas! Let us bewail their arrival!

"From the east they came, when the bearded men arrived in this land, the messengers of the sign of divinity, the foreigners of the earth, the red-bearded men…the beginning of the Flower of May.

"Alas, Itza, Sorcerer-of-the-water, for the white cowards come from the sky, the white sons of heaven! The blow of the white man shall come down, it shall come from the sky, everywhere it shall come, at dawn you shall see the sign that announces it.

"Alas! Let us bewail their coming, the arrival of the great pilers of stones, the great pilers of beams for building, the false *ibteeles* of the earth

who shoot fire at the ends of their arms, who muffle themselves up in their blankets, those with ropes to hang the lords!

"A different tribute shall you pay tomorrow and the day after; this is what comes, my children. Prepare to bear the weight of misery that comes to your villages, for this *katun* that sits is the *katun* of misery, the katun of strife with the devil, strife in the 11th Ahau.

"Oh, you younger brothers and sisters, oh, you elder brothers and sisters, the word of the God of the sky and the earth, receive your visitors, the bearded men, the messengers of the sign of God, who come to establish themselves as your elder brothers, the lords who shall mark the stone from now on, the *Ah Tantunes*, those who shall ask you for many generations of gods."

The conquest silenced the shell horns and drums of the Aztec temples. A deathly silence took possession of the pre-Columbian cities before the new Hispanoamerican cities arose out of their ashes.

225

Bibliography

There are numerous accessible volumes on pre-Columbian America for the general reader. *Atlas of Ancient America* (Facts On File, 1986), by Michael Coe, Dean Snow and Elizabeth Benson provides a good introduction to the many cultures that rose and fell in this region. See also *Mysteries of the Ancient Americas: The New World Before Columbus* (Reader's Digest, 1986); *The Art of Mesoamerica* (Thames & Hudson, 1986), by Mary E. Miller; *Pre-Columbian Art* (Abrams, 1983), by Jose Alcina Franch; and *Sweat of the Sun and Tears of the Moon: Gold and Silver in Pre-Columbian Art* (Hacker, 1977), by Andre Emmerich. More advanced are Muriel P. Weaver's *Aztecs, Maya and Their Predecessors: Archaeology of Mesoamerica* (Academic Press, 1981); Richard E. Blanton's *Ancient Mesoamerica: A Comparison of Changes in Three Regions* (Cambridge University Press, 1982); *Ancient North Americans, Ancient South Americans* (Freeman, 1983, 2 vols.), edited by Jesse D. Jennings; and *Archaeology of West and Northwest Mesoamerica* (Westview Press, 1985), edited by Michael S. Foster. The definitive text, at least in scope, is the 16-volume *Handbook of Middle American Indians* (University of Texas Press), edited by Robert Wauchope.

To learn more about the Olmec, Mesoamerica's first complex culture, see Roman Pina Chan's *Olmec: Mother Culture of Mesoamerica* (Rizzoli, 1989); Ignacio Bernal's *Olmec World* (University of California Press, 1969); Robert J. Sharer's *The Olmec and the Development of Formative Meso-american Civilisation* (Cambridge University Press, 1989); and the two-volume *Land of the Olmec* (University of Texas, 1980), by Michael D. Coe and Richard A. Diehl, which focuses specifically on recent archaeological excavations in Tenochtitlan.

For more on the Toltec culture, which served almost as an inspiration to the Aztec, Richard A. Diehl's *Tula: The Toltec Capital of Ancient Mexico* (Thames & Hudson, 1983) and *The Toltec Heritage: From the Fall of Tula to the Rise of Tenochtitlan* (University of Oklahoma Press, 1980), by Nigel Davies, are useful.

There's no lack of books on the Aztec themselves, and the reader is referred to the volumes *The Aztecs* (Rizzoli, 1989), by Eduardo Matos Moctezuma; *Daily Life of the Aztecs on the Eve of the Spanish Conquest* (Stanford University Press, 1961), by Jacques Soustelle; *The Aztec Empire: The Toltec Resurgence* (University of Oklahoma Press, 1987), by Nigel Davies; *The Aztec Arrangement: The Social History of Pre-Spanish Mexico* (University of Oklahoma Press, 1985), by Rudolf van Zantwijk; and *Aztec Thought and Culture: A Study of the Ancient Nahuatl Mind* (University of Oklahoma Press, 1982), by Miguel Leon-Portilla.

The incredible bureaucracy and structure of the Inca is covered in detail in Sally F. Moore's *Power and Property in Inca Peru* (Greenwood Press, 1973), and in *The Inca and Aztec States, Fourteen Hundred to Eighteen Hundred: Anthropology and History* (Academic Press, 1982), edited by George Collier. The scholar Burr Cartwright Brundage has written numerous studies of Mesoamerican cultures, including *Empire of the Inca* (University of Oklahoma, 1985) and *Lords of Cuzco: A History and Description of the Inca People in Their Final Days* (University of Oklahoma Press, 1985), and a comparative study, *Two Earths, Two Heavens: an Essay Concerning the Aztecs and the Incas* (University of New Mexico, 1975).

For more information about the Maya, see *Blood of Kings: Dynasty and Ritual in Maya Art* (Braziller, 1986), by Linda Schele and Jeffrey H. Miller, which includes important new information on the deciphering of the Maya hieroglyphic code in 1960; *Lords of the Underworld: Masterpieces of Classical Mayan Ceramics* (Princeton University Press, 1978), by Michael D. Coe; *Ceremonial Centers of the Maya* (University of Florida Press, 1974), by Roy C. Craven Jr., William E. Bullard Jr., and Michael E. Kapne; and *The Ancient Maya* (Stanford University Press, 1983), by Sylvanus G. Morley and George W. Brainerd (4th edition, revised by Robert J. Sharer).

Because the early inhabitants of North America worked in wood instead of stone and inscribed their written records on perishable buffalo hides, our knowledge of them is scanty compared to what we know of their southern neighbors. For information on Indian tribes of North America in general, see Carl Waldman's *Atlas of the North American Indian* (1985) and *Encyclopedia of Native American Tribes* (1988), both published by Facts On File; *Man's Rise to Civilization: The Cultural Ascent of the Indians of North America* (E.P. Dutton, 1978), by Peter Farb; *A History of the Indians of the United States* (University of Oklahoma Press, 1984), by Angie Debo; the two-volume *Reference Encyclopedia of the American Indian* (Todd Publishing, 1986), edited by Barry Klein; and *Indians of the United States* (Doubleday, 1966), by Clark Wissler and revised by Lucy Wales Kluckhohn.

A fuller appreciation of many early cultures can be gained through a study of their religious beliefs. This is especially true of the Aztec, though their reliance on human sacrifices and blood offerings may be too grim for some readers. See Ake Hultkrantz's *Religions of the American Indians* (University of California Press, 1979) and *Belief and Worship in Native North America* (Syracuse University Press, 1981), the latter edited by Christopher Vecsey; *North American Indian Mythologies* (P. Bedrick Books, 1985), by Cottie Burland; *Olmec Religion: A Key to Middle America and Beyond* (University of Oklahoma Press, 1978), by Karl W. Luckert; *The Fifth Sun: Aztec Gods, Aztec World* (University of Texas Press, 1979), by Burr Cartwright Brundage; *The Aztec Cosmos* (Celestial Arts Publishing Company, 1984); and *Archaeoastronomy in the New World: American Primitive Astronomy* (Cambridge University Press, 1982).

In primitive cultures, medicine and religion often went hand in hand, and the shaman's herbal collections and lore had ritualistic as well as healing purposes. For more on this relationship, see *The Smoking Gods: Tobacco in Maya Art, History, and Religion* (University of Oklahoma Press, 1978), by Francis Robicsek; *Plants of the Gods: Origins of Hallucinogenic Use* (Van der Marck, 1987), by Richard Schultes and Albert Hofmann; and *Hallucinogens and Shamanism* (Oxford University Press, 1973), edited by Michael J. Harner. *The Pre-Columbian Mind* (Seminar Press, 1971), by Francisco Guerra presents a good overall view of how these cultures saw their world.

The general reader who wants to get an idea of what day-to-day life was like for the pre-Columbian Indian should consult Jeremy A. Sabloff's excellent *Cities of Ancient Mexico: Reconstructing a Lost World* (Thames and Hudson, 1989). Also, Dorset Press has a very readable Everyday Life Series, of which three titles are relevant here: *Everday Life of the Aztecs*

(1987), by Warwick Bray, *Everyday Life of the Maya* (1987), by Ralph Whitlock, and *Everyday Life of the North American Indians* (1988), by Jon Manchip White; the latter includes a separate chapter on reservation life.

For a taste of pre-Columbian literature, several translations exist of early texts. The Maya account of the creation of the world is beautifully related in *Popol Vuh: The Mayan Book of the Dawn of Life* (Simon & Schuster, 1985), translated by Dennis Tedlock. The *Codex Magliabechiano*, the 16th-century Aztec pictorial manuscript, is reproduced in the two-volume *Book of the Life of the Ancient Mexicans* (University of California Press, 1982), with text and commentary by Zelia Nuttall and Elizabeth Hill Boone. Also, a number of early American creation myths are included in *This Country Was Ours: A Documentary History of the American Indian* (Harper & Row, 1972), edited by Virgil J. Vogel, and *Voices of the Winds: Native American Tales* (Facts On File, 1989), by Margot Edmonds and Ella E. Clark.

Serious students who contemplate reading some of the existing Mesoamerican texts in the original are referred to *Maya Glyphs* (University of California Press, 1989) by S.D. Houston; *An Outline Dictionary of Maya Glyphs* (Dover Publications, 1978), by William Gates; *Mayan Language Dictionary* (Garland Publishing, 1981), by Robert W. Blair; and *A Dictionary of the Huazalinguillo Dialect of Nahuatl with Grammatical Sketch and Readings* (Tulane University Press, 1980).

Contemporary Spanish accounts of the Conquest are numerous. See Bernal Díaz del Castillo's *Conquest of New Spain* (Penguin, 1963), translated by John M. Cohen; Bernardino de Sahagún's *War of Conquest: How It Was Waged Here in Mexico* (University of Utah Press, 1978), translated by Arthur J. Anderson and Charles E. Dibble, and his 13-volume *Florentine Codex: A General History of the Things of New Spain*, also translated by Anderson and Dibble and published by the University of Utah Press; Diego De Landa's *Yucatan Before and After the Conquest* (Dover, 1978); Garcilaso de la Vega's *Florida of the Inca* (University of Texas Press, 1957), edited by John and Jeannette Varner, and *Royal Commentaries of the Incas* (B. Franklin, reprint of 1869 edition), translated and edited by Clements R. Markham.

The relationship between Old and New World cultures and the inevitable comparisons—the similarity of the pyramids of Egypt to those in Mesoamerica, for instance—has inspired a number of transatlantic colonization theories, which date back at least to the 19th century: Lord Kingsborough (*Antiquities of Mexico*) believed the Maya to be descended from the 10 lost tribes of Israel, while Augustus Le Plongeon (*Maya-Atlantis; Queen Moo and the Egyptian Sphinx*) argued that the Maya colonized the Nile. In more modern times, Thor Heyerdahl has demonstrated that reed boats of the type commonly used in Egypt could withstand the rigors of ocean travel, and his experiences are well documented; Heyerdahl's own account is contained in *RA Expeditions* (Chronica Botanica India, 1971). Harvard professor Barry Fell has carried Heyerdahl's ideas a step further in books like *America B.C.* (Simon & Schuster, 1989), which places ancient Phoenicians in Iowa and Celtic Druids in Vermont.

For information about the effects of Spanish exploration on the ancient native civilizations, the catalog to an extensive exhibition mounted at the Florida Museum of Natural History, *First Encounters: Spanish Explorations in the Caribbean & the United States, 1492-1570* (University of Florida Press, 1990), edited by Jerald T. Milanich and Susan Mulbrath, is an up-to-date survey. The reader should see also *The Columbian Exchange: Biological and Cultural Consequences of 1492* (Greenwood Press, 1973), by Alfred W. Crosby.

The best way to study anything, of course, is firsthand, and those lucky enough to actually visit ancient sites of importance to pre-Columbian Americans should carry along Joyce Kelly's *Complete Visitor's Guide to Mesoamerican Ruins* (University of Oklahoma Press, 1982); C. Bruce Hunter's *Guide to Ancient Maya Ruins* (University of Oklahoma Press, 1974); or *A Guide to America's Indians: Ceremonials, Reservations and Museums* (University of Oklahoma Press, 1975), by Arnold Marquis.

Chronology

100,000 B.C. Possible, though doubtful, arrival of settlers on the continent.

40,000 B.C. Doubtful arrival of settlers. Nodular and chip cultures appear.

25,000 B.C. Probable arrival of settlers in America.

12,000 B.C. Paleo-Indian or megalofauna hunter cultures appear.

9000 B.C. Paleo-Indian Folsom culture.

7000 B.C. The Recent period begins. First attempts to domesticate corn, black beans, pumpkin and avocado in Mesoamerica.

6000 B.C. Archaic period or Hunter-gatherer period. Altithermal.

5730 B.C. Black beans cultivated in the Andean region.

5000 B.C. Corn cultivated in Mesoamerica.

4000 B.C. Black beans and chili peppers cultivated in Mesoamerica.

3500 B.C. Cotton cultivated on the coast of Peru (Chilica).

3150 B.C. Ceramics appear in Valdivia (Ecuador) and soon after in Puerto Hormiga (Colombia).

3000 B.C. Llamas domesticated and corn cultivated in the Andean region.

2500 B.C. Ceremonial centers appear in the Andean region.

2000 B.C. Potatoes domesticated in the Andean region.

1200 B.C. The Formative period or spread of agriculture. Yucca domesticated in the north of South America. Olmec culture lasting until 400 B.C. (will contribute calendar and hieroglyphic writing).

850 B.C. Beginning of the development of the Chavín culture of Huantar, which will reach its height between 400 B.C. and 200 B.C.

100 B.C. Classic period in Mesoamerica and central Andean region (appearance of first urban centers). This period will last until 900 A.D.

150 A.D. Development of the Teotihuacan culture; will last until the 7th century.

250 Beginning of the Maya Classic period, (calendar, writing, accounting, etc.), which will reach its height between 600 and 800. Its major cities (Tikal, Palenque, Copán, Yaxchilán, Quirigua) will survive until 900.

292 Tikal begins to take on the form of a great urban center.

450 Tiahuanaco at its height.

600 End of cultural hegemony of the Mochica and Nazca, which had developed since 200 A.D..

615 Pacal the Great becomes king of Tikal.

900 The Huari empire at its height (had been important since 500 A.D.). Its decline will begin toward the 12th century.

960 Tula, the Toltec capital, is founded. Will retain its hegemony until the 12th century.

987 The Toltec invade Yucatán. The Post-Classic Maya period begins with Chichén Itzá, which will dominate Yucatán until the 12th century.

1100 Ruled by the first emperor, Sinchi Roca, a descendant of the legendary Manco Capac, the Inca settle in Cuzco. The Maya of the Post-Classic found Mayapán, their last great city.

1168 Fall of Tula.

1200 Flight of the Itzá to Peten.

1299 The Aztec arrive in Chapultepec.

1323 Culhuacan declares war on the Aztec and expels them from the territory.

1325 Founding of Tenochtitlan.

1367 Acampichtli, prince of Culhuacan, agrees to rule the Aztec in the city of Tenochtitlan.

1428 The Triple Alliance is forged by the cities of Tenochtitlan, Texcoco and Tlacopan.

1438 Pachacutec is crowned king and he begins a series of conquests. He is the first Inca king in recorded history.

1440 Motecuhzoma Ilhuicamina, the great Aztec reformer, is elected *tlatoani* of Tenochtitlan.

1441 End of the hegemony of Mayapán and the beginning of the Maya decline during the Post-Classic period.

1471 Tupac Inca Yupanqui is elected the successor to Pachacutec. With his conquests, he founds the empire.

1473 Axayacatl, *tlatoani* of Tenochtitlan, defeats and annexes the twin city of Tlatelolco.

1500 Floods in Tenochtitlan.

1502 Motecuhzoma Xocoyotzin, called Moctezuma by the Spaniards, ascends the Aztec throne. Christopher Columbus reaches the island of Guanaja and meets a Maya merchant boat.

1519 Motecuhzoma invites Cortés into Tenochtitlan.

1521 The Spaniards invade Tenochtitlan. End of Aztec supremacy and imprisonment of Cuitlahuac, the last *tlatoani* of the Aztec capital.

1524 Cortés crosses Maya territory on his way to the Hibueras and sees the remains of the ancient Maya civilization.

1527–1532 Civil war between the factions of Huascar and Atahualpa for control of the Inca empire.

1532 Defeat of Atahualpa by the Spaniards in the Battle of Cajamarca puts an end to Inca supremacy.

Biographies

Acamapichtli Prince of Culhuacan who went to Tenochtitlan in 1367 to become the ruler of the Aztec.

Achitometl *Tlatoani* of Culhuacan, whose daughter was sacrificed by the Aztec in 1323, causing the war between the two peoples.

Ah Ban Grandson of Ah Kulel. He is believed to have compiled the book *The Songs of Dzibilchaltun*, which contains 15 Maya songs from the Colonial period.

Ahuitzotl (1486–1502) First *tlatoani* of Tenochtitlan, whose reign saw the beginning of Aztec supremacy. He conquered the southern portion of the Isthmus of Tehuantepec, advancing as far as Xoconochco, which was the best cocoa-producing area in all of America. He undertook a number of great public works, among which were the aqueduct of Tenochtitlan (which flooded the city) and the Great Temple, inaugurated in 1487 with a ceremony of human sacrifice. Toward the end of his reign, he failed in his attack on Tlaxcala.

Atahualpa (1527–1533) Overshadowed by the greatness of his father, Huayna Capac, he lived in Tomebamba (modern-day Cuenca, Ecuador) and then in Caranqui, at the northern frontier of the *Tahuantinsuyu*. He met all the great Inca generals, such as Chalcuchima, Rumiñahui and Quisquis, who served under him. After the death of his father, Atahualpa rose up in arms against his brother, Huascar, who had been proclaimed emperor in Cuzco. Atahualpa's army won a major battle fought near Tomebamba and then went on to Cajamarca to face some strange bearded invaders (the Spaniards). On the way to Cajamarca, news reached him that General Chalcuchima had defeated Huascar, taken him prisoner, and was on his way to join him. In 1532, after Pizarro's victory at Cajamarca, Atahualpa secretly ordered the death of his brother, in order to prevent him forging an alliance with the Spaniards. He was executed for his crimes the following year, in accordance with Spanish law.

Axayacatl (1469–1481) Grandson of Motecuhzoma Ilhuicamina, whom he succeeded as *tlatoani* of Tenochtitlan. He conquered Tlatlauhquitepec and, in 1473, using as a pretext the rough treatment given by its ruler to his Mexican wife, defeated and annexed the twin town of Tlatelolco. A great warrior, he subdued the rebellious province of Cuetlaxlan and conquered Tollocan, Ocuillan and Malinalco. In 1478, he was beaten by the Tarascos but later managed to win back his prestige with a victory over Xilotepec.

Cauac Caan Lord of Quirigua, a Maya city that reached its height under him. In 725 he ascended the throne, waging a war against Copan, which he defeated. He enlarged the city and was supreme over the whole Valley of Motagua, whose jade mines account for the importance of Quirigua. He died in 785, and was succeeded by his son, Caan Xul.

Cocom A dynasty of Maya rulers of Mayapán that, until 1441, ruled supreme over the city in Yucatán with the aid of mercenaries.

Cuauac Vinal I First lord of Palenque, who ruled between 501 and 524. He was succeeded by Hok I, who ruled from 528 to 565, after which Palenque was ruled by his sons, the governors Cuauac Vinal II (565–570) and Bahlum (572–582). The latter was succeeded by a queen or governess, Kan Ik, who ruled from 583 until 604.

Cuitlahuac (1520–1524) Succeeded Motecuhzoma Xocoyotzin. He defended Tenochtitlan from the Spanish invaders, leading the famous Sad Night campaign of June 20, 1520, and the final battle against the conquistadores. He was held prisoner under Cortés until the latter marched to the Hibueras, when he was murdered under the pretext of having planned a native uprising.

Chan Bahlum Son of Pacal the Great, who ruled Palenque from 683 until 701. He renovated the city's Great Palace, having three temples built: the Temple of the Sun, the Temple of the Cross and the Temple of the Foliated Cross, whose bas-reliefs are a masterpiece of Maya art. He was succeeded by Hok II, under whose rule Palenque rapidly declined.

Chimalpopoca Succeeded Huitzilihuitl. The aqueduct of Chapultepec was built during his reign. He warred against Azcapotzalco and Tenayuca.

Chuquillanto A young noblewoman, *acllawasi* or "chosen one," the main character in a beautiful love story with a shepherd named Acoitapia, which ended in tragedy and with the lovers changed into hills.

Fluted Nose Succeeded Jaguar Claw I in Tikal in 378. During his reign, he established relations with Teotihuacan. He died at the end of the 4th century.

Huascar (1527–1532) Natural heir of Huayna Capac, he was proclaimed Inca emperor in Cuzco on the death of his father but had to confront his rebellious brother, Atahualpa. He was defeated and taken prisoner in the battle of Cotabamba by Chalcuchima. While Atahualpa made for Cajamarca to fight the Spaniards, Huascar was murdered to prevent him from forging an alliance with Pizarro.

Huayna Capac (1493–1527) Son of Tupac Inca Yupanqui. Under his rule, Inca conquests stretched to the empire's natural limits in every direction except the north, which decided him to transfer the capital from Cuzco to Tomebamba (Cuenca, Ecuador), a town he had ordered built. He overcame the Chachapoya and the Moyopampa on the edge of the jungle and ordered fortifications to be built in the gorges leading to Amazonia, an area from which he feared invasion. He put down a rebellion in Quito in 1524 and fought off an invasion by the Chiriguano. He spent the last few years of his life in Tomebamba, where he had established a second court. He died in 1527, probably of smallpox, an illness brought to Mexico by the Spaniards, who by then had reached the Andes.

Huitzilihuitl He succeeded Acamapichtli, and married the daughter of Tezozomoc, Lord of Azcapotzalco, thus allowing the Aztec to pay less tribute.

Itzcoatl (1426–1439) Succeeded Chimalpopoca and took advantage of the internal conflicts of the Azcapotzalco dynasty to free the Aztec. In 1428, he established the Triple Alliance of Tenochtitlan, Texcoco and Tlacopan, enabling them to win a major victory over Azcapotzalco. Itzcoatl conquered Xochimilco, Teotihuacan, Otompan, Coyoacan, Mizqujiz, Cuitlahuac y Cuaunahuac (Cuernavaca). During his reign, the Aztec were divided into *pipiltin* or lords and *macehualtin* or serfs. His nephew, Tlacaelel, was his greatest counselor, and in 1427 he ordered a purge of all the books written on old Aztec historical traditions and legends, so that people could not learn other than an official version of the truth.

Jaguar Bird The most important ruler of Yaxchilán. Born in 709, he ascended the throne in 752 after defeating numerous enemies. He made alliances with many powerful neighboring lords, put down rebellions, submitted to a marriage of convenience with a princess from Peten and ordered many buildings to be constructed. He died in 768. After his death, Yaxchilán began to decline.

Jaguar Claw I Became the ruler of Tikal in 330 after a military victory and introduced a new dynasty. He died around 378. His tomb, known as number 22, was desecrated in the 7th century.

Jaguar Claw II Ruler of Tikal at the time of its decline. He is portrayed on stele number 29. He possibly had to fight against Pecari Kan, another ruler, portrayed in stele number 9.

Jaguar Shield Ruler of Yaxchilán from 682 until his death at the age of 90. He defeated the lord Ahau and other enemies in numerous battles. He is portrayed next to his wife on stele number 11 of the town.

Kak Cacabil One of the most outstanding rulers of Tikal at the time of its decline. he ruled from 682, when he was proclaimed successor to Stormy Sky. He reinforced the divinity of his position and as-

229

sumed the highest religious authority, merging the civil and the religious. He died around 730.

Manco Capac First ruler of Inca legend. The god-creator, Viracocha, called him out of a mountain cave, together with his sister, Mama Ocllo, and another four brothers who were married to four sisters (whose descendants would be the 10 *ayllu incas*). On their long wanderings to Cuzco, all died except Manco and his sister-wife. They conquered Cuzco and brought civilization to the Inca, giving them a moral code of conduct. He was succeeded by seven legendary kings: Sinchi Roca, Lloque Yupanqui, Mayta Capac, Capac Yupanqui, Inca Roca, Yahuar Huacac and Viracocha Inca.

Moquihuixtli Ruler of Tlatelolco, murdered by the Aztec in 1473 when they took over the city on the orders of his brother-in-law, Axayacatl.

Motecuhzoma Ilhuicamina (1440–1469) Brother of Tlacaelel, he made great political, social and religious reforms, creating a bureaucracy to rule the realm. The great famine of 1450–1454, brought about by floods and frosts, forced him to conquer good arable land in Chalco, Oaxaca and Tepeyec, cities that, in turn, were to play an essential part in the forming of the empire.

Motecuhzoma Xocoyotzin (1502–1520) Son of Axayacatl, he succeeded Ahuizotl as *tlatoani* of Tenochtitlan. He fought against Huexotzinco, Tlaxcala and the Tarascans but was primarily a great reformer. He strengthened the role of the *tlatoani*, giving it a sacred character, and introduced great pomp into his court. He also carried out his policies for transforming his nobles into palace courtiers. Motecuhzoma, whom the Spaniards called Moctezuma, was obliged to open the city of Tenochtitlan to Hernán Cortés, who subsequently took him prisoner. He died in 1520 in an accident.

Netzahualcoyotl *Tlatoani* of Texcoco and contemporary of Izcoatl. He was a great poet, philosopher and legislator (he wrote the regulations named after him). He embellished his city with beautiful gardens and had a gigantic wall built around it to protect it from frequent flooding.

Netzahualpilli Poet and *tlatoani* of Texcoco. His name is associated with curious love stories. His favorite was the lady of Tula, for whom he went so far as to sacrifice his own son. He condemned his daughter to death for having a lover smuggled into the palace inside a carpet. One of his wives (of whom there were 2,000) committed adultery, and,

finding her with three noble lovers, he had her executed. This upset relations with Tenochtitlan, since the woman in question was the daughter of the *tlatoani*.

Ollantay Main character in a play of the same name. A fictitious general under Pachacutec who fell in love with the king's daughter, Star of Joy, whom he finally managed to marry after many adventures.

Pacal the Great Most important ruler of Palenque, he was born on March 6, 603, and died on August 3, 684. He ascended the throne in 615, at 12 years of age, the grandson of Kan Ik, the founder of the dynasty. Pacal married his sister, Ahpo Hel, and during his reign Palenque had lordship over the whole of the southwest of the Maya territory. While still alive he ordered his burial chamber built. It was discovered in 1957 and contained an enormous number of funeral objects. The slab covering his tomb is carved with the great works of this ruler.

Pachacutec (1438–1471) An Inca general who became lucky during the war against the Chanca. He was proclaimed emperor in 1438, thus becoming the first Inca in recorded history. His conquests extended as far as the Titicaca region and to Pachacamac in the west. He left military matters to his son Tupac and devoted himself to the organization of the empire, beginning with the reconstruction of Cuzco. He established units of production and consumption based on the decimal system. He died in 1471.

Quetzalcoatl Legendary king of a Toltec people who invaded Maya territory around 987 and gave rise to the origin of Chichén Itzá.

Rabinal Achi Main character of a Quiche play copied in 1850 by Abbot Brasseur de Bourbourg.

Sinchi Roca One of the legendary Inca emperors, he was the son and successor of Manco Capac. *Sinchi* means "warrior hero," and during his reign the Inca conquered the area around Cuzco.

Stormy Sky Succeeded Fluted Nose (and was perhaps his son or grandson) at the end of the 4th century as ruler of the Maya city of Tikal. He forged strong ties with Teotihuacan, whose warriors are frequently found depicted in local art. His majestic figure appears on stele 31, a recently discovered monument. He died in 455, in the last year of the city's splendor.

Tacayahuatzin Lord of Huexotzinco, he gathered poets and wise men around him in his house.

Tizoc (1481–1486) Succeeded his brother Axayacatl. Not a great warrior-king; was defeated at Metztitlan and had great difficulty in suppressing the rebellion of Tollocan. According to the chronicles, he was poisoned by some of his warriors, who believed him to be inept in matters of war.

Tlacaelel Counselor of Itzcoatl, Motecuhzoma Ilhuicamina and Axayacatl. He was the brain behind the reform of Mexico, organizing the Triple Alliance, dividing social classes and purging the old books in which the Aztec were seen in an unfavorable light.

Tupac Amaru The last of the Inca, he was the son of Manco Inca. The last to hold out against the Spaniards, he was captured and decapitated in 1572. A character of the same name, the brother of Tupac Inca Yupanqui, was at the center of a love story with the *ñusta* Cusi Chimpo.

Tupac Inca Yupanqui (1471–1493) Succeeded Pachacutec. He was a great conqueror, winning most of his campaigns while his father was still alive. This Inca went from Piura and Tumbez to the region of Quito. He conquered the Cañari, the Cara and the Quito, extending the northern border of the *Tahuantinsuyu* to the Ancasmayo River in southern Colombia. He also extended the eastern borders to the north of Chile and on the coast conquered the Chimú. He explored the sea (possibly reaching the Galapagos Islands and even Oceania), leaving Tumbez with a fleet of rafts. He had artisans brought to Cuzco from the coast in order to introduce official traditions. He is also throught to have founded Sacsahuaman to defend Cuzco. He died at over 80 years of age in 1493.

Yac-Pac One of the last governors of Copán, who, together with Governors I and II, is portrayed in a bas-relief dating from 776.

Yax Akab Kin Lord of Tikal from 734, he died in 760. During his reign many public works were carried out, and trade brought food and luxury items sent by the chieftains of the conquered lowlands.

Yax Macaw Son of Jog 18th, he ascended the throne of Copán in 763 and died in 775. He had numerous luxurious villas and temples built. The most outstanding temple is that called number 22, which is considered the masterpiece of Copán architecture.

Zac Kuk Queen of Palenque, who married a foreigner, Kan Bahlum Mo'o, establishing a long line, of which her son Pacal the Great (615–683) was the most outstanding descendant.

Glossary

Abipon An Amerindian ethnic branch of the Guaicuru, inhabitants of all of southeastern El Chaco and now almost extinct.

Achiote A dye extracted from the seeds of the plant of the same name.

Achira An herbaceous plant with a knotty stem and sword-shaped leaves. It is found in the wetlands and in water.

Alacaluf The language spoken by the tribes living in the southernmost part of South America.

Algonquian Amerindian natives of North America. A great number of tribes belonging to this ethnic group live all over Canada and part of the United States. Before the arrival of the Europeans, they inhabited most of the land east of the Mississippi.

Amautas Inca sages and philosophers whose epic poems described the imperial conquests.

Anon An arboriform plant with alternating, simple leaves and without stipules, ending in either a single flower or carpels, which become fleshy and form a ball-like mass.

Arawak Numerous tribes belonging to this ethnic group currently live in the area between the coast of Venezuela and Pilcomayo and also Paraguay.

Arracacha An edible plant of similar characteristics to those of the parsnip but having a longer, thicker root.

Arequipa A Peruvian city, army headquarters and supreme court of justice, situated at the foot of the western Andes.

Aribalo A vessel from Peru made during the Inca period.

Atole A Mayan gruel made of cornmeal.

Ayllu The primary social group or community in Inca society.

Bochica The Chibcha god of civilization and the arts. His legend has much in common with that of Atlas and the Flood.

Bohio A hut or primitive house in America. It is square-shaped and built with tree trunks or branches on posts holding it above ground, away from the damp. The roof is thatched and has air-vents in the sides serving as windows or doors.

Boleadoras A weapon commonly used by South American Indians consisting of ropes tied together with balls at the end.

Bonampak A Maya word meaning "painted walls." An archaeological center in Chiapas (Mexico), near Yaxchilán.

Bororo A group of languages spoken in South America, the two most important ones being Bororo and Otuke. The Bororo people were divided into six smaller tribes, two of which are now completely extinct. Surviving Indians, who total about 2,500, live from hunting and fishing and use poisoned arrows and spears as weapons.

Cacamatzin Succeeded Netzahualpilli as lord of Tezcoco in 1516. Hernán Cortés was his ally for a short time before having him imprisoned. He died in prison, apparently on the orders of Cortés.

Cajamarca A Peruvian city situated in the heart of the western Andes, in the southern region. Cajamarca stands on a vast pampa surrounded by mountains, the Cajamarca River dividing the city in two.

Calca A Peruvian city situated in the Vilcanota mountain range. The Urubamba River flows through it.

Calpulli Land where a particular clan or family line lived. Each *calpulli* covered an area of arable land belonging to the group.

Camana A Peruvian city situated on the Pacific Coast, at the mouth of the Majes River.

Canella An arboriform or bushy plant with alternating leaves. Two types are found in tropical America. Its leaves are used to make a very low-quality oil.

Cañahua A type of millet. It is fermented and made into *chicha*.

Caripuna An Amerindian tribe, belonging to the Pacaguara branch of the Pano family, who live in the Beni River valley where the Guapore and Madre de Dios (Bolivia) meet.

Casma A Peruvian city, situated at the mouth of the Casma River. There are remains of the Mochica culture in the Casma River valley.

Cayapo An Amerindian tribe and the main group of the Ge people (Brazil). They are tall, brachycephalic and have light-colored skin. They cultivate the land and practice basket-making.

Cempoala One of the most important Totonaca cities, dependent on Teotihuacan. It was a crossroads on the trade routes between the coast, the highlands and the Yucatán Peninsula.

Chachapoya An Amerindian tribe belonging to the Chinchasuyu group, who lived on the banks of the Marañon River (Peru).

Chan Chan A central Andean region of Ecuador.

Chanacay A Peruvian city situated on the coastal plains of the Pacific.

Chapultepec The ancient city of the Toltec that was later taken over by the Aztec and became a city of leisure for the kings of Tenochtitlan.

Chavin de Huantar A Peruvian city situated on the ridges of the Blanca mountain range.

Charqui Meat that has been dried under the sun or in the open air.

Charrua A tribe that occupied a vast territory, from the banks of the Uruguay River to Panama, the Atlantic and the Plata River.

Chasqui Messengers of the Inca empire.

Chesapeake A great bay on the east coast of the United States.

Cheyenne An Amerindian tribe belonging to the Algonquian group.

Chicama A Peruvian city situated in the Chicama River valley.

Chicha An alcoholic beverage obtained through fermenting corn in water and sugar.

Chichicaste A thorny bush, its fibrous stem is used in rope-making.

Chimú Pre-Inca kingdom on the northern coast of Peru. Its capital was Chan Chan. Chimú ceramics, made with molds, are of extraordinary richness.

Chinanteca A tribe living in the border mountains between the Mexican states of Veracruz and Oaxaca.

Chinchorro A hammock made of knotted string.

Chorrera The name of the culture of the Indian tribes living on the coastal plain of the Pacific from Panama to Ecuador.

Cinteotl The god of corn, son of Tlazolteotl and husband of Xochiquetzal, goddess of flowers.

Coatlinchan A city near Texcoco. Outside the city, there is a massive Teotihuacan statue representing the water god.

Comal An Aztec earthenware plate.

Crow An Amerindian tribe belonging to the Sioux group, which lived on the banks of the Yellowstone River.

Cuicalli Aztec "houses of song" where Aztec children received their training in the arts, including poetry, song and dance.

Curaca Chief or governor of a tribe of the Inca empire.

Dakota An Amerindian tribe of the Sioux language group that used to inhabit the upper Mississippi area.

231

Diaguita An extinct Amerindian tribe from Argentina. They inhabited a vast territory southeast of Salta, Cajamarca and the Tucuman and Riojo valleys. They developed a very interesting culture, well-known due to the archaeological excavations carried out there.

Fox An Amerindian tribe belonging to the Algonquian group, who originally lived on Green Bay (Wisconsin) and in 1842 moved to Iowa.

Frijol The kidney bean, one of the major crops domesticated in the Mexican region around 4000 B.C.

Guanabana The fruit of the guanabana tree. It is heart-shaped, green on the outside and white inside, having a pleasant, sweet and refreshing taste.

Guayaqui An Amerindian people speaking a language belonging to the Tupi-Guarani group, who live in the jungle in the east of Paraguay.

Haida An Amerindian tribe who speak a language related to the Nadene. They are inhabitants of Queen Charlotte Archipelago and the southern portion of Prince of Wales Island (Canada). They developed a very interesting culture based on the exploitation of their fishing resources and of the wood from the vast forests of their habitat.

Hopi An Amerindian people belonging to the Sosohou who speak a language of the Uto-Aztec group. They live on the banks of the Little Colorado River in northwestern Arizona and belong to the Pueblo cultures.

Huanca An Amerindian tribe belonging to the Inca group whose language belongs to the Quechua group. They lived on the banks of the Jauja River and shores of Lake Juumun (Peru).

Huipilli A type of blouse worn by Aztec women.

Inkario The immense Inca highway system connecting southern Columbia with Chile.

Iroquois North American Indian tribes composed of Seneca, Oneida, Onondaga, Cayuga, Mohawk and Tuscarora. Natives of the southeast of the United States, a number of migrations took them to their present habitat. The Iroquois Confederation is considered the most developed among all the North American Indians.

Itzamna Kauli A benevolent Maya deity, son of Hunabku, god of creation. He is usually represented in the codices in the likeness of an old toothless man with a hooked nose and a beard.

Kero Inca wooden vase.

Kotosh A pre-Inca archaeological area situated on the eastern slope of the Andes. Excavations have proved that the main temple was rebuilt five times during the first period. It is dated ca. 1450.

Macehualli A member of the lower classes of Aztec society. Class was inherited through birth. The macehualli provided for the ruling classes, filling all kinds of posts.

Maidu An Amerindian tribe related to the Permitiana living in the northwest of California.

Mamey A tree (*Mammee americana*) both medium-sized and large, whose fruit is edible, brown in color, of between 4 and 6 inches (10 and 15 centimeters) in diameter, with a taste similar to that of the apricot.

Manioc A type of flour made from the pulp of the bitter yucca.

Metate The mortar and pestle used throughout South America.

Mixtec An Amerindian people whose language belongs to the Otomi-Mangue group, which lived in pre-hispanic Oaxaca.

Muskogee An Amerindian tribe whose language belongs to the Algonquian family and who belong to the Creek group. They lived in the southwestern United States.

Natchez An extinct Amerindian tribe whose language belongs to the Muskogee group. Living on the left bank of the Mississippi River, their culture reached a high degree of development.

Nopal A thorny and fleshy cladocarpous cactus, with large many-petaled flowers that give edible berries with a green skin. Also known as the "prickly pear."

Ñusta The name given in Peru to daughters of the Inca emperor and of noble lineage who were married to the Inca.

Olmec A group of pre-Hispanic Mexican tribes who inhabited the coast along the Gulf of Mexico. It is believed that it was they who introduced civilization in Mesoamerica.

Omaha An Amerindian tribe belonging to the Sioux group who inhabited the northwest of present-day Nebraska. What is left of this tribe now live on reservations.

Orejon Inca noble who had pierced ears and qualified for high office in the empire.

Panche An Amerindian tribe speaking a language related to the Karibe group who live on the left bank of the Magdalena River (Brazil).

Papa The potato, first domesticated in the Peru area.

Piaroa An Amerindian tribe whose language belongs to the Saliva group, living on the right bank of the Orinoco River.

Piapoco An Amerindian tribe whose language belongs to the Arawak group, living on the lower and middle reaches of the Guaviare River (Venezuela).

Pilli The Aztec noble class.

Pima An Amerindian tribe belonging to the Pima-Nahua whose language belongs to the Yuto-Aztec group. They live on ranches in the Mexican state of Sonora.

Pochteca Travelling Aztec merchants who dealt in valuable goods, including cloth, jewelry, and semi-precious stones. They were part of the upper class within Aztec society.

Puelche An Amerindian tribe belonging to the Pampeane who lived on the Argentinian pampas. They included the Serrano, the Qurandi and the Chechelet.

Pulque An Aztec alcoholic drink made from fermented maguey juice. Also known as octli.

Quichua An Amerindian ethnic group and language belonging to the Maya-Quiche group. During the pre-Colombian period they spread along the Yucatán Peninsula. The origins and development of their culture are recorded in the *Popol Vuh*.

Quiua An annual plant of some 6 inches (15 centimeters) in height with triangular leaves whose seeds can be eaten boiled or as flour. Although native to Peru, it grows all over America, where its leaves are eaten as a main vegetable.

Quipu Knotted strings used in pre-Columbian Peru for recording information.

Quipucamayoc Inca accountants who kept records on all aspects of Inca society, using the quipu.

Rucana An Amerindian tribe whose language belongs to the Queche group who lived on the slopes of the western *cordillera* in Peru.

Saliva Belonging to the Amerindian group, their culture is very primitive, and they live on both sides of the rivers Meta, Guaviare and Meta del Orinoco.

Sinú A pre-Columbian culture that developed on the Gimi River basin.

Taclla An Inca wooden tool used for tilling soil.

Tairona An extinct Amerindian tribe of an unrelated language who once inhabited the coastal area of the Gulf of Santa Marta (Colombia).

Telpochcalli Aztec public schools set up by district, for teaching Aztec doctrine.

Tenquedama A Colombian waterfall along the Bogota River.

Tierra del Fuego Indians Made up of three different Amerindian tribes (the Ona, the Alacaluf and the

Yaghen), who spoke different languages but developed very similar primitive cultures. They inhabited the southernmost part of South America, the Isla Grande de Tierra del Fuego, from where they received their name. They are currently on the verge of extinction.

Tlacauilo   Venerated artisans responsible for illustrating the Aztec codices.

Tlachtli   An Aztec sport played with a rubber ball on an H-shaped court.

Tlatoani   An Aztec king or emperor. Every large city had a tlatoani, the one in the capital being called the huey tlatoani or "great orator."

Tlaxcalteca   An extinct Amerindian tribe belonging to a branch of the Nahuatl people, whose language belonged to the Uto-Aztec group. During the pre-Hispanic period, they inhabited the Mexican *meseta*.

Tonalpohualli   The sacred calendar governing the life of each Aztec.

Tonalpouhqui   The Aztec reader of destinies who deciphered the tonalpolualli.

Totonaca   A pre-Columbian Amerindian tribe whose language belongs to the Maya-Zoque group living in the central area of present-day Veracruz (Mexico).

Tucano   A language group spoken by numerous Amerindian tribes—the Tucano included—living in the Amazon basin, mainly between the rivers Putumayo and Napo.

Ulua   An Amerindian tribe belonging to the Sumo group, whose language belongs to the Mosquito-Sumo-Matagalpe group. They live northwest of Lake Nicaragua.

Wichita   A grouping of Amerindian tribes whose language belongs to the Caddo group living on the banks of the Canadian and Trinidad rivers and also the Red River (northeast Texas).

Xipe Totec   A pre-Hispanic Mexican deity, worshiped since early times, who is usually represented as a young man dressed in the skin of a human sacrifice. For this reason, he was often known as "Our Lord, the Flayed One."

Xochipilli   A pre-Hispanic Aztec god of spring and vegetation, originally the god of the morning sun.

Yaqui   An Amerindian tribe of the Pima-Nahua whose language belongs to the Uto-Aztec group. They live on the banks of the Yaqui River in Sonora (Mexico).

Yucca (Manihot)   A major crop grown in South America and the Caribbean. There were two varieties: the sweet (manihot utilissima) and the bitter or hot (manihot esculenta).

Index

234

235

Photo Credits

AISA: 16 (Heitmann), 21, 32, 44 (bottom), 72, 73, 96, 119, 120, 144, 157, 158, 159, 162, 164, 184 (top right and bottom left), 194, 199, 221. **Archivo Anaya:** 162, 166, 188, 190, 219. **Archivo Anaya/Museo Naval:** 9, 33 (left, middle and right), 38, 39, 54, 55, 72 (top), 113, 118, 126, 170, 173, 179, 198 (top and bottom), 211. **M. Arribas:** 53. **C. Caillouet:** 18. **L. Castedo:** 77 (top and bottom), 121 (top right and bottom left), 122 (left and middle), 161, 174-175, 176, 195, 201. **Martin Chambi/Erika Billeter/Fotografía Latinoamericana:** 28. **Ediestudio:** 2, 17, 22, 48 (top right, bottom left and bottom right), 76, 81, 88 (top, bottom left and bottom right), 90-91, 92, 93, 127, 134 (left and bottom right), 135 (top left, top right and bottom), 155 (top left and bottom left), 187 (top left, top middle and bottom left). **Fototeca:** 150, 161, 171. **Index:** 20, 148, 149, 165, 199. **Justin Kerr, 1987:** 6-7, 62, 63, 69, 80, 109, 112, 123, 124, 125, 128 (top right and bottom), 129, 140 (top, bottom left and bottom right), 141, 144, 145, 161, 172, 192, 202, 203, 209, 216, 220. **Jorge Montoro:** 156. **Cristina Morató:** 1989: 61 (top), 120, 122, 123, 127, 128, 144. **Oronoz:** 11, 36, 37, 51, 64, 99, 131, 133, 182, 183, 225. **Jorge Provenza**, 1989: 34, 35, 38 (bottom), 39 (bottom), 44 (top), 45, 56 (bottom), 74 (top left and bottom right), 118 (top middle and bottom right), 130, 151 (top and bottom), 170, 178, 199, 200 (top and bottom), 210 (bottom left, bottom middle and bottom right). **Mireille Vautier:** 14, 15, 26, 27, 29, 30, 31, 42, 46, 47, 50 (top right, bottom left and bottom right), 58, 59, 65 (top left and top right), 66, 67, 68, 75 (top and bottom), 78 (top and bottom), 82, 83, 94 (top and bottom), 95, 97, 98 (left and right), 99 (bottom left), 100, 101, 102 (left, top right and bottom left), 103 (top right, bottom left and bottom right), 104, 105, 110, 111, 114, 115, 121, 127, 132 (top right and bottom right), 133 (top right and bottom right), 136, 137, 138, 139 (top and bottom), 146, 155, 163, 166-167, 169, 176, 195, 204, 205 (top right, bottom left), 206, 207, 208, 212 (right and left), 213. **Patrick Rouillard:** 1988: 8, 166, 214, 215. **Vautier-Decool:** 19, 84, 177, 185.

Sources:

Museums: Museo Amano (Lima): 100, 207; Museo de América (Madrid): 11, 36, 37, 41, 51 (top right), 64, 99 (right), 106, 116, 119, 130 (top right), 133 (left), 157 (top right), 158, 159, 164 (bottom left), 182 (bottom right), 183, 201 (top right). Museo de América/Gabinete de Bibliofilia: 48 (top left), 70 (bottom left), 74 (bottom), 89 (top, bottom left and right), 222 (bottom), 223 (top and bottom); Museum of American Indian (New York): 63, 140 (bottom left); American Museum of Natural History (New York): 144 (top middle) Ref. 30.3/2521, 209 Ref. 30.3/2524; Museo Nacional de Antropología (Lima): 42, 50 (top, bottom right and left), 51 (top left and bottom), 52 (top, bottom left and right), 58, 59, 66, 67, 73, 78 (top right and bottom left), 101, 102 (left), 104, 105, 114, 115, 121 (bottom), 127 (bottom right), 146, 163, 169, 176 (bottom right), 177, 195 (top right), 204, 205 (top right), 208, 212 (right and left), 213; Museo Nacional de Arqueología (Mexico): 17, 19, 21, 93 (right), 120 (right), 131 (bottom left), 144 (bottom right), 147, 148, 149, 152 (right and left), 153 (top right and left, bottom right), 154 (right and left), 157 (bottom right), 174-175, 184 (bottom left), 185, 191, 194, 221; Museo Nacional de Antropología de San José (Costa Rica): 122 (right), 123 (top left); Museo de Arqueología y Etnología (Guatemala): 14, 18, 68, 128 (left); Museo Arqueológico de Oaxaca (Mexico): 93 (left); The Art Museum, Princeton University: 123 (left), 124, 145, 203; Museo de Arte Precolombino (Santiago, Chile): 77 (top right), 121 (top left and right), 122 (middle), 161 (bottom left), 176 (bottom left), 195 (top left); Museo del Banco Central (Quito): 72, 184 (top right); The British Museum (London): 6-7, 20, 112, 140 (top), 141, 220; Museo Brüning (Lambayeque, Peru): 30, 102 (top right and bottom right), 103 (top, bottom left and right), 138, 139 (top and bottom left); Cleveland Museum of Art: 62, 192 (James Albert and Mary Gardiner Ford Memorial Fund), 216; Colección Chávez Ballón (Lima): 132 (top and bottom right); Dallas Museum of Art: 109; Denver Art Museum: 140 (bottom right), 192; Detroit Institute of Art: 69; Dumbarton Oaks (Washington, D.C.): 128 (top right); Archivo histórico de la ciudad (Barcelona): 96; Museo de la Iglesia de la Compañía de Jesús (Cuzco): 136; Palacio del Gobierno (Mexico): 84, 85; John Frederic Lewis collection (Philadelphia): 150; Kimbell Art Museum (Fort Worth): 125, 128 (bottom), 172, 202; Colección Leoncio Arteaga (Yucay, Peru): 75 (top right and bottom left); Metropolitan Museum of Art (New York): 122 (left); Munson-Williams-Proctor Institute (New York): 129; Museo Nacional (Colombia): 127 (top); Museo Naval (Madrid): 9, 33, 38 (top right), 39 (top right), 54, 55, 79 (top right), 113, 118 (bottom left), 126 (bottom left), 170 (top right), 173, 179 (bottom right), 187 (top right), 198 (top), 200 (bottom), 211; New Orleans Museum of Art: 80, 161 (top right); Museo del Oro (Bogota): 2, 8, 76; Museo de Pedro de Osma (Lima): 97, 136, 137, 155 (top right); Museo Popol Vuh (Guatemala): 61 (bottom right), 120 (top left), 127 (bottom left), 128 (top middle), 144 (bottom left); Museo Postal (Madrid): 162 (bottom left); Museo R. Tamayo de Oaxaca (Mexico): 77 (bottom left), 92; Museo de la Universidad (Cuzco): 26, 27, 31, 65 (top left and top right), 99 (bottom left), 133 (top and bottom right), 205 (left).

Libraries: Biblioteca Arcaya (Caracas): 38 (bottom left), 39 (bottom left), 44 (top right), 56 (bottom left), 74 (top left and right), 130 (bottom left), 151 (top left and bottom right), 170 (bottom left), 178 (bottom left), 199 (bottom left), 200 (top right), 210 (bottom left, middle and right); Det Kongeligi Bibliotek (Copenhagen): 162 (top right), 166 (bottom left), 219 (bottom right and left); Library of Congress, Washington, D.C.: 32, 157 (top left), 160, 171 (bottom left), 199 (top right and bottom right); John Carter Library (New York): 210 (bottom left); Biblioteca Laurenziana (Florence): 48 (top right and bottom left and right), 81, 88 (top and bottom left and right), 155 (top and bottom left), 187 (bottom left and middle and top right); Biblioteca Nacional (Caracas): 34, 35, 45, 118 (top, middle and bottom right); Biblioteca Nacional (Madrid): 40 (top and bottom), 57 (right and left), 60, 79 (bottom right), 96, 131 (top right), 142 (top and bottom right), 143 (top and bottom), 168 (bottom left), 179 (top right), 182 (top right), 186, 189 (top right and bottom left), 190, 224, 225; Biblioteca Nacional (Mexico): 134 (left and bottom right), 135 (top right, top left and bottom); Bibliothèque Nationale (Paris): 22, 44 (bottom left), 194, 218 (bottom left and right); Biblioteca de la Real Academia de la Historia (Madrid): 156; Biblioteca Nazionale Centrale (Florence): 168 (top and bottom right), 223 (top right); Assamblee Nationale Bibliothèque Palais Bourbon (Paris): 49 (bottom), 61 (top), 70 (top), 71, 90-91, 107, 108, 222 (top right); Biblioteca del Palacio Real (Madrid): 12, 13, 23, 43, 49 (top), 56 (right), 65 (bottom), 187 (top right), 188, 218 (top right), 219 (top right and left), 222 (top left); Vatican Library: 117.

Acknowledgments:

The author would like to thank Concepción González del Río, Ernesto Nakandakari, Chávez Ballón and Justo Cáceres at the Museo Nacional de Antropología y Arqueología in Lima; Justin and Barbara Kerr in New York; Maria Luisa López Vidriero and Elena de Santiago at the Biblioteca Nacional in Madrid; Pilar Ruiz and Pilar Pardo at the Gabinete de Bibliofilia in Madrid; and Erika Billeter at the Museum of Fine Arts in Lausanne.

Sources for illustrations in boxes

pg. 17 Illustration of the hierarchical structure of Classic Maya society.
pg. 49 Basket of ears of corn. Detail from the Bourbon Codex.
pg. 60 Indians from New Spain (Mexico) making cacao, 17th-century engraving (Biblioteca Nacional de Madrid).
pg. 65 Cactacea plant from the Venetian Codex (Biblioteca del Palacio Real de Madrid).
pg. 66 Erotic Mochica figure (Museo de Arqueología y Antropología de Lima).
pg. 68 Painting by Antonio Tevendaf depicting the Maya marriage ceremony (Museo de Arqueología y Etnología de Guatemala).
pg. 93 Detail from the Mendoza Codex depicting Aztec craftsmen.
pg. 100 Fragment of a Chancay textile (Museo Amano de Lima).
pg. 126 Funeral ceremony of a cacique in the Amazon jungle from *Historia de América* by Belloc, 1844.
pg. 130 Image from the Biblioteca Arcaya de Caracas.
pg. 146 Mochica figure (Museo de Arqueología y Antropología de Lima).
pg. 147 Fragment of the Mendoza Codex (Museo Nacional de Antropología y Arqueología de Mexico).
pg. 155 Portrait of Mama Huaco, detail from a painting illustrating the geneology of the Inca. (Museo Pedro de Osma de Lima).
pg. 163 Part of a *quipu* (Museo Nacional de Antropología y Arqueología de Lima).
pg. 171 Photograph taken during the second half of the 19th century of a Snake Dance, practiced by the Hopi.
pg. 187 From the Venetian Codex, depiction of a ritual Aztec dance dedicated to the god Huctehutf, protector of vagabonds.
pg. 202 Fragment of a ninth-century Maya polychrome vase depicting a group of Maya warriors leading a prisoner with his hands bound, possibly to be sacrificed.
pg. 206 Partial view of the Inca fortress of Sacsahuaman, a protective wall defending the city of Cuzco.

los ᵃ
cᵃ̃a
poᵃ